IFRS
FOR
DUMMIES®

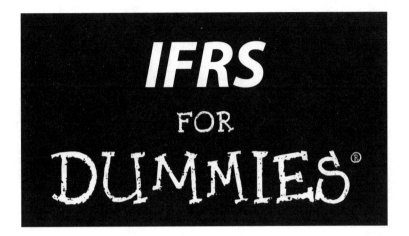

by Steve Collings

A John Wiley and Sons, Ltd, Publication

IFRS For Dummies®

Published by
John Wiley & Sons, Ltd
The Atrium
Southern Gate
Chichester
West Sussex
PO19 8SQ
England
www.wiley.com

For general information on our other products and services, please contact our Customer Care Department within the U.S. at 877-762-2974, outside the U.S. at 317-572-3993, or fax 317-572-4002.

For technical support, please visit www.wiley.com/techsupport.

Wiley publishes in a variety of print and electronic formats and by print-on-demand. Some material included with standard print versions of this book may not be included in e-books or in print-on-demand. If this book refers to media such as a CD or DVD that is not included in the version you purchased, you may download this material at http://booksupport.wiley.com. For more information about Wiley products, visit www.wiley.com.

British Library Cataloguing in Publication Data: A catalogue record for this book is available from the British Library

ISBN 978-1-119-96308-0 (pbk); ISBN 978-1-119-96652-4 (ebk); ISBN 978-1-119-96653-1 (ebk); ISBN 978-1-119-96654-8 (ebk)

Printed and bound in Great Britain by Bell & Bain Ltd., Glasgow, United Kingdom

10 9 8 7 6 5 4 3 2 1

WILEY

About the Author

Steve Collings, FMAAT FCCA, is the audit and technical director at Leavitt Walmsley Associates, a firm of Chartered Certified Accountants based in Sale, Manchester in the United Kingdom. Steve trained and qualified with the firm, for which he is also Senior Statutory Auditor. He qualified with the Association of Accounting Technicians in 2000 and then went on to qualify as an Associate Chartered Certified Accountant (ACCA) in 2005. In 2010, he became a Fellow of the Association of Chartered Certified Accountants (FCCA). Steve also holds the Diploma in IFRS from ACCA which he obtained in 2008, as well as their Certificates in IFRS and Certificates in International Standards on Auditing.

Steve specialises in financial reporting and auditing issues, and has been writing professionally for several years. He is the author of *The Interpretation and Application of International Standards on Auditing* (published by John Wiley & Sons, Ltd. in March 2011) and of other publications on the subjects of UK accounting standards, International Financial Reporting Standards and International Standards on Auditing. He is also the author of several articles which have been published in the various accounting media, primarily *AccountingWEB.co.uk*. Steve also lectures to professional accountants on financial reporting, auditing and Solicitors Accounts Rules.

Steve won *Accounting Technician of the Year* at the British Accountancy Awards in November 2011.

Author's Acknowledgements

Many people believe that writing and producing a book is a one-person project. Believe me, it is anything but! I have been writing about accounting and auditing issues for many years now but writing *IFRS For Dummies* has proved to be one of the biggest (but best) challenges I have faced. My most sincere thanks and gratitude must therefore go to the Commissioning Editor, Claire Ruston, who helped to get this project off the ground. There has not been one instance where I have not enjoyed writing this book, and it has been an absolute pleasure to write.

Every author of a book needs a strong and supportive publishing team behind them and I feel honoured to have people like Steve Edwards (my project editor), Charlie Wilson (my development editor), and Caroline Fox (my technical reviewer) to have worked with during the writing of this book. My heartfelt thanks and gratitude must go to these guys as well as the other guys on the publishing team who have helped to bring this book to market.

The support I have received from my family and friends over the years does not go unnoticed, especially when deadlines are approaching and the pressure kicks in (you all know who you are). My thanks also must go to Les Leavitt, my friend and colleague, who has shown a huge amount of enthusiasm and support for this project and accommodated my deadlines in with work projects.

Finally my thanks go to you, the reader who has picked up this book. I sincerely hope you find it informative, helpful and a good reference guide to the world of IFRS. Keep it close to hand to guide you through complex issues on IFRS and IAS.

Dedications

I am fortunate to know so many influential and special people, both in my personal and professional life, and to name every individual who has influenced my career and writing would be impossible. For every member of my family and each one of my friends (many of whom feature in the illustrative examples in this book), this book is for you. I would also like to dedicate this book to all my peers in the world of financial reporting (particularly Roger Bryant, Lisa Weaver, Clare Finch and Annette Smyth).

Publisher's Acknowledgements

We're proud of this book; please send us your comments at http://dummies.custhelp.com. For other comments, please contact our Customer Care Department within the U.S. at 877-762-2974, outside the U.S. at 317-572-3993, or fax 317-572-4002.

Some of the people who helped bring this book to market include the following:

Acquisitions, Editorial, and Vertical Websites

Project Editor: Steve Edwards

Commissioning Editor: Claire Ruston

Assistant Editor: Ben Kemble

Development Editor: Charlie Wilson

Copy Editor and Proofreader: Kim Vernon

Technical Editor: Caroline Fox

Production Manager: Daniel Mersey

Publisher: David Palmer

Cover Photo: © iStock/CGinspiration

Cartoons: Rich Tennant (www.the5thwave.com)

Composition Services

Project Coordinator: Kristie Rees

Layout and Graphics: Claudia Bell, Corrie Neihaus, Julie Trippetti

Proofreader: Melissa Cossell

Indexer: Sharon Shock

Special Help

Brand Reviewers: Rev Mengle and Jennifer Bingham

Publishing and Editorial for Consumer Dummies

    Kathleen Nebenhaus, Vice President and Executive Publisher

    Kristin Ferguson-Wagstaffe, Product Development Director

    Ensley Eikenburg, Associate Publisher, Travel

    Kelly Regan, Editorial Director, Travel

Publishing for Technology Dummies

    Andy Cummings, Vice President and Publisher

Composition Services

    Debbie Stailey, Director of Composition Services

Contents at a Glance

Table of Contents

Introduction

*W*elcome to *IFRS For Dummies*. This book introduces you to the complex world of international financial reporting that's now gathering faster pace as International Financial Reporting Standards (IFRS) become more prevalent around the globe. Many countries still use their own domestic accounting standards, such as UK Generally Accepted Accounting Practice (GAAP) and US GAAP. However, many countries are also considering the switchover from their own national standards to IFRS.

If you're a student accountant, you may have financial reporting papers on your syllabus that examine IFRS. If you're an accountant in practice, you may have a client, or a number of clients, that choose to, or already, report under IFRS. And if you work for a company that's considering becoming listed, the company may be mandated to prepare its financial information using IFRS.

The method of preparing financial reports has evolved considerably over the last few years and this evolution has led to an increasing demand for more transparent reports to meet the needs of investors, analysts, employees, tax authorities and other stakeholders – *users* of the financial statements. The principles contained in IFRS and International Accounting Standards (IAS) recognise these needs.

About This Book

I've written *IFRS For Dummies* to convey the complex world of international financial reporting in an easy-to-understand, fun and down-to-earth manner. I look at the way the standards work and the objectives each standard is trying to achieve, and illustrate the standards in operation by looking at practical examples to demonstrate how an IFRS or IAS works in real life. I believe the only way to show people how something works is to put it into practice.

This book has a practical approach. In other words, chapters don't run in order of each IAS or IFRS, but instead each chapter is self-contained. You may read the book from cover to cover, or you may jump to the chapters you consider are more relevant than others; whichever method suits you, I advise that you have a quick glance at each chapter in isolation to make sure that you don't miss any important points that may apply to your circumstances.

Conventions Used in This Book

Because the world of financial reporting is complicated and some points throughout the book are more important than others, I've set up a few conventions to help you on your way through this book:

- ✔ I use *italics* to emphasise key points and terms.

- ✔ I use **bold type** to highlight keywords. Such terminology is vital to ensure correct application of the standards.

- ✔ I alternate pronouns between chapters.

- ✔ The double underlining you find in illustrative statements of financial position (balance sheets) and statements of comprehensive income (income statements) shows a final monetary amount; for example, net assets. Single underlining demonstrates that I'm completing a calculation.

- ✔ Numbers in brackets are negative numbers that you subtract from totals or sub-totals.

- ✔ The currency unit used in this book is the dollar (simply a currency unit; not a US or other specific dollar), other than when I make a country-specific reference.

What You're Not to Read

Throughout this book, I include information that may be of interest to some readers but may not be appropriate to others. The grey boxes (sidebars) contain information that you can ignore without incurring any serious consequences. But I do encourage readers to digest the information contained in the sidebars – they explain some country-specific issues, illustrate why an accounting standard was introduced and show you how a standard interacts with other standards, legislation or taxation issues.

Foolish Assumptions

While writing this book I kept in mind some assumptions about you, the reader, and what I want you to get out of this book:

- ✔ I assume that you've knowledge of double-entry concepts and that you're comfortable with some accounting jargon, such as depreciation, amortisation, net assets, retained earnings and so on. The Glossary at the back of the book defines terms I use; and if you need a basic grounding, take a look at *Bookkeeping For Dummies* by Paul Barrow and Lita Epstein (Wiley).

✔ I assume that some of you have worked in some areas of accountancy, whether it be in industry, commerce or general practice. I also assume that you've had some sort of involvement in the preparation of financial statements, even if limited to areas such as accruals and prepayments.

✔ I assume that some readers of this book may never have worked in accountancy, but may be considering a career change or starting out in accountancy and be enrolled on an accountancy course (whether for professional qualifications or at degree level). If so, this book is very much for you.

✔ I assume that you've a knowledge of the importance of accounting standards. Although I don't assume that you've detailed knowledge of how IFRS and IAS work, I've worked on the premise that you know why accounting standards exist and why they're important in the preparation of financial information.

✔ I assume that the main reason for you reading this book is to gain a *basic* understanding of IFRS and IAS. I've kept in mind the fact that students may read this book to help them in their financial reporting papers, which examine IFRS and IAS. I've considered that professional accountants may want to broaden their understanding of IFRS and IAS. Therefore, my assumptions have led me to write this book at an introductory–intermediate level of understanding, rather than striving to make users of this book technical experts in what is a hugely complex subject.

How This Book Is Organised

IFRS For Dummies is split into five major parts. Each part looks at a different area in the world of financial reporting under IFRS and IAS. I divide each part into chapters that relate to the part's theme; each chapter then sub-divides into individual sections. You can see how this division works by referring to the Table of Contents at the start of the book.

Part 1: Concepts and Basic Standards

This part introduces you to the world of IFRS. I look at who creates the standards and how, and which countries have decided to take the plunge and adopt IFRS as their framework for financial reporting. What you start to see quite soon in *IFRS For Dummies* is that the standards are very much principles-driven, and for this reason I also look at why you must stick to the principles to keep people like the auditors and tax people happy, but I also look at instances in which you may depart from a principle. Finally, I take you through how to prepare financial statements under IFRS and look at some of the simpler standards in an attempt to ease you into the book.

Part II: Looking at the Key Components of Financial Statements

In this part, I examine some important characteristics of the financial statements: assets, liabilities, income, equity and expenses. I examine how you account for various assets and liabilities and when you account for income in the financial statements. And in this part, you also get an insight as to what a company's equity is made up of and how equity arrives in the financial statements.

Part III: Consolidating and Investing

This part looks at some of the more complicated areas of financial reporting. Many companies own other companies, or have an investment in other companies, and they have to prepare consolidated financial statements for their subsidiary companies, or deal with the complex accounting for companies they've invested in but aren't subsidiaries. This part considers what gives rise to a subsidiary, an associate or a joint venture as well as how the parent or the investor must account for them.

Part IV: Disclosing Information in the Financial Statements

If you've ever read a set of financial statements, or been involved in the preparation of general purpose financial statements, you know that companies have to make extensive disclosures in addition to the usual primary financial statements such as the statement of comprehensive income (income statement), statement of financial position (balance sheet), statement of cash flows (cash flow statement) and the statement of changes in equity. In this part, I take you through some of the most important disclosure issues, covering related parties, segmenting information and earnings per share. And I give you an idea as to why users place a huge amount of emphasis on disclosure notes.

Part V: The Part of Tens

One characteristic of *For Dummies* books that distinguishes them from other books is the Part of Tens. *IFRS For Dummies* contains three chapters, each of which considers ten 'need-to-know' points. I tell you about ten pitfalls you must avoid, and ten of the most important disclosure requirements you need to know about when preparing financial statements under IFRS. Finally, because nothing stands still in the world of accountancy, I take a look at ten future IFRS developments to keep an eye on to make sure that you're up to speed.

Part VI: Appendixes

Here I include some additional material you may find useful. First, I give guidance on websites and books to check out for further information on IFRS. Then, I take a look at IFRS for SMEs – the mini IFRS for small and medium-sized organisations. And finally, I include a handy glossary offering simple-to-grasp definitions for key IFRS terminology.

Icons Used in This Book

As you go through each chapter, you see various icons I use to help you understand the book and its contents more succinctly:

This icon marks warnings that you must heed; failing to do so may land you in hot water.

Signals a friendly reminder of points that you must keep in mind. I use this icon quite a lot in this book, primarily because in the real world many standards interact with other standards. The knowledge I impart here is important.

This icon indicates that the text to follow is somewhat technical, and if you're struggling to grasp the detail, you can move on.

A key feature of *IFRS For Dummies* is the examples I use to bring technical issues to life. When you see this icon, you know that I'm about to show you how to apply a particular concept.

This icon helps you identify a time-saving mechanism or something that helps in your accounting studies or professional life.

Where to Go from Here

You can use this book in many different ways. Some readers may choose to start from the beginning and work their way through it at their own pace, and doing so is a good way to get a sound understanding of how IFRS works.

Some of you may already have some knowledge of IFRS and just simply want to refresh your memory on certain issues, or simply look up a particular subject. I've structured this book in such a way that you can skip straight to the relevant section. For example, if you're not sure about consolidated financial statements, you can simply jump to Part IV. If you've just adopted IFRS for the first-time (or are about to), you may want to understand about first-time adoption and the process you've got to go through; in this case, flick over to Chapter 3.

I've written this book for *you* – to guide you through the murky world of IFRS, and I try to make it a fun subject even though it's a crucially important topic. I've really enjoyed writing this book and I sincerely hope that you find it provides useful insights and helps you in your day-to-day working life.

Part I
Concepts and Basic Standards

In this part . . .

*F*inancial reporting has become increasingly complicated over the years. Many trainee and professional accountants find the sheer size of the accounting standards, as well as trying to figure out just exactly what the standards want you to do, problematic.

In this part, I introduce you to the conceptual framework and examine some of the more basic standards. Understanding how and why the standards are created is crucial in actually understanding the world of financial reporting. I start with the basics, introducing you to the standard-setting process, and then move on to how a company develops its accounting policies and how a first-time adopter of IFRS deals with the switchover from domestic accounting standards to IFRS.

Chapter 1

Introducing IFRS

*M*any organisations use International Financial Reporting Standards (IFRS) and International Accounting Standards (IAS) in preparing their *general purpose financial statements* – the year-/period-end statements prepared for *users*: shareholders and external stakeholders like employees, tax authorities, banks and financiers. The IFRS and IAS tell accountants and other preparers of financial statements how to account for transactions and events, and what to disclose, within the accounts.

Over recent years, the IFRS have become more and more prevalent throughout the world, but a frequently asked question is why? Well, many countries like the idea of being able to produce financial information comparable to that of other companies that report under IFRS – for example, comparing against other companies in the same industry but in a different country. Think from a potential investor's point of view: if you're planning to pump money into a company, you need to see clear and comparable financial information. And because IFRS is now gathering pace all around the world, you can compare financial information far more easily now than, say, 20 years ago.

In this chapter, I move beyond telling you what standards are to helping you understand what they do. To start, I explain how the standards are created and amended, and then I take a look at the scope of IFRS worldwide. Finally, I introduce you to the important financial statements that you must present to conform with IFRS: the statement of financial position, statement of comprehensive income and the statement of changes in equity. By the end of this chapter, you've a good grounding in IFRS.

Creating and Amending the Standards

The standards don't create themselves – someone has to produce them – and this unenviable job belongs to the International Accounting Standards Board (IASB). The Board began work in 2001 and took over from the International Accounting Standards Committee (IASC), which was originally set up in 1973. The IASB doesn't have the authority to impose its standards on any country – this decision is left to the various countries themselves. A major breakthrough came in 2002 when the European Union (EU) adopted legislation that requires listed companies in Europe to apply IFRS in their consolidated financial statements and this applied to more than 7,000 companies in 28 countries.

When the IASB sets the accounting standards, it has a clear objective in mind: that companies reporting under IFRS and IAS produce general purpose financial statements that are of a high quality, clear and transparent nature and allow the financial statements to be comparable. The objective is that the user (the shareholder or the external stakeholder) can make rational decisions about the company based on the information contained in the financial statements. The IASB also promotes the IFRS and IAS globally with the aim that eventually all countries report under the standards. The Board works with other national standard-setters (for example, the US Financial Accounting Standards Board) to converge national accounting standards to IFRS.

The following sections take you through the IASB's *Conceptual Framework*, and how it sets and amends standards.

Understanding the Framework

When the IASB develops or changes an accounting standard, it does so with reference to their *Conceptual Framework for Financial Reporting*. The *Conceptual Framework* considers the theoretical and conceptual issues that surround financial reporting and its objective is to form a coherent and consistent basis upon which accounting standards are developed.

The differences between IFRS and IAS

A common question I hear is, 'Why are there IFRS *and* IAS?' When the IASB had its first meeting, it took on all the IASC's standards (which were all IAS). The IASB amended quite a lot of the standards, but also issued new standards, known as IFRS. The abbreviation IFRS has become a generic term to refer to all the standards (for example, when you hear people say 'the company reports under IFRS' what they mean is that they adopt all the IFRS and IAS in preparing their financial statements). Throughout this book, I refer to IFRS and IAS for consistency and simplicity.

Knowing who does what at the IA

The structure of international financial reporting isn't exactly straightforward. You don't just find one senior person at the head of the IASB directing a load of accounting standard writers/editors underneath. Instead, you find a fairly complicated structure consisting of:

- Advisory Committee (appointed by the IASC Foundation, advises on activities of the IASB)

- Director of operations and non-technical staff (report to the IASC Foundation)

- Director of technical activities and technical staff (report to the IASB and IFRIC)

- International Accounting Sta mittee Foundation (22 trustees)

- International Financial Reporting I tations Committee (IFRIC, appointed b IASC Foundation)

- National standard-setters and other interested parties (link to the Standards Advisory Council and the Advisory Committee)

- Standards Advisory Council (advises on activities of the IASB)

- The IASB itself (16 Board members appointed by the IASC Foundation)

The *Conceptual Framework* is a vital tool used by the IASB in setting and updating standards. Its purpose is to:

- Assist in the development of future IFRS as well as assist the IASB when it reviews existing standards by setting out the underlying concepts

- Promote harmonisation of accounting regulation and standards by reducing the number of permitted alternative accounting treatments

- Assist other standard-setters in setting their own national standards

- Assist auditors to form an opinion as to whether (or not) financial statements have been prepared in accordance with IFRS

- Assist users in interpreting financial information contained in a set of IFRS financial statements

- Allow those interested in the work of the standard-setting process at the IASB to have an insight as to the IASB's approach to standard-setting

The *Conceptual Framework* itself is *not* an accounting standard. If conflicts exist between an IFRS or IAS and the *Conceptual Framework*, the standard always prevails.

The *Conceptual Framework* deals with various aspects of a set of IFRS financial statements as well as setting out the overall objective of why general purpose financial statements are prepared. In a nutshell, the objective of financial reporting is to help users to make informed decisions about a company – in particular whether (or not) to invest in it.

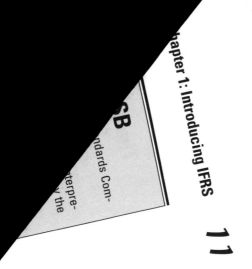

onceptual Framework

has changed considerably because the needs
f users have changed considerably. So, in
eptember 2010, the IASB decided to revise
e Framework to take into account the revised
ectives of general purpose financial report-
and the qualitative characteristics of useful
rmation.

...utive characteristics

The *Conceptual Framework* sets out certain characteristics of useful financial information. These characteristics are split into two bits:

- ✔ **Fundamental qualitative characteristics:** Financial information is:

    - **Relevant:** The information is capable of making a difference in the decisions made by users.

    - **Faithful in its presentation:** The information is complete, neutral and free from error.

- ✔ **Enhancing qualitative characteristics:** Financial information is enhanced when it is comparable, verifiable, timely and understandable.

The *Conceptual Framework* also includes materiality as a sub-section of relevance. An item is *material* if the financial information's omission or mis-statement may cause the user of the financial statements to arrive at the wrong conclusion. For example, if you forget to make an accrual for a late invoice amounting to $20, the chances are that this omission is immaterial and the user will still make the same conclusions he would have done had the $20 accrual been made. However, in contrast, if you missed a $20,000 accrual then this mistake may lead the user to the wrong conclusion about the company.

Where materiality is concerned, be especially careful. Sometimes (particu-larly in auditing), you can calculate materiality using a variety of methods. Something that may be immaterial in numerical terms may become material in nature; for example, if it turned a profit into a loss.

Laying out the elements of the financial statements

A key feature of the *Conceptual Framework* document is that it outlines the elements of the financial statements:

✔ **Assets:** Basically, things that belong to the organisation. The full definition of assets is quite complex; turn to Chapter 4 for details.

✔ **Capital maintenance adjustments:** Occur when a company revalues a building or another *non-current asset*, which is an asset not easily turned into cash and not expected to be turned into cash within a year (see Chapter 4 for more on revaluations). They're essentially gains and losses and you don't take them directly to the income statement but to the equity section of the statement of financial position as 'capital maintenance adjustments' or 'revaluation reserves'.

✔ **Equity:** The bit left over in the assets of a company when you deduct all its liabilities (flick to Chapter 9 for more on equity).

✔ **Expenses:** Cost of sales, payroll costs, bank charges, depreciation and the like. Expenses can also include things like exceptional items, such as if a building burns down, and you usually show these expenses as a separate line item in the income statement so the user is aware of them.

✔ **Income:** Relates to funds received from the selling of goods or rendering of services (*revenue*, which I cover in Chapter 8). Income also relates to *gains*: things that don't usually occur in the ordinary course of business, such as when a company sells a non-current asset (for example one of its buildings) at a profit; the profit on disposal is the gain.

✔ **Liabilities:** Basically, what a company owes to another person or another company. Chapters 6 and 7 explore liabilities in detail.

✔ **Performance:** Relates to income and expenses and the measure of income and expenses through the resulting profit (or loss as the case may be), the calculation of gross profit margins (gross profit/revenue), net profit margins (net profit/revenue) and trade receivables days (trade receivables/revenue x 365, or 366 if a leap year). (*Trade receivables* are customers who still owe you money.)

Going through the IFRS-setting steps

Here's what happens when a new accounting standard is about to hit the streets. The IASB follows these six steps to setting an IFRS:

1. **Set the agenda.**

2. **Plan the project.**

3. **Develop and then publish the discussion paper.**

4. **Develop and then publish the Exposure Draft.**

5. **Develop and then publish the standard.**

6. **Meet with interested parties and other standard-setters after the standard is issued, to weed out any unanticipated issues.**

When the IASB issues an *Exposure Draft* (which sets out a specific proposal in the form of a standard), anyone can comment on the proposals. The comment period for international Exposure Drafts is generally 120 days, though (in exceptional circumstances) this comment period may be reduced to 60 days or less if the matter is urgent. The IASB publishes all comment letters received on its website (www.ifrs.org) as well as detailing how it has responded to comments in the 'Basis for conclusions' section, which is attached to the published standards.

Changing the standards

After a standard has been issued, that's not necessarily the end of the story. The IASB often needs to amend standards for a variety of reasons, and it makes necessary but not urgent changes through the *Annual Improvements Project* (IFRIC deals with the more pressing issues; see the next section).

The IASB looks at feedback from the IFRS Interpretations Committee, which interprets any ambiguities in the IFRS/IAS, and feedback from staff at the IASB and accountancy practitioners. The IASB focuses on areas of inconsistency within the standards themselves, or looks at the wording of the standards to see whether it needs to be clarified in any way to make the standard more transparent and easier to apply.

During the third quarter of every year, the IASB publishes an Exposure Draft of all the proposals for public comment (the comment period is open for 90 days). When the comment period closes, the IASB goes through all the comments it has received and then aims to issue the amended standards in their final form in the following second quarter (usually with an 'effective from' date of 1 January of the next year).

Generally, the IASB makes two types of amendments to IFRS/IAS:

- ✔ To *clarify* a standard, usually because of ambiguous wording within the standard or because gaps appear in it. The effectiveness of a new standard is only apparent when the standard is put into practice.

- ✔ To *correct* a minor (and unintended) consequence, conflict resolution and deal with any oversights. The correction doesn't introduce, or change, the existing principles.

Understanding IFRIC

IFRIC is an abbreviation for the IFRS Interpretations Committee. It was previously known as the Standing Interpretations Committee (SIC), which is why on the IASB website (www.ifrs.org) you see reference to IFRIC and SIC interpretations (described as IFRIC-1, IFRIC-2 and SIC-1, SIC-2 and so on).

Sometimes when an IFRS is put into practice, issues emerge. It may also be the case that an IFRS is worded in such a way that clarification is needed. The IASB can't deal with all these emerging issues when they suddenly arise; so IFRIC must give the emerging issues attention before the standard can be amended, or even issued. IFRIC deals with conflicting or unsatisfactory interpretations of the standards when they emerge, and issues its interpretations of the standards.

IFRIC doesn't issue standalone standards, but IFRICs *are* authoritative as per IAS 1 at paragraph 7.

The *IFRIC Handbook* outlines the seven-stage process for how it applies the requirements of transparency and consistency:

1. **Identify the issues.**
2. **Set an agenda.**
3. **Hold the IFRIC meeting and vote.**
4. **Draft an interpretation.**
5. **The IASB releases the draft interpretation.**
6. **Comment period and deliberation.**
7. **The IASB releases the interpretation.**

When the IFRIC Committee issues draft interpretations for comment, the comment period isn't less than 60 days, and anyone can comment.

Spreading IFRS Worldwide

IFRS is fast becoming one of the most used financial reporting frameworks around the world. Many countries adopt IFRS because they want consistency in financial reporting and believe that adopting IFRS gives access to more sources of capital because investors, creditors, financial analysts and other users of the financial statements welcome standards that require high-quality, transparent and comparable information. Without common standards, it's inherently difficult to compare financial information prepared by companies located in different parts of the world, particularly in an increasing global economy.

The following sections outline which countries are on board with IFRS, and which are on their way.

Countries that have taken the plunge and adopted IFRS

More than 120 countries around the globe are reported to be allowing, or mandating, the use of IFRS. The following must report under IFRS:

- ✔ All domestic listed companies in the European Union and European Economic Area member states
- ✔ All listed companies, including domestic companies, in Estonia, Brazil, Bangladesh, the Czech Republic and Canada (private sector companies in Canada are permitted to use IFRS, including those in the not-for-profit sector)
- ✔ Banks in Russia, Ukraine, Kazakhstan and the United Arab Emirates

IFRS is gathering momentum at a rapid pace and the number of countries that permit, or mandate, organisations to use IFRS as a financial reporting framework is constantly changing. The list highlights just exactly how quickly IFRS is gathering momentum throughout the world.

Countries that are planning to take the plunge

Some countries do not permit IFRS (at present), including Pakistan, Saudi Arabia and Malaysia. But many other countries are aware of the existence of IFRS and are considering adopting it, purely because of the consistency it offers.

What usually happens is that countries 'converge' their standards to IFRS so that no fundamental gaps exist between domestic standards and IFRS (a bit like the UK has done). A convergence project is currently ongoing with Indonesia and convergence over to IFRS is expected in 2012. China has undertaken a convergence project to substantially converge all its domestic standards to IFRS, so China will probably take the plunge eventually.

Mexico is going to require all listed companies to report under IFRS in 2012, whereas Japan has introduced a roadmap for adoption of IFRS and is to decide on this roadmap in 2012, with adoption likely to occur in 2015 or 2016.

The country that seems to hold the key to the vast majority of countries converging to IFRS is the US. The US Securities and Exchange Commission (US SEC) is a prominent member of the International Organisation of Securities Commissions (IOSCO). The members of IOSCO are securities commissions and other stock exchange regulators. The global harmonisation of financial reporting standards has been high on their agenda for quite a long time. However, the US has been reluctant to adopt IFRS because of the major gaps between IFRS and US Generally Accepted Accounting Practice (GAAP), some of which still exist, as shown in Table 1-1.

Table 1-1	Conflicts between IFRS and US GAAP
IFRS	**US GAAP**
Prohibits the last-in, first-out method of inventory valuation	Permits the last-in, first-out method of inventory valuation
Uses a single-step method for write-offs in respect of impairment losses	Uses a two-step method (so impairments are more likely for US companies if they adopt IFRS in its current form)
Permits a breach of a loan covenant to be recognised as non-current provided the lender gives their agreement and a covenant breach is unlikely to occur again within 12 months from the end of the reporting period	Requires current presentation in such cases

The IASB and the US standard-setters (the Financial Accounting Standards Board (FASB)) are working to come to an agreement so that eventually the US may adopt IFRS, but for now it's just a case of sitting back and seeing what happens.

Dealing With the Numbers: The IFRS Financial Statements

The following sections explain the different types of performance and position statements that a company reporting under IFRS has to present in their *general purpose* financial statements (not to be confused with internal financial statements, such as internal management accounts, which may be produced monthly). The complete set of IFRS financial statements is as follows:

- ✔ A statement of financial position as at the end of the accounting period
- ✔ A statement of comprehensive income
- ✔ A statement of changes in equity

✔ A statement of cash flows (see Chapter 2 for more on the statement of cash flows)

✔ Notes to the financial statements that summarise the company's significant accounting policies, break down the information contained within the primary financial statements and show other disclosures required under the IFRS/IAS

At the heart of these statements is the numbers, which convey a lot of information to the user, some of which isn't always immediately apparent (for example, the gross profit margin of a company and whether the gross margins have fluctuated from one year to the next). You may prepare management accounts for internal use that follow a company-specific style (a house style). However, you have to prepare IFRS financial statements in a specified way to comply with the principles in IFRS.

IAS 1 *Presentation of Financial Statements* deals with the presentation of financial statements. It requires a minimum amount of information, but in general the standard is fairly permissive and offers great flexibility in terms of the order and layout.

Translating terminology

Back in September 2007, the IASB issued a revised IAS 1, which changed the names of the primary financial statements as accountants have always known them.

The following table outlines the differences between the old and new terminology.

Traditional Terminology	IFRS Calls It
Balance sheet	Statement of financial position
Cash flow statement	Statement of cash flows
Debtors/creditors	Receivables/payables
Fixed assets	Non-current assets
Minority interest	Non-controlling interest
Movement on reserves	Changes in equity
Profit and loss account	Statement of comprehensive income/ income statement
Profit and loss reserves	Retained earnings
Stock	Inventories
Turnover (or sales)	Revenue

Be careful with the layouts – many jurisdictions have legislation that governs the way you lay out financial statements. So although IAS 1 may be fairly relaxed, legislation may dictate how a company sets out its financial statements.

If your company is adopting IFRS for the first time, then, as well as reading the following sections, take a look at Chapter 3. This chapter is an important one if your company (or one of your clients) is adopting IFRS for the first time because you've a lot (and I mean a lot) of extra things to take into consideration.

Presenting the statement of financial position

The *statement of financial position* is a snapshot of the financial state of a company at any one point in time. Many companies produce monthly management accounts, in which case the statement of financial position is at the close of business on the last working day of the month. The statement of financial position at the year-end shows details of the company's assets, liabilities and equity at the close of play as at the year-end or period-end.

IAS 1 says that, as a minimum, the statement of financial position should include the line items that present the following amounts:

- ✔ Property, plant and equipment
- ✔ Investment property
- ✔ Intangible assets
- ✔ Financial assets, excluding amounts shown under:
  - • Trade and other receivables
  - • Cash and cash equivalents
  - • Investments accounted for using the equity method
- ✔ Investments accounted for using the equity method
- ✔ Biological assets
- ✔ Inventories
- ✔ Trade and other receivables
- ✔ Cash and cash equivalents
- ✔ The total of assets classified as held for sale and assets included in disposal groups classified as held for sale in accordance with IFRS 5 *Non-Current Assets Held for Sale and Discontinued Operations*
- ✔ Trade and other payables
- ✔ Provisions

✔ Financial liabilities, excluding amounts shown under:

  • Trade and other payables

  • Provisions

✔ Liabilities and assets for current tax, as defined in IAS 12 *Income Taxes*

✔ Deferred tax liabilities and deferred tax assets, as defined in IAS 12

✔ Liabilities included in disposal groups classified as held for sale in accordance with IFRS 5

✔ Non-controlling interests, presented within equity

✔ Issued capital and reserves attributable to the owners of the parent

IAS 1 says that the statement of financial position must contain the items in the list 'as a minimum'. So, for example, if a company has investment property, it needs to report it. It's worth pointing out that not every company that reports under IFRS has every one of those items, but if it does it must report them under the relevant line.

Figure 1-1 shows how a typical statement of financial position looks.

When you first started out as a novice in the world of accountancy, you probably discovered the accounting equation:

Assets = Liabilities + Owners' equity

However, if you look at the format of the statement of financial position, you see that it starts with assets, then equity and finally liabilities, so under IAS 1 the equation becomes:

Assets = Owners' equity + Liabilities

At the end of the day, the presentation of the equation may be slightly different, but the objective under IAS 1 is still the same as in any other GAAP – the statement of financial position shows the state of the company's financial position as at a point in time; in other words, a snapshot of the financial position.

Understanding the statement of comprehensive income

The *statement of comprehensive income* shows the trading/financial performance of the company during the accounting period. For example, a company's year-end may be 31 December 2011. This means that the accounting period starts on 1 January 2011. The statement of comprehensive income, therefore, shows the trading/financial performance of a company from the start of the year (1 January) to the end of the year (31 December).

Typical Co Limited

Statement of Financial Position as at 31 December 2011

	31/12/11 $	31/12/10 $
ASSETS		
Non-current assets		
Property, plant and equipment	X	X
Goodwill	X	X
Other intangible assets	X	X
Investments in associates	X	X
Available-for-sale investments	X	X
	X	X
Current assets		
Inventories	X	X
Trade receivables	X	X
Other receivables	X	X
Cash and cash equivalents	X	X
	X	X
Total assets	Y	Y
EQUITY AND LIABILITIES		
Equity attributable to equity holders of the parent		
Share capital	X	X
Other reserves	X	X
Retained earnings	X	X
	X	X
Non-controlling interest	X	X
Total equity	X	X
Non-current liabilities		
Long-term loans	X	X
Deferred tax	X	X
Provisions	X	X
Total non-current liabilities	X	X
Current liabilities		
Trade and other payables	X	X
Short-term borrowings	X	X
Current tax payable	X	X
Provisions	X	X
Total current liabilities	X	X
Total liabilities	X	X
Total equity and liabilities	Y	Y

Figure 1-1:
A statement
of financial
position.

Under the revised IAS 1, you can split the statement of comprehensive income into two separate statements, showing:

- ✔ The income statement itself
- ✔ A second statement starting with profit (or loss) for the year from continuing operations (or loss for the year from discontinuing operations as the case may be) and then disclosing the separate components of other comprehensive income

So, what exactly is *other comprehensive income*? Well, essentially this income is any gains or losses that you take directly to the equity section of the statement of financial position (for example, a gain on revaluation of property, plant and equipment, which I cover in Chapter 4). You can also put in other comprehensive things like actuarial gains (or losses) when a company has a defined benefit pension plan (I explain actuarial gains and losses in Chapter 7). The upshot of other comprehensive income is that anything that goes here is a re-measurement as a result of movements in a price or valuation.

The objective of the statement of comprehensive income is to show the *inflows* (resources coming into the company) from the company's assets from sales of goods or services during the period. It also shows the *outflows* (resources going out of the company) of those assets that occur due to expenses, which is how you arrive at profit (or loss, as the case may be).

Figure 1-2 shows how a typical statement of comprehensive income prepared under IAS 1 looks.

You don't have to have the statement of comprehensive income running all in one statement if you prefer not to. The standard allows you to present the normal income statement in the traditional way and then show the bottom bit (the other comprehensive income bit) in a separate statement.

Unravelling the statement of changes in equity

In addition to the statement of comprehensive income, the statement of financial position and the statement of cash flows (see Chapter 2 for more on the statement of cash flows), a company also has to produce a statement of changes in equity. The statement of changes in equity shows the capital that has been invested in the business from the shareholders as well as the profit earned by the business from its ordinary course of business and the amount of profit it has retained.

Typical Co

Statement of Comprehensive Income for the year ended

31 December 2011

	31/12/11 $	31/12/10 $
Revenue	X	X
Cost of sales	(X)	(X)
Gross profit	X	X
Other income	X	X
Distribution costs	(X)	(X)
Administrative expenses	(X)	(X)
Other expenses	(X)	(X)
Finance costs	(X)	(X)
Profit before tax	X	X
Income tax expense	(X)	(X)
Profit for the year from continuing operations	X	X
Loss for the year from discontinued operations	(X)	(X)
Profit for the year	X	X
Other comprehensive income:		
Exchange differences on translation of foreign operations	X	X
Available-for-sale financial assets	X	X
Cash flow hedges	X	X
Gains on property revaluation	X	X
Actuarial gains (losses) on defined benefit pension plans	X	X
Share of other comprehensive income of associates	X	X
Income tax relating to components of other comprehensive income	(X)	(X)
Other comprehensive income for the year net of tax	X	X
Total comprehensive income for the year	X	X

Figure 1-2:
A statement of comprehensive income.

When a company has worked out its *post*-tax profit, this profit is then 'distributable' to the shareholders in the form of a dividend. I say 'distributable' because in real life many companies won't distribute the entire amount of post-tax profit to its shareholders, but instead pay a certain amount in dividends and then retain some of this profit. The bit that's retained is called the *retained profit* and is put into *retained earnings* and you see it in the equity section of the statement of financial position. It consists of accumulated retained profits from when the company first started in business, and provided the company has sufficient funds available in this account, a company that makes a loss in one year may still be able to pay a dividend because of sufficient retained earnings.

For companies that are stand-alone companies and have a simple structure (usually referred to as *owner-managed businesses* or *OMBs*), the statement of changes in equity is a fairly straightforward statement to make. However, the statement itself gets complicated and more detailed when the company is large, quoted on a recognised stock market and has hundreds of shareholders.

The statement of changes in equity isn't just about the changes that have arisen directly through profits and dividends. If you look at the other comprehensive income section of the statement of comprehensive income (see 'Understanding the statement of comprehensive income', earlier in this chapter), you see that other matters affect the statement of changes in equity, such as gains that arise when a company revalues some of its property, plant and equipment or when a defined benefit pension plan has an actuarial gain or loss. You don't report these items directly through the income statement as profits or losses; you report them in the statement of changes in equity.

Figure 1-3 shows how the statement of changes in equity may look.

	Share capital	Retained earnings	Revaluation reserve	Total
Balance at 1 January 2011	X	X	X	X
Dividends		(X)		(X)
Issue of shares	X			X
Total comprehensive income for the year		X	X	X
Gain on revaluation of building			X	X
Balance at 31 December 2011	Y	Y	Y	Y

Figure 1-3:
A statement of changes in equity.

Figure 1-3 shows a simple illustration that is applicable to a small, stand-alone company (though larger companies may also have a statement of changes in equity as simple as this one).

When a company is an owner-managed business, the only things that may affect the statement of changes in equity are the resulting profit or loss that is transferred to retained earnings and any dividends that the directors may have taken in their capacity as shareholders. So, in this situation, the statement of changes in equity simply consists of:

Opening balance at the start of the year	X
Less dividends paid	(X)
Plus profit for the year	X
Closing balance at end of the year	X

Chapter 2

Getting to Grips with Some Basic IFRS

*I*n this chapter I get you started by examining some of the more routine, day-to-day standards that affect all companies reporting under IFRS. These are the standards that you can expect to come across frequently, so understanding them is important.

More businesses fail because of cash flow issues than because they can't achieve a profit, which is why the first basic standard to get to grips with is IAS 7 *Statement of Cash Flows*. Cash is king, and understanding the statement of cash flows is essential so that you can be sure that cash is backing profit.

Next, I take you through IAS 8 *Accounting Policies, Changes in Accounting Estimates and Errors*, which covers big issues governing a company's financial statements. I examine what to do if IFRS doesn't permit a company's policies and show you how to deal with changes in accounting policies, accounting estimates and (deep breath) errors.

And because many companies find year-end accounting tricky, I finish up with IAS 10 *Events After the Reporting Period*, and show you what to do about events that occur *after* the company's year-end but whose conditions existed already at the year-end.

Finding Out Where the Money Has Gone in the Statement of Cash Flows

You often hear accountants referring to the *primary financial statements*, which comprise:

- ✔ The statement of comprehensive income (the income statement)
- ✔ The statement of financial position
- ✔ The statement of changes in equity
- ✔ The statement of cash flows (also known as the cash flow statement, especially in the UK)

This section looks at the statement of cash flows. (If you want to have a look at how the other primary statements are typically laid out, flip to Chapter 1.)

In certain Generally Accepted Accounting Practices (known as GAAP), for example UK GAAP, the statement of cash flows is optional if you're classed as a 'small' company in the eyes of legislation. But if you're reporting under IFRS, you've no option – the statement of cash flows is mandatory (boo!).

You prepare financial statements using the *accruals* basis of accounting; that is, you account for goods or services as they're received even if the bill hasn't arrived yet. The accruals concept allows users of the financial statements to understand the profitability (or loss) and the financial position of the company at the end of the accounting period. When I talk about *users* of financial statements, I mean anyone looking at the accounts: shareholders, financiers, potential investors, suppliers, employees – basically, any stakeholders. You also find this terminology in the *IFRS Conceptual Framework*, which is the document the International Accounting Standards Board (IASB) uses when developing accounting standards or amending existing standards.

Seeing the importance of the statement of cash flows

An organisation prepares the statement of cash flows so that users of the accounts can see both how the organisation has generated and spent its cash. Now, that description sounds like an income and expenditure statement, but actually the statement of cash flows is different because it takes account of different things. The statement of cash flows can reveal things in the financial statements that may not be apparent due to the accruals concept (I show you how this works in the later section 'Preparing the statement of cash flows'). So, the statement of cash flows is the only primary financial statement that you prepare on a cash (receipts and payments) basis.

The statement of cash flows is an extremely useful primary statement. It can tell the user an awful lot about the company that the statement of financial position and the statement of comprehensive income may not. For example, if a company has run into difficulties and is paying its tax in instalments, the income statement merely shows the tax charge on that year's profit and the statement of financial position shows the total liability due to the tax authority, but the statement of cash flows actually shows the taxation *paid* in the year. Therefore, anyone who has an awareness of how the statement of financial position, statement of comprehensive income and the statement of cash flows all interact can easily conclude that a company may (or may not) have cash flow difficulties.

A lot of people also like to look at the statement of cash flows because it simply shows how a company has generated and spent cash; as a result, it eliminates a lot of the weird accounting treatments found in the statement of comprehensive income and the statement of financial position.

Negative operating cash flows always signal that danger is ahead! A company can make profits but still go bust. Profits must be cash backed, so watch out if the operating cash flows are negative, because if they are then clearly problems exist.

Preparing the statement of cash flows

The IAS that tells you how to prepare the statement of cash flows is IAS 7 *Statement of Cash Flows*. The standard itself is fairly user-friendly and goes into a lot of detail about how to go about preparing the statement. So here I stick to the basics.

Choosing between the direct and indirect method

The starting point is to decide how you'll prepare the statement of cash flows. You choose between two methods: the 'direct' method and the 'indirect' method.

The direct method isn't as popular as the indirect method, and I think that the indirect method is actually easier.

With the *direct method*, you take the major classes of gross receipts (such as money in from your customers) and payments and disclose them on the main body of the statement of cash flows. IAS 7 actually encourages companies to use the direct method, but on the grounds that it provides information that's not available under the indirect method and that may be useful in estimating future cash flows. Here's an illustrative example of how the direct method works:

	2011 $,000	2010 $,000
Operating activities		
Received from customers	7,046	6,665
Payments to suppliers	(4,742)	(4,426)
Payments to and on behalf of employees	(928)	(783)
Other payments	(567)	(547)
Net cash inflow from operating activities	**809**	**909**

Net cash inflow is how much cash you've had in purely from your day-to-day trading.

The *indirect method* works differently. First, you take your *operating profit* (the net income or loss reported in the income statement). Then, you *adjust* the operating profit, which means adding back non-cash expenses and deducting non-cash gains. You adjust for:

- ✔ Non-cash items: such as depreciation

- ✔ Changes in:

    - • Working capital: inventory, trade receivables (customers)

    - • Trade payables (suppliers)

An illustrative example of how this works is as follows:

	2011 $,000	2010 $,000
Operating activities		
Operating profit	940	897
Adjustments for:		
Depreciation	160	151
Loss on sale of non-current assets	100	110
Profit on sale of non-current assets	(50)	–

Cash flow from operating activities before		
changes in working capital	1,150	1,158
Decrease in inventory	130	110
Increase in trade receivables	(80)	(119)
Increase in trade payables	120	75
Cash generated from operations	1,320	1,224
Interest paid	(75)	(95)
Tax paid	(234)	(190)
Net cash inflow from operating activities	**1,011**	**939**

If the inventory value had *increased* from the previous year, you'd deduct this increase from the operating profit because this means more money is tied up in inventory, which equates to a cash *outflow*. If the trade receivables had *decreased*, you'd add this decrease onto the operating profit because this means more money has been collected in from receivables, giving rise to a cash *inflow*. Finally, if trade payables had *decreased* you deduct this decrease from operating profit because this means that you paid out more to payables than the previous year, which equates to a cash *outflow*.

Select the method that allows your financial statements to present fairly the state of your company's affairs. Don't simply select one method because you're more comfortable with it than the other – users want to see relevant and reliable information, and if you can supply such info by adopting the direct method as opposed to the indirect method then you must prepare the statement of cash flows under the direct method.

Understanding the format for preparation

After you master the method you're going to prepare the statement of cash flows by, you need to prepare it in accordance with IAS 7 requirements. Many companies have their own house style when it comes to preparing management information (such as management accounts), but when it comes to preparing the annual financial statements, you have to follow a set format.

IAS 7 prescribes the format in which you must prepare the statement of cash flows. You split the statement into three sections as follows:

  ✔ **Operating activities:** Your day-to-day revenue-producing activities that aren't investing or financing activities (see the examples in the previous section). This category is essentially a default category, encompassing all cash flows that don't fall within the investing or financing classifications.

  ✔ **Investing activities:** Those activities that involve the acquisition and disposal of long-term assets; for example, you include monies used for purchasing *non-current assets* (those not easily turned into cash and not expected to be turned into cash within a year), cash receipts when you sell non-current assets and cash payments for buying another company.

✔ **Financing activities:** Those activities that change the equity and borrowing composition of the company. So, for example, if a company issues shares in the year to raise cash, you classify the proceeds from this issue as a financing activity. Similarly, if the company takes out a loan, this is a financing activity.

Working through an example

In this section, to help you get to grips with preparing your statement of cash flows, I work through an example, taking each section of the statement (operating, investing and financing activities) in turn.

Right, so I'm going to assume that you've decided that the indirect method of preparing the statement of cash flows is the best one for you (see the earlier section 'Choosing between the direct and indirect method'). What you need now is the following:

✔ The statement of comprehensive income for the current year

✔ The statement of financial position for both the current and the previous financial year

When you've got your hands on the statements, you're ready to start. Here's your income statement for the year ended 31 December 2011:

	$,000
Revenue	31,461
Cost of sales (including depreciation of $2,172)	16,304
Gross profit	15,157
Loss on disposal of non-current assets	183
Distribution costs	5,663
Administrative expenses	3,681
Profit from operations	5,630
Finance costs	800
Profit before tax	4,830
Tax	919
Profit after tax	3,911

And here's your statement of financial position as at 31 December 2011:

	2011 $,000	2010 $,000
ASSETS		
Non-current assets		
Property, plant and equipment*	29,882	19,100
Current assets		
Inventories	4,837	4,502
Trade receivables	5,244	4,978
Bank accounts	64	587
	10,145	10,067
Total assets	40,027	29,167
EQUITY AND LIABILITIES		
Equity		
Share capital	8,000	5,000
Share premium	2,500	1,000
Retained earnings**	15,570	12,359
Total equity	26,070	18,359
Non-current liabilities		
Bank loan	10,000	7,000
Current liabilities		
Trade payables	3,038	2,954
Tax	919	854
	3,957	3,808
Total liabilities	**13,957**	**10,808**
Total equity and liabilities	**40,027**	**29,167**

Workings:

* The net book value of non-current assets sold in the year is $692.

** Retained earnings at 1 January	12,359
Dividends	(700)
Profit for the year	3,911
Retained earnings at 31 December 2011	15,570

The next step is to turn all this into a statement of cash flows under IAS 7. What you're essentially doing is taking the operating profit and the two statements of financial position and showing how your opening cash balance of $587 (see the statement of financial position for 2010) has turned into a closing cash balance of $64 (see the statement of financial position for 2011).

IAS 7 states that you have to prepare the statement of cash flows in the order of operating activities, then investing activities and then financing activities.

Step 1: Calculating cash flow from operating activities

You need to reconcile the operating profit to the net cash inflow from operating activities.

You're doing this calculation under the indirect method so you take profit from operations (operating profit) from the income statement and adjust this for the non-cash items you've included within this operating profit. See the earlier section 'Choosing between the direct and indirect method' for clarification of the indirect method.

First, take the income statement and find the 'profit from operations' line (sometimes known as *operating profit*), which shows a profit of $5,630. Included in this figure is stuff like depreciation and the loss on disposal of non-current assets – these aren't cash transactions, they're simply 'paper' transactions to arrive at an operating profit.

To reconcile operating profit to the net cash inflow from operating activities, you take your operating profit (profit from operations) and add back the *non-cash* transactions, such as depreciation and the loss on disposal of non-current assets. You then compare the current year's inventory, receivables and payables to the previous year and work out whether these have increased or decreased (check out the previous section 'Preparing the statement of cash flows' to see when you add or deduct increases or decreases in these amounts). Here's an example:

	$	$
Profit from operations		5,630
Adjustments for:		
Depreciation	2,172	
Loss on disposal of non-current assets	<u>183</u>	
		<u>2,355</u>
Operating cash flows before movements		
in working capital		**7,985**
Increase in inventories	(335)	
Increase in trade receivables	(266)	
Increase in trade payables	<u>84</u>	
		<u>(517)</u>
Cash generated by operations		**7,468**
Income taxes paid*	(854)	
Interest paid	<u>(800)</u>	
		<u>(1,654)</u>

Net cash from operating activities		5,814
* Workings for income taxes paid:		
Tax liability brought forward	(854)	
Tax charge per income statement	(919)	
Tax liability carried forward	<u>919</u>	
Balancing figure = tax paid	<u>854</u>	

You've done the hardest bit. After you reconcile your operating profit to net cash from operating activities, the other bits are fairly simple.

Step 2: Considering investing activities

Work out how much cash you've spent on investing activities (things like buying new non-current assets such as a van, or selling a non-current asset). Keep in mind the following:

- ✔ Increases in inventories mean that more cash is locked up in inventory, representing a cash outflow. So be sure to deduct cash outflows. You add decreases to operating profit to represent cash inflows because you've turned inventory into receivables (*trade receivables*, also known as debtors, are amounts owed to you by your customers) or receivables have paid you, representing an increase in cash.

- ✔ Increases in trade receivables mean less cash has been brought in from customers than the prior year, representing an outflow, so deduct these from operating profit.

- ✔ Decreases in trade receivables represent an inflow of cash because you've collected more cash in than the prior year so be sure to add decreases on to operating profit.

- ✔ Increases in *trade payables* (also known as creditors, these are amounts you owe to your suppliers) represent an inflow of cash because you've paid less to your suppliers than in the prior year, so you add increases in payables, but you deduct decreases because more cash has gone out to pay trade payables than the prior year.

Now you're ready to work out how much cash you've used in *investing activities*, like disposing of non-current assets and buying property, plant and equipment. You need to work out how much cash you've received in when you sell a non-current asset, and then work out how much cash you've paid out when you buy a non-current asset. Here's how it works. (I bring forward the net cash from operating activities to keep a running total.)

Net cash from operating activities		5,814
Investing activities		
Proceeds from disposal of non-current assets*	509	
Purchases of property, plant and equipment**	(13,646)	
Net cash used in investing activities		(13,137)
		(7,323)

* Workings for proceeds from disposal of non-current assets:

Book value of assets sold	692
Loss on sale per income statement	(183)
Proceeds = balancing figure	509

** Workings for purchases of property, plant and equipment:

Opening balance = \$19,100 less depreciation of (\$2,172) less net book value of assets sold (W2) (\$692) plus additions (?) = closing balance of \$29,882, therefore (?) = \$13,646.

Step 3: Focusing on financing activities

You're nearly there. The third step is to work out how much you've raised and spent in the year on *financing activities* – things like raising bank loans, or raising finance from a share issue. Here's the example. Again, I bring forward your running total so you know where you're up to.

		(7,323)
Financing activities		
New bank loans raised	3,000	
Proceeds from share issue*	4,500	
Dividends paid	(700)	
Net cash used in/from financing activities		**6,800**
		(523)

* Workings for proceeds from share issue

Share capital brought forward	(5,000)
Share premium brought forward	(1,000)
Share capital carried forward	8,000
Share premium carried forward	2,500
Balancing figure = proceeds	4,500

Step 4: Balancing the figures

Phew! You're not quite there yet, but nearly. Now you need to see whether the numbers actually balance. (I bet you can feel the nerves kicking in.)

Remember, the whole point of the statement of cash flows is to reconcile the opening cash position with the closing cash position in the statement of financial position to see how you've generated and spent cash. The opening cash at bank balance was $587 and you closed at the end of December 2011 with $64. Does the figure you've generated in Steps 1 to 3 balance with the figures from the statement of financial position for 2010 and for 2011? (See the introduction to this section 'Working through an example' for these statements.)

Net increase (decrease) in cash and cash equivalents	(523)
Cash and cash equivalents at beginning of year	**587**
Cash and cash equivalents at the end of the year	**64**

Deducting the cash and *cash equivalents* (short-term, highly liquid investments that are readily convertible into a known amount of cash) at the start of the year ($587) from the cash and cash equivalents at the end of the year ($64) exactly equals the net increase (decrease) in cash and cash equivalents ($523) that you calculated in Steps 1 to 3.

Hooray! So what you've done here is shown how your day-to-day operations have generated an operating profit and how this profit has contributed to the cash you've generated and spent.

Coming Up with Appropriate Accounting Policies

In the world of accountancy, you're not given free reign and told to come up with numbers that suit your particular circumstances. In fact, this couldn't be farther from the truth! IFRS is very much a principles-based framework and you have to stick to those principles because otherwise everyone would be in a complete mess. *Principles-based* (as opposed to rules-based) means that accountants make their own judgements. So an organisation must select suitable *accounting policies* (the specific principles, bases, conventions, rules and practices applied by an organisation in preparing and presenting its financial statements) that are in line with IFRS principles.

The good news is that the IFRS provides specific guidance on accounting policies in IAS 8 *Accounting Policies, Changes in Accounting Estimates and Errors*, and in this section I look at what IAS 8 has to say about selecting appropriate policies. (I address the other part of the IAS 8 – errors – in the later section 'Putting Mistakes Right').

Selecting policies best suited to individual circumstances

IAS 8 requires an organisation to select accounting policies appropriate to its individual circumstances, not simply because one policy may be easier to apply than another alternative policy (remember that you prepare general purpose financial statements for the user, not the management).

Here's an example of policy that focuses on the method of inventory valuation (IAS 2 *Inventories* deals with this subject; flick to Chapter 4 for more information on this topic). Badger Inc operates in the retail clothes industry and has a large retail outlet in the middle of a vibrant city centre. The directors of Badger Inc have decided that it would be a good idea to value their inventory (their stock) using the *retail method* (this method converts the selling price of a retailer's inventory back to cost by using a ratio known as the *cost-to-retail* ratio, which is calculated by dividing the cost of goods available for sale by the retail value of the goods available for sale), which gives a more relevant and reliable inventory valuation at their financial year-end. Badger Inc's *accounting policy* is therefore to use the retail method of inventory valuation (rather than other methods such as first-in, first-out (FIFO) or a weighted average basis of inventory valuation; see the later section 'Knowing how to change accounting policies' for definitions of these methods).

Some accounting policies are *critical* (and also require disclosure, by the way), which means that they've a material effect on the financial statements. A typical example of a critical policy is the policy of revenue (turnover) recognition. Usually, in a set of financial statements, revenue is the biggest number and is therefore vital, so organisations need to have an accounting policy for revenue recognition. Surely that's perfectly simple? Well, yes – but think beyond sales in general.

Different companies have different sorts of sales; a restaurant, for example, recognises a sale when the customer pays, so this accounting policy may be relatively straightforward to disclose in the financial statements. However, consider a mail-order company that may receive payments in advance before the customer receives her goods. Can the company recognise the payment in advance as a sale? Well, not really because the mail-order company has to prepare the goods for despatch and then despatch the goods, which may take a few weeks. So until the goods have been despatched and signed for by the customer, the mail-order company can't recognise the payment as a sale (the payment in advance is a liability by the mail-order company that represents the goods owed to the customer). The mail-order company's policy is therefore to recognise payments in advance as a liability until such time as the goods have been despatched and signed for by the customer, at which point the policy is to recognise the payment in advance as revenue.

You've a lot to think about when it comes to accounting policies, but the main objective is that the organisation selects the policies best suited to its individual circumstances.

Dealing with transactions and events not covered by an IFRS/IAS

Only two certainties exist in life: death and taxes! Life is otherwise uncertain, and sometimes unexpected things crop up that you have to deal with. Transactions and events that aren't covered by an IFRS/IAS are quite rare, but they do occur occasionally.

So, you've gone through the painstaking process of selecting your accounting policies, you're plodding along just nicely and then along comes a transaction or event that isn't covered by an accounting standard. How do you deal with that? Well, burying your head in the sand is one option, but that won't solve the problem. The good news is that IFRS does recognise that the path of true accounting doesn't always run smoothly and it tells you what to do when the unexpected lands on your desk. The bad news is that IFRS doesn't spoon-feed you the solution – you have to use the old grey matter.

When something isn't covered by an IFRS/IAS, management has to come up with an appropriate accounting policy to deal with the transaction or event. Now, this situation isn't an excuse to just write the transaction off to profit or loss or to ignore disclosure of a certain event; no, management develops an appropriate accounting policy in accordance with the IFRS *Conceptual Framework*.

Management needs to look at the transaction and consider whether it meets the definition of an asset, a liability, income, expense or equity and treat it accordingly. For an event, management needs to decipher the impact on the financial statements; for example, could it be an adjusting or a non-adjusting event (see the later section 'Adjusting your accounts')?

Knowing how to change accounting policies

Nothing stays the same and the world of accountancy moves at a fast pace – no sooner is there a new accounting standard than another one appears to replace it or it gets changed to meet the needs of the world. And even at individual company level, things change frequently. What people working in accountancy have to consider is the effect that such changes have on a company's accounting policies.

Consider a company that has always used UK GAAP to prepare its financial statements and has always used the *last-in first-out (LIFO)* inventory method (it sells, uses or disposes of the most recently produced items first) as a basis for arriving at a cost formula. This is permissible under the UK's accounting standard SSAP 9 *Stocks and Long-Term Contracts*, though admittedly SSAP 9 doesn't really like this method of cost formula. The company has now decided to report under IFRS, but immediately the company stumbles upon a problem. Under IAS 2 *Inventories*, a company is prohibited from using LIFO as a cost formula. It can only use *first-in first out* (FIFO; inventory produced or acquired first are sold, used or disposed of first) or *weighted average cost* (which divides the total cost of goods available for sale by the total amount of goods from opening inventory and purchases). As a consequence, the company has to change its accounting policy to comply with IFRS.

So, as you can see, change can substantially affect your accounting policies – and not just mandatory change. A company reporting under IFRS is required to change its accounting policies if the revised policies are going to result in more relevant and reliable information being provided in the general purpose financial statements. Don't forget – IFRS is all about the user!

Changing a company's accounting policy can be a bit fiddly. This is because you have to apply the change in policy retrospectively. In other words, you've got to go back to the earliest set of financial statements presented and apply the change to those, so it looks like the revised policy has always been in existence. Boo! So if you've two years' financial statements presented (say 31 December 2011 and 31 December 2010), you go back to the 2010 financial statements and restate these. In some circumstances, a company may have three years' financial statements presented; again, you go back to the earliest period reported (so the 2009 accounts if three years are presented).

The reason you have to go back to the earliest period presented in the financial statements is to achieve consistency. Think about how inconsistent it would look if you had a closing inventory figure in the current year valued under FIFO, but in the previous year it was valued under weighted average cost. That's hardly a basis for users to make rational decisions on.

Here's an example in practice of how you change your policy. In 2010, the Big Bed Company valued its inventory at $10,000 using the average cost method. But, during 2011, the directors decided that FIFO would produce more relevant and reliable accounting information, so they decided to adopt FIFO for inventory valuation. This is a change in accounting policy, so Bob, the company accountant, has to apply the change retrospectively (the financial year-end is December 2011). Bob has calculated that if FIFO had been used last year, the inventory valuation would have been $9,000 (instead of $10,000). To apply the change retrospectively, he reduces (that is, credits) the inventory in the 2010 financial statements by $1,000. Clearly, if the Big Bed Company had used FIFO last year the profit would have been $1,000 less, so the corresponding debit would go to *retained earnings* (net profit left in the company from accounting period to accounting period). Because the closing balances in 2010 become the opening balances in 2011, Bob has to reduce opening inventory (that is, credit) and debit retained earnings because otherwise the opening inventory and retained earnings won't agree with last year's closing inventory and retained earnings.

Fiddly? Yes, but not rocket science and the key is to remember the reason that you're applying the change retrospectively: to achieve consistency.

When you change an accounting policy, you must make various disclosures in the financial statements themselves such as:

- ✔ The nature of the change in accounting policy

- ✔ The reasons why the new policy provides more relevant and reliable information

- ✔ The amount of the adjustment for each financial statement line item

- ✔ The amount of the adjustment relating to periods before those presented (to the extent practicable)

- ✔ (For each component of equity) the effect of changes in accounting policies, disclosed for each prior period and the beginning of the period

Understanding estimation techniques

Hand in hand with accounting policies are *estimation techniques*: management's best estimate of various things in the financial statements, such as estimating how long an item of machinery used in the business will last (how long to *depreciate* the machine over, which means writing off the cost over its estimated useful life).

You can handle estimation techniques really easily, but like everything to do with general purpose financial statements, they must be appropriate to a company's individual circumstances. It wouldn't exactly be reasonable to depreciate a company van over 50 years when (realistically) 3 to 5 years is more like a best estimate.

In the previous section, 'Knowing how to change accounting policies', I explain that you apply changes to accounting policy retrospectively. But a change in estimation technique is *not* a change in accounting policy. As a result of this, you apply changes in estimation techniques *prospectively* (going forward).

So how do you differentiate between a change in estimation technique and a change in accounting policy?

Depreciation is an estimation of how long an item of non-current asset is going to last – hence depreciation is an estimation technique. Management may think that a computer should last for three years, but it may only last for two. Changes in depreciation rates are the most common change in estimation technique. If a company decides that changing the depreciation of its plant from five years on a straight-line basis to three years on a straight-line basis is a more appropriate consumption of its plant (and therefore providing more relevant and reliable information), then the company applies this change prospectively because this is a change in estimation technique – it is still consuming the original cost of the asset, but at a faster pace than originally anticipated.

A change in accounting policy, however, typically occurs when a company changes from valuing its inventory from weighted average cost to FIFO. Here the policy of accounting has changed and to achieve consistency, management must go back to the earliest period presented and restate the company's previous year's inventory valuation to what it should be under FIFO. This is so that the financial statements are consistent because how odd would it look having two inventory valuations presented that have both been calculated under different valuation methods?

Putting Mistakes Right

Everyone makes mistakes – in life, and so of course in accountancy. What's important is both learning from those mistakes and trying as hard as you can to put them right. IFRS recognises that accountants make mistakes and therefore it covers the issue within IAS 8.

As well as mistakes, you have adjustments to make. Financial statements always contain figures that are subject to varying degrees of estimation, such as inventory valuations, provisions, accruals and costs and revenues relating to construction contracts. In many cases, some may be under- or over-provided for in the current and/or previous year's financial statements. If the under- or over-provisions are insignificant (that is, immaterial or trivial), then you simply adjust for the under- or over-provision in the current year and carry on as normal. But if they're significant, you need to take action.

Correcting mistakes in previous years' accounts

Unfortunately, when mistakes or under- or over-provisions occur, you can't always just adjust for them in the current year and carry on as normal. Sometimes a mistake is so significant to the financial statements that it would be misleading to the user to simply correct it and not draw the user's attention to the error. You make such a disclosure in the notes to the financial statements. These notes break down the information in the primary financial statements (statement of comprehensive income, statement of financial position, statement of cash flows and statement of changes in equity) and tell the reader extra things about the company.

Imagine that you work for an accountancy firm that's putting together the end-of-year 2011 financial statements for a company called Lovely Lilos. A different firm prepared the 2010 financial statements, and you discover that the other firm made a mistake: it omitted the sales invoices from the last four months (all of which remained unpaid as at 31 December 2010) in the 2010 financial statements. You've totalled the sales invoices up and found that 2010 revenue was understated by $40,000 (which is significant to the financial statements). You can't just uplift 2011 revenue by $40,000. Instead, you have to do more or less the same as you do when you instigate a change in accounting policy (see the earlier section 'Knowing how to change accounting policies'). You have to go back to the previous year and adjust the financial statements to reflect how they should have looked had the mistake not been made. So you go back to the 2010 financial statements and add (credit) $40,000 to the retained earnings and increase (debit) trade receivables by $40,000. You increase retained earnings because the profits in 2010 should have been $40,000 higher than originally reported. (Note: this simple illustration ignores the tax effects of such an omission.)

Disclosing your mistakes in the accounts

The user of the financial statements has to be made aware of all material issues relating to the financial statements. Prior-period errors are no exception. Where you correct errors or under- or over-provisions by way of a prior-period adjustment, you have to make relevant disclosures to enable the user to understand the significance of the prior-period error and the effect such an error has had, not only on the prior year, but also on the current year (significant errors can have a double whammy by increasing/reducing retained earnings (and net assets) accordingly).

IAS 8 requires that when you correct a prior-period error, you note the following in the disclosure notes in the financial statement:

✔ The nature of the prior-period error

✔ To the extent practicable, the amount of the correction for each financial statement line item affected

✔ The amount of the correction at the beginning of the earliest prior period presented

✔ If retrospective restatement is impracticable for a particular prior period, the circumstances that led to the existence of that condition, and a description of how and from when the error has been corrected

Dealing With Events After the Reporting Period

In this section I look at IAS 10 *Events After the Reporting Period*, which deals specifically with events (favourable to the business, or not) that occur between the reporting date (the year-/period-end) and the date on which the financial statements are approved.

Adjusting your accounts

Bolting the door after the horse is gone is pointless, right? Well, in the world of accountancy you do, actually, sometimes go back and apply present understanding to the past.

Picture the scene. The clock strikes midnight and the office is empty, but you're putting the finishing touches on the final draft year-end financial statements for the company, XYZ. You've been slaving over the figures for the last month to get them ready for the Board meeting in three weeks. You're feeling pretty good because results are good, and so profit-related bonuses look healthy. Job done, and you're off for a well-deserved fortnight in the Bahamas.

You arrive back in the office after your holiday; everyone's looking extremely sombre, but you put it down to the Monday blues. You check your emails and you find one there from the finance director requiring an urgent meeting. Off you go to the meeting.

The finance director tells you that a major customer has gone into liquidation. This customer owes XYZ $100,000 and this amount is extremely material to the financial statements. The financial director asks you to do everything in your power to make sure that this year's accounts don't take the hit of a bad debt provision.

You're facing Events After the Reporting Period, which calls into play IAS 10. The question you face now is: do you need to adjust your financial statements in light of this information? Is this an adjusting event or a non-adjusting event?

✔ An *adjusting event* occurs between the reporting date (the year-end) and the date on which the financial statements are approved and authorised for issue that *provides evidence of conditions that existed at the reporting date*. You have to adjust the financial statements accordingly. Examples include

- Discovery of fraud or errors that show the financial statements to be incorrect at the reporting date

- Settlement of a court case after the reporting date that confirms the company had a present obligation at the reporting date

- Receipt of information after the reporting date that indicates that the sale of inventory after the reporting date was below cost price (hence a write-down of inventory would be required)

✔ A *non-adjusting event* is the opposite of an adjusting event. Such events arose after the reporting period but didn't exist at the year-end. By definition, you don't have to adjust financial statements to take account of non-adjusting events, which include

- Announcing a plan after the reporting date to restructure the business

- A change in tax rates or laws after the reporting date

- Commencing major legal cases arising solely out of events that occurred after the year-end

In the example, a major customer has gone into liquidation while owing a material sum. The bankruptcy of a customer so soon after the reporting period is a condition that existed at the reporting date, and is now evidence that at the reporting date XYZ wasn't going to get paid from the customer because of the customer's financial difficulties. So you have to adjust the XYZ financial statements to take account of this potential bad debt (bad news for the financial director). If you failed to make a provision, you'd be overstating XYZ's current assets (because trade receivables would still recognise the bad debt) and profitability (because you'd make no provision against the $100,000 bad debt). Not only would this be misleading to the user of the financial statements, but the auditors would also have a problem with XYZ not making a provision against the bad debt and they would almost certainly make reference to this issue in their auditors' report – which would not be doing XYZ any favours at all. This is a typical adjusting event.

Although you only need to adjust for adjusting events, you need to disclose in the notes to the financial statements the following for *both* non-adjusting and adjusting events:

- The circumstances and nature of the event
- An estimate of the financial effect, or a statement that estimating the financial effect isn't possible

Dishing out dividends

Shareholders are the people who own the company. *Directors* manage the company on behalf of the shareholders and the directors prepare the financial statements, but the shareholders expect a return on their investment (as would anyone who'd invested money into a company). The shareholders' return on their investment is given in the form of dividends.

Dividends are appropriations of profit and are always issued out of post-tax profits (the tax authorities won't let you give dividends out of pre-tax profits, before they've had a slice of the pie). The company can also pay dividends out of *accumulated profits*: profits that have been made in previous years and have built up. So it may be the case that, in a particular year, the company has made a post-tax loss but has still paid out dividends. Provided the company has enough in accumulated profits (retained earnings), this isn't really a problem.

The issue for financial reporting purposes concerns the timing of the proposed dividend. Consider the two examples below:

- **Bricks and Mortar Inc** has a year-end of 31 December 2011 and is in the process of preparing its financial statements for the year then ended. Today's date is 4 April 2012 and the draft figures have been more or less finalised and the AGM is about to take place. In that meeting, the directors have decided to declare a dividend in the financial statements for the year ended 31 December 2011 amounting to $4 per share and this dividend is to be included in the 31 December 2011 year-end financial statements.

- **Sand and Ballast Inc** also has a year-end of 31 December 2011 and produces monthly management accounts, which the Board discusses. The November 2011 accounts showed a healthy profit and the directors decided on 10 December 2011 that a dividend should be proposed in the year-end financial statements of $5 per share because there would be more than sufficient profit to meet the payment of this dividend to the shareholders.

Bricks and Mortar Inc has approved the paying of a dividend after the year-end. The problem here is that there was no constructive obligation at the year-end to pay the dividend (a *constructive obligation* arises by way of a Board resolution that is documented and approved). Therefore, in this example, because no constructive obligation arises (as defined in IAS 37 *Provisions, Contingent Liabilities and Contingent Assets*; see Chapter 7), Bricks and Mortar Inc can't go back and retrospectively recognise the dividend in the year-end financial statements. The dividend must be recognised in the 2012 financial statements.

Sand and Ballast Inc has foreseen that profitability is more than sufficient in order to pay a dividend and they've passed the proposal in the Board meeting on 10 December 2011 (well before the year-end of 31 December 2011). A constructive obligation (as defined in IAS 37) arises because the passing of this resolution in the AGM gives rise to a liability to the shareholders. As a result, Sand and Ballast Inc is able to include the dividends in the financial statements as at 31 December 2011.

Whether you can include dividends in the financial statements at, or after, the year-end depends on whether a constructive obligation has been met. In other words, dividends declared after the reporting date (in the eyes of IAS 10) are, in fact, non-adjusting events (see the previous section 'Adjusting your accounts').

Approving your accounts

The final stage in the financial statement preparation process is the approval of the financial statements, and in many cases the signing of an auditors' report by the company's external audit firm.

You may think it obvious that the director(s) signs the financial statements to authorise them for issue and dates them. But don't forget about IAS 10's requirement to consider all events, both favourable and unfavourable, before approving the financial statements.

Given the definition of events after the reporting period, the date on which the financial statements are authorised for issue is clearly important. IAS 10 recognises two particular instances that give rise to differences in the meaning of *authorised for issue*:

 ✔ An organisation may be required to submit its financial statements to its shareholders for approval (as in France, for example) after the financial statements have been issued. In such cases, the financial statements are considered authorised for issue *on the date of issue*, not the date when the shareholders approve them.

✔ The management of an organisation may be required to issue its financial statements to a supervisory Board (made up solely of non-executive directors) for approval. Under IAS 10, such financial statements are considered authorised for issue *when management authorises them for issue to the supervisory Board.*

So, you can see that the date on which the financial statements are signed and dated is fairly important. But what if a company re-issues financial statements because of errors? It may well be that a mistake is discovered fairly soon after the financial statements have been authorised for issue, as opposed to when the next year's financial statements are being prepared. (I cover error correction in the section 'Putting Mistakes Right', earlier in the chapter.)

If an organisation re-issues its financial statements because of error, or even to include events that occurred after the financial statements were originally authorised for issue, clearly you need a new date of authorisation for issue. The financial statements must then properly reflect all adjusting and non-adjusting events (as defined in IAS 10), which also includes those that occurred during the interim period between the original and the new date of authorisation.

Considering whether the company is a going concern

The legwork has been done, the financial statements have finally been audited, the tax provisions have been calculated and agreed and the shareholders are laughing all the way to the bank following the approval of their dividend before the year-end. You're not quite at the end of the story, though! Management must look to the future (that is at least, but not limited to, 12 months from the reporting date) and decide whether the company can continue in business for the foreseeable future or not (in other words whether the company is a *going concern*).

So what's going concern all about then?

To be classed as a *going concern*, management must presume that a company is able to continue in business for the foreseeable future. IAS 1 *Presentation of Financial Statements* considers *the foreseeable future* to be a period of 12 months after the reporting date, though in many jurisdictions this period is 12 months from the date of approval of the financial statements. Some countries require you to do the going concern assessment for a period of 12 months from your year-end. Other countries (like the UK) require you to do a going concern assessment for a period of 12 months from the date the financial statements are approved.

Under IAS 1, companies must prepare financial statements on a going concern basis, provided that management doesn't intend to liquidate the organisation, or to cease trading, or has no realistic alternative but to do so. If management is aware of *material uncertainties* (significant events that may occur in the future) that could cast significant doubt upon the organisation's ability to continue as a going concern, the financial statements must include those uncertainties. For example, say that the organisation is dependent on a large contract being renewed and the renewal date is some months after the accounts are approved. You disclose the uncertainty in the notes to the financial statements, because if the contract isn't renewed, the company may be forced to close.

In the event that financial statements are *not* prepared on a going concern basis, you disclose that fact, together with the reasons why the organisation isn't considered a going concern and the basis on which the financial statements are prepared – for example, the *break-up basis*, which means that you restate all assets at the amounts they could be realistically sold for (*net realisable value*) and reclassify all non-current assets and liabilities to current.

The going concern presumption is an assertion made by the management that the company is to continue in business for the foreseeable future. In assessing the going concern presumption, management need to consider

- ✔ The economic conditions the organisation is operating in
- ✔ The state of the company's cash flow
- ✔ Whether borrowing facilities are going to be renewed
- ✔ Whether external factors such as interest rates or customers' abilities to pay are likely to affect the company as a going concern

A company can't prepare its financial statements on the going concern basis if events after the reporting period indicate that the going concern assumption isn't appropriate.

Various conditions may indicate that a company isn't a going concern, including:

- ✔ A net liability or net current liability position on the statement of financial position
- ✔ Adverse key financial ratios
- ✔ Arrears or discontinued dividends

- ✔ Deteriorating relations with suppliers

- ✔ Inability to comply with terms of loan agreements

- ✔ Loss of major market, franchise, license or principal supplier

- ✔ Major debt repayments falling due where refinancing is necessary to the organisation's continued existence

- ✔ Major restructuring of debt

- ✔ Significant operating losses or significant deterioration in the value of assets used to generate cash flows

This list is by no means exhaustive: many other factors may indicate that a company isn't a going concern.

Here are two examples to help you understand going concern.

Mark's Mechanics has been in business for 40 years and has always been profitable. The financial statements for the year-end 31 December 2011 have been prepared and are going to be approved on 17 April 2012. On 16 April 2012, Mark received a huge contract to service the fleet of vehicles for a large, well-known supermarket chain. This contract is highly profitable and is going to last Mark five years.

In this example, no going concern issues exist: the company is profitable and has secured a large contract for additional services for a period longer than 12 months (subject to any national requirements that require otherwise).Chris's Caravans has also been in business for 40 years but over the last three years demand for caravans has fallen because of the recession. The financial statements for the year-end 30 April 2012 are about to be prepared. On 4 April 2012, Chris's Caravans received notification that its major customer operating in the holiday home industry has ceased to trade because of financial difficulties. The customer owes Chris's Caravans $175,000 and the liquidator isn't hopeful that the debt is going to be recovered. The directors of Chris's Caravans have decided that they've no alternative but to close down.

In this example, you'd prepare the financial statements of Chris's Caravans on the break-up basis. You reclassify all non-current assets as current assets (because they will be sold off to generate some cash). You class all non-current liabilities as current liabilities and disclose that the going concern presumption isn't appropriate and that the financial statements are prepared on the break-up basis.

Chapter 3

Taking the Plunge: Adopting IFRS for the First Time

In This Chapter

▶ Knowing the IFRS policies and how they can differ from domestic ones

▶ Seeing what to put in the opening statement of financial position

▶ Examining some exemptions

▶ Making the statement of compliance with confidence

. . . .

Many countries still use their own domestic accounting standards (Generally Accepted Accounting Practices, or GAAP) but are looking at the potential to change over to IFRS. Why? Because more and more countries are using IFRS, and that means if your country's on board, you can access more capital markets. IFRS have been created to produce high-quality financial information that facilitates investment and other economic decisions across borders, resulting in market efficiency and a reduction in the cost of capital.

The standard that deals with first-time adoption of IFRS is IFRS 1, aptly named *First-time Adoption of International Financial Reporting Standards.* The principal aim of IFRS 1 is to ensure that a company adopting IFRS for the first time produces financial statements, and interim financial statements, that provide high-quality and transparent information where the cost of producing this information doesn't outweigh the benefits.

When a country adopts IFRS as its financial reporting framework for the first time, the chances are that all the companies within that country must switch to IFRS. Sometimes, though, only certain companies have to switch. For example, when the EU adopted IFRS in 2005, only *listed companies* (those that trade their shares on a recognised stock market) had to report under IFRS, though since 2007 this has been rolled out to those companies listed on the Alternative Investment Market.

So, with so many countries moving to IFRS, accounting professionals need to know how to adopt IFRS for the first time – and that's the focus of this chapter. I take you through the steps, from examining the issues you need to address in terms of your accounting policies and getting your opening statement of financial position right, to considering some exemptions that may be of use to you. Then I round off by helping you ensure that the auditors give you a cheery thumbs-up on your first IFRS financial statements.

Checking That Your Accounting Policies Fit with IFRS

When a company adopts IFRS for the first time, it has to produce an opening statement of financial position under IFRS. But in order to do that, companies first need to examine their accounting policies. Accounting policies form the basis of how financial statements are prepared, and I look at these in Chapter 2. The issue facing first-time adopters is whether their policies are IFRS compliant, because what may be permissible in domestic GAAP may not be permissible in IFRS. Some accounting policies may need to change.

A company can't mix and match domestic GAAP with IFRS. If a company moves over to IFRS it does so in its entirety. If a company isn't mandated to report under IFRS, but wishes to do so anyway, it needs to consider the appropriateness of IFRS to its particular circumstances because you can't go back to domestic standards if things don't quite go according to plan – the move is one-way, I'm afraid.

Recognising how IFRS differs from domestic GAAP

Table 3-1 outlines some of the differences between policies under domestic GAAP and IFRS.

Table 3-1	Policies: GAAP versus IFRS	
Policy	*Under Some GAAP*	*Under IFRS*
Recognition of a defined benefit pension plan surplus or deficit	You can't bring a defined benefit pension plan surplus or deficit onto the statement of financial position.	IAS 19 (see Chapter 7) requires that you recognise such a surplus or deficit.
Recognition of deferred tax assets or liabilities	You don't recognise a deferred tax asset or liability.	IAS 12 (see Chapter 6) requires that you recognise deferred tax assets and liabilities.
Recognition of intangible non-current assets (those non-current assets that don't have a physical form – in other words, you can't kick them)	You write off the cost of intangible assets to the income statement.	IAS 38 (see Chapter 4) requires that you recognise items of expenditure as an intangible non-current asset if it meets the recognition criteria.
Share-based payment transactions	You don't recognise the expense arising on a share-based payment transaction.	IFRS 2 (see Chapter 9) requires a company dealing in share-based payments to reflect the effect of such payments in its income statement.
Provisions for liabilities when a legal or *constructive* (an obligation to pay that arises out of conduct and intent rather than contractual) obligation exists	You don't recognise a 'constructive' obligation, only a legal obligation.	IAS 37 (see Chapter 7) requires you to recognise both legal and constructive obligations that fulfil the recognitions criteria of a provision.
Assets and liabilities in respect of finance leases	You don't recognise finance leases and instead write off all leasing payments to the income statement.	IAS 17 (see Chapter 6) requires that you capitalise (bring on to the statement of financial position) an asset obtained under a finance lease (where the risks and rewards of ownership of the asset subjected to the lease pass to the lessee) and recognise a corresponding lease creditor in the statement of financial position.

(continued)

Table 3-1 *(continued)*

Policy	Under Some GAAP	Under IFRS
Borrowing costs	You can choose not to capitalise borrowing costs (interest charges on a loan) on qualifying assets (those that take a substantial amount of time to construct).	IAS 23 (see Chapter 5) requires you to capitalise the costs.
Transaction costs of buying another company	You can include transaction costs (like legal fees and accountancy fees) for buying another company in the cost of the transaction (the domestic policy sees the costs as 'directly attributable' to the cost of the acquisition).	IFRS 3 (Chapters 10 and 11) requires that you expense transaction costs immediately.
Statement of cash flows	You can be exempt from preparing and presenting a statement of cash flows in the financial statements. (This is the case in the UK for small companies.)	IAS 1 (Chapter 2) requires you to produce a statement of cash flows.
Valuing inventories	You can use the last-in, first-out (LIFO) method of valuing the cost of inventories (you sell, use or dispose of the most recently produced items first).	IAS 2 (Chapter 4) only permits the other cost valuation models – first-in, first-out (FIFO; you sell, use or dispose of the first produced items first) and weighted average cost (calculated by taking the cost of goods available for sale and dividing this figure into the total amount of opening inventory plus purchases).

Be careful when reviewing accounting policies on transition from domestic GAAP to IFRS because many more little differences exist than I have room to outline here. Remember, getting the accounting wrong can be quite embarrassing and could get you into trouble with the authorities!

Changing policies as required

So you've gone through the painstaking process of identifying your allowable and disallowable policies and have established those policies that you're going to continue using and those that you have to change in order to comply with IFRS. The question is, what to do with the stuff that's not allowable? You need to follow these three steps:

1. **Understand how the initial accounting affected the financial statements.**

2. **Consider what the treatment under IFRS should have been.**

3. **Make the required changes.**

Bright Sparks Inc is a nationwide firm of electricians with a year-end of 31 December 2011. The 2010 financial statements were prepared under domestic GAAP. GAAP permits staff training costs to be capitalised in the statement of financial position as an intangible non-current asset. Bright Sparks has decided to report under IFRS and is in the process of preparing its opening statement of financial position as at 1 January 2010.

The issue that Bright Sparks face is that it can't capitalise such training costs under the provisions in IAS 38 *Intangible Assets* (which I cover in Chapter 4); instead, they must be written off to profit or loss as they're incurred. IFRS 1 requires a company to de-recognise items as assets or liabilities if IFRS doesn't permit such recognition. In this instance, therefore, Bright Sparks must de-recognise and expense the training costs.

When you recognise assets and liabilities on adoption of IFRS, there may well be changes in the values of these assets and liabilities because of the changes in the accounting policy for the relevant assets and liabilities. You need to recognise any changes in these values in retained earnings. For example, before you adopted IFRS you may well have accounted for your building in the statement of financial position using the *revaluation model* (showing the building at each reporting date at its fair value). But when you adopt IFRS, you may decide that this model doesn't show enough relevant and reliable information, so you switch to showing the value of the building in the statement of financial position using the *depreciated historic cost model* (writing the cost of the building off over the building's estimated useful life).

Demystifying retained earnings

Profit is the residual of income less expenses. *Retained profit* is income less expenses, less income tax expense and less any dividends paid to shareholders. The balance left over is then put into *retained earnings* – the bit you see in the statement of financial position in equity (shareholders' funds).

Think about what happens every year – a company sells products or services, it incurs expenses and throughout the year the income statement builds up. Unlike the statement of financial position, the income statement shows the trading activity throughout, from the start of the accounting period to the end of the accounting period. The statement of financial position is only a snapshot of the state of the company's affairs as at the close of business on the day of the year-end. On the first day of the next financial year, the income statement is cleared out and the retained profit is put into retained earnings and the process starts all over again.

This is perfectly acceptable. When you adopt IFRS for the first time, you aren't under any obligation to make sure that your IFRS policies are as close as possible to what you did under your old accounting standards. The authorities don't mind a first-time adopter switching. But you need to take into consideration the requirements in IAS 8 *Accounting Policies, Changes in Accounting Estimates and Errors* (I look at IAS 8 issues in Chapter 2). You also need to move the balance on the revaluation reserve account, which is shown in the equity section of the statement of financial position, into retained earnings (shareholders' funds) because you won't be using the revaluation reserve account any more under the depreciated historic cost model.

Therefore, if domestic GAAP permits an asset or liability, but IFRS says the opposite and requires the transaction to otherwise be expensed, you remove any such assets and liabilities from the statement of financial position and put them into retained earnings after you switch over to IFRS (see the sidebar 'Demystifying retained earnings'). Profits in the year the transaction occurred reduce (or losses increase) and such reductions and increases increase (or reduce, in the case of losses) the value of retained earnings. By debiting retained earnings with the disallowable asset, or crediting retained earnings with the disallowable liability, you're effectively increasing or reducing the value of retained earnings (retained profits).

Disclosing the accounting policies

A crucial part of a set of general purpose financial statements is the notes to them, which are required under IAS 1 *Presentation of Financial Statements* (see Chapter 1). One of the disclosures within the notes is the company's accounting policies in areas like revenue recognition policies, inventory valuation policies and accounting for non-current assets. The policies take prominence because they're so important: they form the basis of how the company accounts for stuff.

IAS 8 *Accounting Policies, Changes in Accounting Estimates and Errors* deals with accounting policies, and I cover these policies in Chapter 2. IAS 8 defines accounting policies as the specific principles, bases, conventions, rules and practices applied by an organisation in preparing and presenting its financial statements. You can see from the IAS 8 definition that the selection and application of accounting policies is absolutely critical in the preparation of financial statements. IAS 8 and IAS 1, therefore, have a close relationship; IAS 8 deals explicitly with accounting policies, but IAS 1 deals with the overarching or general principles.

Many companies have to disclose their accounting policies relating to the following:

- **Deferred tax:** How deferred tax is recognised and the basis on which it is recognised.

- **Financial instruments:** How financial instruments are classified as *debt* or *equity instruments* (financial instruments recognised as liabilities or in the equity section of the statement of financial position) among other things.

- **Hire purchase and leasing commitments:** Disclosing the company's policy for recognising finance leases and *depreciating* (writing off the cost of the asset over its economic useful life) assets obtained under such leases.

- **Inventories (stock):** How the company values its inventories and how it arrives at *net realisable value* (how much a company could get for an item(s) of inventory).

- **Non-current assets and depreciation policies:** How the company recognises and measures its non-current assets and the rates at which these assets are being depreciated.

- **Pension plans:** How the company accounts for company pension plans, such as defined contribution plans or defined benefit plans (see Chapter 7).

- **Revenue (sales):** How and when the company recognises revenue and whether this revenue is stated net of any sales taxes and discounts.

IAS 1 only requires that a company discloses the *significant* accounting policies in the notes to the financial statements. Therefore, only disclose those accounting policies that are fundamental in the preparation of your financial statements. If the company doesn't have any non-current assets that are subject to finance leases, it doesn't have to disclose the accounting policy for the treatment of finance leases. You don't disclose every conceivable accounting policy because doing so confuses the users of the financial statements.

Preparing and Adjusting Your Opening Statement of Financial Position

After you've got your policies done and dusted, it's time to get into the nitty gritty of IFRS 1 as you prepare your opening statement of financial position (balance sheet). As a first-time adopter, you previously prepared financial statements under your own domestic GAAP. Now you need to go back to the *earliest* period presented in the financial statements that you are preparing (remember, normally a set of financial statements shows the current year's results and the previous year's results as comparatives) and rework those financial statements so that they comply with IFRS.

The objective is that you prepare the current year and the previous comparative year under the same accounting framework. When you're looking at a set of general purpose financial statements prepared to IFRS, you often see two sets of data. You see the current year's results and the preceding year's results, because IAS 1 requires comparative information. If you think about it logically, if the preceding year's financial statements were prepared under domestic GAAP and the current year's prepared under IFRS, they're not exactly going to be comparable, are they? Don't forget that some GAAPs permit certain accounting treatments that may not be acceptable under IFRS. Therefore, to achieve consistency and comparability, the comparative year is always restated to IFRS.

The following sections take you through what you need to know to prepare the opening statement.

Getting your head around the date of transition

You prepare the opening statement of financial position as at the date of transition to IFRS. You can easily confuse the date of transition to be the year-end in which the financial statements are prepared, but this is not the case at all! The *date of transition* is the beginning of the *earliest* comparative period for which the company presents full comparative information under IFRS.

Getting the date of transition to IFRS right is extremely important because if you don't, the financial statements are basically meaningless. This may have all sorts of repercussions, particularly when the auditors arrive. Under IFRS 1, a company's *first* IFRS financial statements must include at least:

> ✔ Three statements of financial position
>
> ✔ Two statements of comprehensive income
>
> ✔ Two separate income statements (if presented)
>
> ✔ Two statements of cash flows
>
> ✔ Two statements of changes in equity

So, as you can see, you must get the date right given the level of information required in the first IFRS financial statements.

Here are two examples to show how you determine the date of transition.

Inner Health Limited is a health food chain that sells health food and vitamin supplements to the general public and started in business on 1 January 2010. It currently reports under UK GAAP. The company's year-end is 31 December and it prepared its December 2010 financial statements to UK GAAP. However, on 1 January 2011, Inner Health decided to use IFRS for the accounts for the year-end 31 December 2011.

Three statements of financial position have to be prepared in a first set of IFRS financial statements, therefore the date of transition is the first day of the *earliest* period presented, so if Inner Health Limited had started in business on 1 January 2007, its date of transition would be 1 January 2009 because it would present the 31 December 2011, 2010 and 2009 statements of financial position in its first set of IFRS financial statements. The date of transition to IFRS is the beginning of the *earliest* comparative period for which the company presents full comparative information under IFRS. The date of transition to IFRS for Inner Health Limited is therefore 1 January 2010.

Sporty Kids Inc sells a range of sports accessories and clothing aimed at children. It has a reporting date of 31 July and local legislation requires two comparative accounting periods to be presented in the year-end financial statements for the first accounting period starting on or after 1 January 2010. In this respect, the first IFRS financial statements are for the period ending on 31 July 2011. The date of transition to IFRS is 1 August 2008, which is the beginning of the earliest comparative period included in the company's IFRS financial statements.

Recognising assets and liabilities

When a company switches to IFRS for the first time, it may have to recognise additional assets and liabilities so that the financial statements are IFRS compliant (Table 3-1 shows some examples of where this is the case). You make adjustments in the opening statement of financial position under IFRS to bring in additional assets and liabilities as required in order that the financial statements give relevant and reliable information to the user.

A company can't make the *explicit and unreserved* statement of compliance with IFRS in their financial statements if they don't comply in *all* respects with IFRS, hence a company must be careful to make sure that its IFRS financial statements are *fully* compliant.

When you have to recognise an asset that was previously written off to the income statement as an expense under domestic standards, you debit the relevant asset account in the statement of financial position and credit retained earnings.

When you have to recognise a liability that was previously written off to the income statement (for example if you received a grant and wrote the full grant off to income under domestic standards), you credit the relevant liability account in the statement of financial position and debit retained earnings.

Here's an example of how you recognise assets and liabilities in the opening statement of financial position. Whitaker Enterprises Limited has decided to switch from domestic GAAP to IFRS as at 1 January 2011 and is preparing the opening statement of financial position as at that date. The following information is relevant to the opening statement of financial position:

- ✔ Under its previous GAAP, Whitaker didn't make a provision for a liability amounting to $25,000 in the financial statements because previous GAAP didn't recognise the concept of a constructive obligation.

- ✔ Whitaker had included advertising expenditure amounting to $10,000 in the valuation of inventories as at 1 January 2011.

- ✔ The company had built its new head office itself but hadn't included legal fees directly attributable to the cost of the building (amounting to $26,000) because previous GAAP didn't allow the capitalisation of such costs.

In preparing their opening statement of financial position, Whitaker Enterprises must change its accounting policies to conform to IFRS as follows:

- ✔ The opening IFRS statement of financial position must contain a provision (a liability) for $25,000 because IAS 37 *Provisions, Contingent Liabilities and Contingent Assets* requires such a provision to be made when a constructive obligation arises.

- ✔ IAS 2 *Inventories* specifically disallows general administrative overheads, which advertising is, so Whitaker Enterprises must remove the cost of this advertising from the inventories valuation.

> ✔ IAS 16 *Property, Plant and Equipment* requires the capitalisation of all costs directly attributable to bringing an asset to its working condition for its intended use, and therefore Whitaker Enterprises should capitalise the legal fees of $26,000 in the opening statement of financial position.

Reclassifying assets and liabilities

Recognising and de-recognising assets and liabilities (see the previous section) is only part of the equation in IFRS – you also have to consider reclassifying assets and liabilities. The following list goes through some of the more common reclassifications that may be required in your opening statement of financial position under IFRS.

✔ **Dividends:** Under the provisions in IAS 10 *Events After the Reporting Period* (see Chapter 2), companies aren't allowed to recognise dividends paid to the shareholders as a liability in the current period if the dividends were declared, or proposed, after the year-end. If you recognised such liabilities under domestic GAAP, you must reverse them in the opening IFRS statement of financial position.

✔ **Identifiable intangible non-current assets:** During the course of a business combination, you may have to reclassify certain identifiable items of intangible non-current assets to goodwill because they fail to meet the definition of an intangible asset under the provisions in IAS 38 *Intangible Assets* (see Chapter 4 for more on intangible non-current assets). It may also be the case that the opposite adjustment is needed where you have to reclassify intangible assets *from* goodwill to other items of intangible assets because they do qualify as an intangible asset under IAS 38.

✔ **Offsetting:** Some domestic GAAPs do allow you to *offset* (counterbalance or net) assets and liabilities or income and expenses. However, IFRS rarely permits the offsetting of such assets and liabilities or income and expenses.

It's not common for assets and liabilities, or income and expenses, to be offset because IAS 1 *Presentation of Financial Statements* doesn't look upon such a practice favourably. IAS 20 *Accounting for Government Grants and Disclosure of Government Assistance* permits grants to be offset against the cost of non-current assets, but some countries prohibit this treatment in company legislation. I discuss grants in Chapter 5.

✔ **Preference shares:** In Chapter 7, I discuss the issue of preference shares, which entitle the holder of those shares to be paid cash (dividends) on those shares on a periodic basis, or where the preference shares are redeemable at a future date. You must recognise preference shares as a liability in the financial statements in accordance with IAS 32

Financial Instruments: Presentation. When domestic GAAP permits preference shares to be recognised in equity (shareholders' funds), you need reclassify them in the opening IFRS statement of financial position in order to comply with IFRS.

Dealing with disclosure issues in the first IFRS financial statements

You simply won't have enough room on the statement of comprehensive income, statement of financial position, statement of cash flows and statement of changes in equity to disclose everything that the user of the financial statements needs. So you have to make extensive disclosures in the notes to the financial statements. The objective of the notes is to give a lot more detail relating to the numbers in the financial statements, as well as other narrative disclosures such as related party transactions (see Chapter 14). Sometimes users are only interested in some of the numerical aspects of the accounts (for example, revenue and profit) and may not even read the notes, but that isn't a get-out-of-jail-free card – the disclosures are as important as the accounting statements themselves.

The list of disclosures you make in the first set of IFRS financial statements by a company is long! A first-time adopter needs to have at least three statements of financial position, two statements of comprehensive income, two income statements (if presented), two statements of cash flows, two statements of changes in equity and all the related disclosure notes.

Investing in a reputable disclosure checklist, which gives you the information that you need to disclose in the financial statements, is advised, particularly on first-time adoption of IFRS. The following list outlines the main disclosures to remember, but it's not exhaustive:

- ✔ A reconciliation of *total comprehensive income* (profit for the year after tax plus other comprehensive income) under IFRS for the latest period in the company's most recent annual financial statements. The starting point here is total comprehensive income under previous GAAP for the same period or, if your company didn't report such a total, profit or loss under previous GAAP.

- ✔ A reconciliation of equity reported under previous GAAP to equity reported under IFRS for both the date of transition to IFRS and the end of the latest period (the current period) presented in the company's most recent annual financial statements prepared under the previous GAAP.

✔ An explanation of the material adjustments to the statement of cash flows, if such a statement had been prepared under previous GAAP.

✔ Where errors were made under previous GAAP, the first two reconciliations in the list must distinguish the correction of these errors from those changes that have arisen due to a change in accounting policy.

✔ Where companies did not present financial statements for previous periods (for example because the company is new), the first set of IFRS financial statements must disclose this fact.

✔ If the company has used *fair values* (the amount for which an asset can be exchanged, or a liability settled, between knowledgeable, willing parties in an arm's length transaction) in the opening IFRS statement of financial position as *deemed cost* (an amount used as a surrogate for cost or depreciated cost at a given date; subsequent depreciation or amortisation assumes that the entity had initially recognised the asset or liability at the given date and that its cost was equal to the deemed cost) for property, plant and equipment, investment property or intangible assets, for each line item in the statement of financial position you must disclose:

  • The aggregate of those fair values

  • The aggregate adjustment to the carrying amount reported under previous GAAP

✔ An explanation of how the transition from previous GAAP to IFRS has affected the company's financial position, financial performance and cash flows.

Getting Away with Some Exemptions

IFRS recognises that a lot of work has to go into switching over from domestic GAAP to IFRS. You have to make a lot of additional disclosures to comply with the IFRS. The good news is that in recognition of the complexities involved in moving across to IFRS, some exemptions available to first-time adopters may be of huge benefit.

In this section, I start off by looking at retrospective application of IFRS, and then take you through some of the more popular exemptions available to companies adopting IFRS for the first time before examining some additional exemptions that only benefit certain companies. I round off the section with a few voluntary exemptions that may benefit you in the move across to IFRS.

Dealing with retrospective application of IFRS: The exceptions

The need to prepare an opening IFRS statement of financial position (under IFRS 1) means that you must apply IFRS retrospectively. However, IFRS 1 does grant some limited exceptions from the general requirement of full retrospective application of IFRS in force at the end of a company's first IFRS reporting period. Prior to 23 July 2009, three exceptions to retrospective application existed. Now, five are in effect that relate to

- ✔ De-recognition of financial instruments (IAS 39) (see Chapter 5)
- ✔ Determining whether an arrangement contains a lease (see Chapter 6 on leases)
- ✔ Full-cost oil and gas assets (beyond the scope of this book)
- ✔ Hedge accounting (IAS 39) (see Chapter 5 on financial instruments, but hedge accounting is beyond the scope of this book)
- ✔ Non-controlling interests (IAS 27) (see Chapters 10 and 11)

You can find more details on these exceptions in Appendix B to IFRS on the International Accounting Standards Board (IASB) website at www.iasb.org.

Using popular exemptions

Many companies that have adopted IFRS as their financial reporting framework have done so because they were mandated to – this situation was particularly the case in 2005 for companies in the EU that are listed companies (PLCs). For this reason, many smaller companies that don't have to adopt IFRS have chosen not to do so, on the grounds that reporting under IFRS would be far too burdensome in terms of disclosures.

The IASB recognises that the cost to switch from domestic GAAP to IFRS is often quite significant, and that it needs to make sure that when companies do switch over, the costs don't outweigh the benefits. For this reason, the IASB introduced some exemptions for first-time adopters. Some, but not all, of the more popular *optional* exemptions are as follows:

- ✔ **Actuarial valuations in defined benefit pension plans:** You prepare three statements of financial position in the first set of IFRS financial statements. So, when a company presents two comparative periods, it has to calculate its obligations under defined benefit pension plans at four different dates, which means obtaining actuarial valuations at four different dates, which would cost an absolute fortune!

The IASB were quite reluctant to give exemptions in this area because their view was that any exemptions may not result in reliable and relevant financial information being produced. Nevertheless, they did agree to a concession whereby if a company obtains a full actuarial valuation at one or two dates, it can roll forward (or backward) to another date, but only as long as the roll forward (or backward) reflects material transactions and other material events between those dates.

✔ **Goodwill in business combinations:** When a company has positive goodwill in its statement of financial position, the value of this goodwill is essentially frozen, and is then subjected to annual impairment reviews (per IAS 36 *Impairment of Assets*; see Chapter 5). When a company has any negative goodwill, this negative goodwill is written off to retained earnings.

✔ **Property, plant and equipment:** When items of property, plant and equipment have been revalued in previous GAAP, IFRS allows you to use a frozen revaluation as deemed cost at the date of transition to IFRS.

✔ **Translation differences:** A first-time adopter doesn't have to comply with full retrospective application of IAS 21 *The Effects of Changes in Foreign Exchange Rates*. This exemption is available to companies that have a foreign operation (for example, a foreign subsidiary). Full retrospective application of IAS 21 would mean that a first-time adopter would have to restate all the financial statements of their foreign subsidiary to IFRS from their date of inception, or later acquisition onwards, and then determine the cumulative translation differences that arose in relation to each of the foreign subsidiaries. Therefore, the cumulative translation differences for all foreign operations may be deemed to be zero at the date of transition to IFRS. Any gains or losses on subsequent disposal of a foreign operation also exclude translation differences that have arisen before the date of transition to IFRS, as well as including any later translation differences.

Look at the complete list of optional exemptions at the IASB website www.iasb.org and check out Appendices B and C to IFRS 1.

Seeing the merits of some not-so-popular exemptions

Some exemptions may only be relevant to certain companies, so not all companies take advantage of some of the not-so-popular exemptions. Here are some of these uncommon exemptions:

✔ **Compound financial instruments:** In Chapter 7, I look at compound financial instruments in a lot more detail. Basically, you need to split a compound financial instrument between the amount that's equity and the amount that's debt. A first-time adopter doesn't have to make this allocation if the debt component is no longer outstanding at the date of transition to IFRS.

✔ **Decommissioning liabilities in the cost of property, plant and equipment:** Under IAS 16 *Property, Plant and Equipment* (see Chapter 5), the cost of an item of property, plant and equipment includes an initial estimate of the costs for dismantling and removing the item and restoring the site on which it is located (these estimates are known as *decommissioning provisions*).

An IFRIC interpretation (*IFRIC* stands for International Financial Reporting Interpretation Committee and these interpretations are issued to clarify a point in an IFRS or IAS) says that a company accounts for changes in decommissioning provisions in accordance with IFRIC 1 *Changes in Existing Decommissioning, Restoration and Similar Liabilities*. However, IFRS 1 allows an exemption for changes that occurred before the date of transition to IFRS. The exemption requires the first-time adopter to recognise the decommissioning liability in accordance with the provisions in IAS 37 (see Chapter 7 for details on provisioning criteria).

The first-time adopter also needs to estimate the amount that would have been included as a decommissioning provision when the liability first arose by discounting the liability to that date using a best estimate of the historical discount rate(s) that would have applied for that liability over the intervening period. Finally, the first-time adopter needs to calculate the accumulated depreciation on that amount as at the date of transition to IFRS using an estimate of the useful life of the asset and the depreciation policy adopted by the company.

Looking at some handy voluntary exemptions

In addition to the limited exemptions available in IFRS 1, additional voluntary exemptions may benefit those in the midst of planning the migration towards IFRS. Nine optional exemptions in Appendix D to IFRS 1 may be applicable to you or your client (you can download Appendix D to IFRS 1 from www.ifrs.org). These relate to:

✔ Assets and liabilities of subsidiaries, associates and joint ventures

✔ Borrowing costs

✔ Designation of previously recognised financial instruments

- Fair value measurement of financial assets or financial liabilities at initial recognition
- Financial assets or intangible assets accounted for in accordance with IFRIC 12 *Service Concession Arrangements*
- Insurance contracts
- Investments in subsidiaries, jointly controlled entities, associates and joint ventures
- Leases
- Share-based payment transactions

Detailed discussion of the exemptions and exceptions contained in IFRS 1 is outside the scope of this book. Head to the IASB's website at www.iasb.org for more information.

Ensuring that Your First Financial Statements Comply with IFRS

When a company first prepares its IFRS financial statements, it has to make an *explicit and unreserved statement of compliance*: an assertion by the directors that the company's financial statements comply in every respect with IFRS.

The explicit and unreserved statement of compliance is very important when it comes to your audit. The auditors express an opinion on whether your company's financial statements give a true and fair view and are free from material misstatement. They give your financial statements a clean (unmodified/unqualified) opinion or an unclean (qualified/modified) opinion. If you make the explicit and unreserved statement of compliance with IFRS but your accounts *aren't* fully compliant with IFRS, the auditors are going to have a problem with this statement and you may not get a clean outcome.

Deal with the move across to IFRS in a carefully planned way. Keep all documentation related to the transition because the auditors will want to see it.

IFRS 1 identifies three situations in which IFRS 1 would *not* apply. These situations are as follows:

- When a company presented its financial statements in the previous year with an explicit and unreserved statement of compliance with IFRS, and its auditors qualify their report on those financial statements.

The previous year's financial statements of Jasper Inc for the year ended 31 December 2011 have been prepared under IFRS. These financial statements were the first IFRS financial statements prepared by Jasper Inc and contain an explicit and unreserved statement of compliance with IFRS. During the audit of these financial statements, the auditors qualified the audit opinion on the grounds that the company had not prepared a statement of cash flows as required by IAS 1 *Presentation of Financial Statements* and prepared in accordance with IAS 7 *Statement of Cash Flows*.

In this example, IFRS 1 doesn't apply to Jasper Inc. If Jasper's financial statements don't fully comply with all aspects of IFRS (which they don't, because Jasper hasn't prepared a statement of cash flows as required under IAS 1) then Jasper isn't considered to be a first-time adopter for the purposes of IFRS 1 in the current year. The disclosed, or undisclosed, departures from IFRS in the previous year's financial statements would be treated as an error under IFRS 1, which would trigger Jasper having to apply the provisions in IAS 8 *Accounting Policies, Changes in Accounting Estimates and Errors* (see Chapter 2 for more about accounting policies, estimates and errors).

✔ When a company, in the previous year, presented its financial statements under domestic GAAP along with another set of financial statements that contained an explicit or unreserved statement of compliance with IFRS, and in the current year it discontinues this practice of presenting its domestic GAAP and presents only under IFRS.

✔ When a company, in the previous year, presented its financial statements under domestic GAAP and those financial statements incorrectly contained an explicit and unreserved statement of compliance with IFRS compliance.

Part II

Looking at the Key Components of Financial Statements

The 5th Wave   By Rich Tennant

"Look—what if we just increase the size of the charts?"

In this part . . .

A set of financial statements has many components, all with very different messages to their users. Assets, liabilities, income, equity and expenses are the major components of a set of financial statements, and the values placed on these have a considerable impact on the financial statements.

In this part of the book, I examine the key components of the financial statements. I start by looking at what assets and liabilities are and how you account for them, and I also cover some of the more uncommon assets and liabilities. Then I examine how you account for revenue (sales), and finish off by considering the equity section of the statement of financial position (balance sheet).

Chapter 4

Accounting for Assets

· ·

In This Chapter

▶ Calculating the cost of your assets

▶ Considering agricultural and biological assets

▶ Selling your assets

▶ Taking stock of your inventory

▶ Interpreting intangible and tangible assets

▶ Investing in investment properties

· ·

*T*his chapter is all about assets. I'm sure that you're familiar with the term. You can describe a person as an asset to her organisation, and you can class personal belongings such as savings and bonds as assets. In the world of financial reporting, an *asset* is something that belongs to an organisation (though the actual definition is a lot more complex than that, as I explain in this chapter). The organisation can have long-term assets that the business uses to help make money (known as *non-current* assets like plant and machinery) and short-term assets (known as *current* assets) that you expect to turn into cash (*realise*) within 12 months of the financial year-end. IAS 1 *Presentation of Financial Statements* specifies when an asset (or a liability; see Chapter 6) is current or non-current.

In this chapter, I take you through the basic elements of an organisation's assets. I show you how a company accounts for its assets, how it measures the components of the cost price and what happens when a company decides to sell an asset. Chapter 5 drills further down into more detail about assets and looks at those assets that aren't as common as the ones you see in this chapter.

Defining an Asset

Some of you who trained in the late 1980s going into the early 1990s may have picked up a dead easy definition of an asset: something the organisation owns. Well, in its *Conceptual Framework*, the IASB has a far more complex definition.

The IASB's definition of an asset is:

> *An asset is a resource controlled by the enterprise as a result of past events and from which future economic benefits are expected to flow to the enterprise.*

Hmmm, so things are a little bit more complicated than just saying an asset is something the organisation owns. Now get someone with absolutely no knowledge whatsoever of accountancy to try to guess what you're talking about when you read that definition to them. The chances are that they glaze over!

If you try to explain assets to non-accountants or those who are attending day one of accounting lectures who may have never have come across the word *asset* before, let alone the IASB's definition of one, you're not going to get far (believe me, I've tried!). Never fear; in this section, I unravel the definition so you clearly understand the term *asset*.

When is an asset an asset?

The main thrust of the IASB definition that I include in the introduction to this section doesn't actually imply ownership – nowhere in the IASB's definition does it say that an asset is something you own. Instead, what the definition is in fact implying is that an asset is something that a company can exercise *control* over and that *future economic benefits* must be expected. Notice that I emphasise *control* and *future economic benefits*. This emphasis is because these two parts of the definition are pivotal. First off, let me clarify these two terms:

- ✔ **Control:** An organisation must be able to exercise control over an asset; in other words, the organisation must be able to restrict the use of an asset; for example, by storing inventories in a locked warehouse. When I explain this situation to accountants, some ask why, then, can employees not be recognised as assets? Why can't their wages be put onto the statement of financial position instead of written off to the income statement (profit or loss)? Well, they can't because an organisation can't control its workforce – they can leave at any time. The ability to control the asset is key in recognising an asset in the financial statements.

- ✔ **Future economic benefits:** Could be viewed as future revenue (sales) or a reduction in future costs.

Think of the definition in terms of some money you've put into a savings account that you can draw out at any time as follows:

An asset is a resource (your savings) *controlled by the entity* (you) *as a result of past events* (from surplus monies received from your wages or a windfall) *from which future economic benefits are expected to flow* (interest from the bank).

There you go – now see whether you can pass on to your non-accountant buddies the definition of an asset.

The grey area: Contingent assets

A *contingency* is something that isn't certain. For the purposes of financial reporting, if you see the word *contingent* then what it means is that a degree of uncertainty surrounds the transaction or event. (Chapter 7 looks at contingencies in more detail.)

You must never recognise a contingent asset until you're virtually sure that it will be settled. For example, if you're involved in a legal dispute and you expect to recover your legal costs from the other party, you can only recognise the recovery of the legal costs if you're virtually certain that you'll receive them back (usually by way of a court order). (Note: don't confuse contingent assets or liabilities with *contingent consideration*, which means that payments of monies have been withheld pending certain future outcomes.)

Clear as mud? Here's an example to help you understand contingent assets.

Cahill Cars has been sued by one of its customers, Scanlon Scooters. The court has found in favour of Cahill Cars because Scanlon Scooters couldn't come up with sufficient evidence to prove their case. Cahill Cars has spent $10,000 in legal fees and the court has ordered that Scanlon Scooters repay these fees back to Cahill Cars.

In this example, Cahill Cars can recognise a contingent asset in respect of the legal fees because they can be virtually certain that Scanlon Scooters will repay them, because the court has ordered them to do so. If it wasn't virtually certain that Cahill Cars would get the legal fees back from Scanlon Scooters, they wouldn't be able to recognise a contingent asset.

Understanding Accounting Treatments for Assets

Some strict rules in IFRS and IAS relate to when you can and can't recognise an asset in the statement of financial position, and how you treat assets. When I say *recognise*, what I mean is put an asset on the statement of financial position. That strict rules exist is quite understandable because if no rules existed and you were more or less left to your own devices then it would cause havoc in the world of financial reporting. There'd be no consistency, no comparability and definitely lots of disagreements among folk like the tax authorities.

The definition of an asset is cited in the *Conceptual Framework*, which I look at in Chapter 1. The *Conceptual Framework* is the backbone of IFRS and IAS, and if you're ever uncertain about whether to recognise an asset or not, default back to the *Conceptual Framework* and consider the transaction in relation to the definitions in the 'elements' of financial statements, which can help point you in the right direction.

Writing off assets as expenses

Sometimes accountants may think that there's an asset to be recognised in the statement of financial position when, in fact, the asset is an expense. This situation usually occurs because the actual substance of the transaction doesn't meet the asset recognition criteria in the *Conceptual Framework*. However, sometimes internal policies within the organisation may mean that certain items of (say) non-current assets that meet the asset recognition criteria may be written off immediately as an expense because this is often based on the concept of materiality. *Materiality* means how significant something is to the financial statements. If it's *material*, it's significant; if it's *immaterial*, it's not significant.

For example, say Sue's Salons Inc has an internal policy that any item of non-current asset purchased under $300 is immediately written off to the income statement rather than capitalised. This policy is also generally accepted by the tax authority in Sue's Salons' country. This example is a common treatment with organisations around the world. Many organisations such as a building company purchase tools (for example, a hammer at $25), which they may use for maybe two to three years. Rather than *capitalise* (bring on to the statement of financial position) $25 and *depreciate* (write off) this amount over three years, the organisation is probably being more realistic to write the whole amount immediately as an expense than to capitalise and depreciate.

Measuring the cost of your assets

When I talk about *measuring* the cost of assets or other stuff such as liabilities, what I mean is the actual amount you put that in the financial statements for an asset, liability, income, expense or item of equity. When you measure the cost of assets, the actual cost isn't necessarily just the purchase price; standards like IAS 16 *Property, Plant and Equipment* and IAS 2 *Inventories* say *cost* can include other bits and bobs as well, such as:

✔ Any irrecoverable taxes (like import duty if you buy a non-current asset from abroad)

✔ Carriage costs (like shipment charges or freight costs)

✔ Any production overhead costs when you come to value your inventories such as direct labour

✔ Any present obligations for future costs (for example, to dismantle and restore a site)

Here's a working example of how you measure the costs of your assets. Stella's Stylish Shoes Inc manufactures high-class ladies shoes. It invested in a machine 15 years ago that puts the shoes together. This machine recently broke down beyond repair, and the directors have sourced a new, and even better, machine from Spain. The supplier's invoice dated 20 September 2011 shows the following:

Cost of machine	$12,000
Freight costs	$2,000
Import duty	$1,000 (not recoverable)

Management have estimated that the annual maintenance costs amount to $750.

Stella's Stylish Shoes Inc has a year-end of 30 September 2011 and you're trying to figure out what to do with all the costs. So you've been given a breakdown of all the costs associated with this brand new, spanking piece of plant. It arrived before the year-end, so the company has no problem with timing issues – it can go into the 30 September 2011 financial statements. The plant is definitely going to bring in sales (economic benefits) and the plant is going to be used for more than one year, so this new piece of plant more than qualifies as a non-current asset. Therefore, IAS 16 is going to apply.

Here's a breakdown of how you handle each cost:

✔ **Cost of the machine:** This cost is quite clearly going to be capitalised because that's what it cost, so you're off!

✔ **Freight costs:** You can capitalise these costs because, as per IAS 16, they're costs that are *directly attributable* to bringing the asset to its present location and condition, so you need to get them onto the statement of financial position as well.

✔ **Import duty:** Hmmm, well, that's a form of tax, isn't it? Nevertheless, this sort of tax isn't recoverable as per the invoice and IAS 16 allows you to capitalise irrecoverable taxes, so you need to get the cost of the import duty in as well.

✔ **Annual maintenance:** The maintenance costs are only *estimated* at $750 per annum. Secondly, maintenance costs, by definition, are routine repairs and servicing costs, which IAS 16 specifically doesn't allow you to capitalise. You write the costs off to the income statement as and when they're incurred. In addition, because the plant is brand, spanking new you won't incur any of the maintenance costs until next year anyway (you hope), so you can ignore them completely.

As you can see, IAS 16 allows you to capitalise a number of additional costs along with the actual cost of the non-current asset, provided that they're *directly attributable* to bringing the asset to its present location and condition.

You can't capitalise stuff like repairs and servicing and routine maintenance and you must write them off to the income statement as and when they're incurred. Also consider that sometimes machinery may need routine servicing, say every five years, and the supplier may throw in an estimate of these costs. Not only can you not capitalise these costs because they're repairs and servicing expenditure, which don't form part of the cost of the asset anyway, but the company may well sell the machine before the five years is up. So, at the point of buying the machine, having it serviced in five years' time is merely an 'intention' as opposed to an 'obligation'.

So in the statement of financial position, you've recognised the cost of the machine at $12,000 plus the freight of $2,000 plus the irrecoverable duty of $1,000 to give you an addition to your property, plant and equipment in the year of $15,000.

Considering agricultural and biological assets

Agricultural and biological assets are subject to IAS 41 *Agriculture*. This standard outlines the accounting treatment for assets related to agricultural produce and biological assets as well as related government grants (I go through grants in Chapter 5). To help you distinguish between a biological asset and agricultural produce, consider a farmer who has a herd of cows. The cows are the biological assets (*biological assets* are living animals or plants), the *agricultural produce* is milk and the harvested product may be cheese. Similarly, sheep are a biological asset, the agricultural produce is the wool and the harvested product is the yarn.

To understand IAS 41, you need to know the meaning of *point-of-sale costs*: things like levies by regulatory authorities, commissions to brokers or dealers or transfer taxes/duties, not things like transport costs or other such costs in getting the asset to market.

IAS 41 is a specialised standard, hence I'm not going to go into a lot of detail on it, but it says that you must

✔ Measure biological assets at fair value, both initially and at each reporting date, less estimated point-of-sale costs

✔ Measure agricultural produce at the point-of-harvest fair value less estimated point-of-sale costs

The following section, 'Understanding how net realisable value affects assets', explains fair value.

Include any changes in fair value less estimated point-of-sale costs in respect of a biological asset in net profit or loss for the period in which the change arises. For agricultural activity, you also include any gain or loss from initial recognition in profit or loss.

When market prices aren't available and alternative estimates of fair value are clearly unreliable, the organisation can value its biological assets at cost, less *accumulated depreciation* (the total amount of depreciation charged against the cost of the biological asset since you bought it) and *impairment losses* (any downward revaluations because the asset isn't worth as much as you could realistically get for it in the open market).

Understanding how net realisable value affects assets

Net realisable value is a term to describe the value at which an asset would be worth in an *arm's-length transaction* – where both parties act independently and have no relationship to each other.

Les has decided to sell his car to Neil for $11,000. The car has actually been valued by a prominent dealer at $20,000. The dealer said he would give Les $20,000 for it, but because Neil is Les's friend, he's letting Neil have it on the cheap. The net realisable value is $11,000. This transaction isn't an arm's-length one because the amount Les is selling it to Neil for isn't what he could get for it if he sold it to the dealer.

I refer to net realisable value a lot in this book (for example, when I talk about the inventories standard in the section 'Inventories and work-in-progress' later in this chapter). Net realisable value is simply how much someone is prepared to give you for a specific asset.

Offsetting assets against liabilities – can you?

You must never offset assets against liabilities, unless an IFRS or IAS specifically allows it, and even then you've got to be careful that you don't breach any rules about offsetting that may sit somewhere in legislation. The following illustrates how some people may try to offset assets and liabilities:

Alicia's Architraves is a company based in the UK and has prepared its financial statements for the year-end 31 December 2011. The following information is relevant to the financial statements:

- ✔ Purchase tax eligible for reclaiming back by the company from the tax authority was in excess of sales tax due to the tax authority by £20,000. This tax was refunded back to the company on 28 February 2012.

- ✔ The company had made tax and national insurance deductions from its employees' salaries in the month of December 2011 amounting to £15,000, which was paid to the tax authority on 19 January 2012.

- ✔ The company's tax liability on its profit for the year amounted to £10,000 and is due for payment on 30 September 2012.

So, what you have here is money due back to the company in respect of sales and purchase taxes amounting to £20,000, which should be shown as an asset (a receivable) because it was refunded back to the company in the next financial year. You then have a liability in respect of the payroll that was paid after the year-end amounting to £15,000 and a further liability in respect of the year-end 31 December 2011, which is the tax due to the tax authority in respect of the profits the company has made amounting to £10,000.

What Alicia's Architraves needs to show in their financial statements is as follows:

Alicia's Architraves
Statement of financial position (extract) as at 31 December 2011
Current assets

VAT recoverable	£20,000
Current liabilities	
Other taxes and national insurance	£15,000
Income tax expense	£10,000

IAS 1 *Presentation of Financial Statements* prohibits Alicia's Architraves off-setting the monies due back to the company in respect of the sales and purchases taxes against the 'other taxes and national insurance' and 'income tax expense' amounts because such offsetting completely distorts the company's statement of financial position and misleads users into thinking that Alicia's Architraves has fewer current liabilities than it has. If you think about it logically, if Alicia's Architraves did offset the tax asset against the liabilities, the statement of financial position would only show a £5,000 income tax expense, which falls due in September 2012. Clearly, this situation isn't the case!

In Chapter 5, I examine the accounting treatment for government grants. You see that the standard that deals with grants (IAS 20 *Accounting for Government Grants and Disclosure of Government Assistance*) allows two types of accounting treatment – and one actually involves offsetting a liability against an asset! – so be sure to take a look at Chapter 5 as well.

Looking at Everyday Assets: Inventories, Work-in-Progress and Non-Current Assets

You find some types of assets frequently in organisations' financial statements. A company that buys and sells goods has inventories, and a company that manufactures goods for resale has both inventories *and* work-in-progress that need to be valued at the year-end. Many companies also have *non-current assets* (not easily turned into cash and not expected to be turned into cash within a year) – both intangible and tangible. This section takes you through the rules that IFRS has for how you account for all these types of assets.

Inventories and work-in-progress

IAS 2 *Inventories* is the accounting standard that deals with inventories.

IAS 2 also deals with work-in-progress issues. Be careful not to get confused over work-in-progress that's attributable to construction contracts, which is dealt with under IAS 11 *Construction Contracts* (see Chapter 8).

Establishing what inventory actually is

Some folk may be more used to the term *stock* when talking about inventories. Take, for example, a supermarket, which buys and sells food and other items to the general public. At the close of business on the last day of the financial year, they've unsold food and other items. This unsold food and other items are what constitute inventories. *Inventories*, therefore, are unsold goods that the company expects to sell in the immediate future as well as those in the process of production.

You need to be careful that you apply the right accounting standard to your inventory. The IAS that I examine in this section of the book is IAS 2. You can't apply IAS 2 to any financial instrument (such as those that are accounted for under IAS 39 *Financial Instruments: Recognition and Measurement*; see Chapters 5 and 7), and nor can you apply IAS 2 to any assets that you would account for under IAS 41 *Agriculture*, such as biological assets and agricultural produce at the point of harvest (which I cover in the section 'Considering agricultural and biological assets', earlier in this chapter).

Valuing your inventory

Net realisable value is the value of goods that a third party is willing to pay you. When you value your inventories, a simple, but extremely important, concept underpins the value at which inventories appear in the financial statements. IAS 2 states that inventories should be valued at *the lower of cost or net realisable value.*

'Well, that's easy!' I hear you say! In fairness, while the concept does seem relatively 'simples', it can get a bit fiddly. The reason is that the word *cost* can encompass a number of things (a bit like what you see when I look at cost in the earlier section 'Measuring the cost of your assets'). You don't simply value some inventories at their purchase price.

Under IAS 2, cost is made up of three elements:

- ✔ **Costs of purchase**, which also includes irrecoverable taxes, transport and handling but stated net of any trade discounts received

- ✔ **Costs of conversion**, which includes fixed and variable manufacturing overheads

- ✔ **Other costs** incurred that are directly attributable in bringing inventories to their present location and condition

IAS 2 specifically excludes some costs, so make sure that you don't include the following when valuing inventories:

- ✔ Abnormal waste

- ✔ Administrative expenditure that isn't related to bringing inventories to their present location and condition

> ✔ Foreign exchange differences that arise because purchased inventory
> has been invoiced in a foreign currency
>
> ✔ Interest charges that may arise when inventory is purchased on terms
> that allow settlement at a later date
>
> ✔ Selling and storage costs

Let me show you how you value inventory in an example.

Jenny's Jeans Limited (Jenny) buys and sells designer jeans for sale to the
general public. The company operates out of a small retail outlet in the middle
of a vibrant city centre in the UK and the target market is young people aged
between 18 and 35. For the purposes of this illustration, assume that Jenny is
registered for Value Added Tax (VAT).

Jenny has a year-end of 31 March 2012 and on that date an inventories count
was undertaken after the shop closed in order to arrive at an inventories valuation. A batch of jeans was bought from Duncan's Designer Denims Ltd (Duncan),
which were unsold on 31 March 2012. The invoice from Duncan shows that the
jeans cost £1,000 plus £50 to ship the jeans to Jenny and because Jenny has
been a long-standing customer of Duncan, Jenny has received a discount of
£100, giving a net figure of £950. Value Added Tax at 20 per cent (£190) has been
charged, giving a total payable on the invoice of £1,140.

Remember, all these jeans were unsold at the year-end and you need to place
a value on them for year-end inventories purposes. To comply with the principles in IAS 2, you value inventories at the *lower* of cost and net realisable
value. For the purposes of this illustration, you need to assume that cost is
the lower value.

Clearly, the cost of the jeans of £1,000 is the starting point, but the constitution of cost under IAS 2 must also be net of trade discount. So, at this point
cost is (£1,000 less £100) £900. IAS 2 also states that cost should include all
transport and handling costs, so the freight cost of £50 should be taken into
account, bringing cost up to £950. In the UK, sales tax (which becomes purchase tax for Jenny) is recoverable from the tax authorities (HM Revenue and
Customs), because Jenny is a registered trader, and therefore this tax doesn't
form part of the cost. If, on the other hand, Jenny had incurred irrecoverable
taxes, you'd include these taxes in the constitution of cost. However, in this
illustration, the value of this inventory at Jenny's Jeans Ltd is £950.

Accounting for obsolete items under IFRS

Sometimes things happen to inventories that cause their value to become
lower than their cost. For example, inventories may become damaged
beyond repair, in which case the chances are that their value will be written
off to zero.

Fabulous Fine Furniture makes bespoke furniture specific to customers' requirements. Their year-end is 31 December 2011, and as at this date the company had an item of furniture that cost $3,000 to manufacture. However, during the manufacturing process, a chemical spillage on the upholstery meant that the fabric was bleached beyond repair. The directors are of the opinion that this item of furniture is now worthless and they decide to scrap it.

The net realisable value is essentially zero because nobody would buy an item of furniture where the fabric has been bleached. The lower of cost or net realisable value is the net realisable value of zero, so zero is the value that Fabulous Fine Furniture assigns to the value of the item.

Sometimes, items of inventories may have a value attached to them, but this value may be less than cost. For example, if Joe Bloggs Joinery has items of wood that cost $100 but it can't sell them, the chances are that Joe Bloggs accept an offer of, say, $50 for someone to take the items of wood off its hands. In this instance, the year-end value placed on the items would be the lower figure of $50. However, if the offer of $50 came *after* the year-end but *before* the accounts are approved, this is what is known as an *adjusting event* as per IAS 10 (see Chapter 2) and Bloggs writes this pile of wood down to $50.

Thinking about work-in-progress

Lots of companies manufacture their own goods for resale. For example, these days double glazing is manufactured by the same company that then sells it on to the end user. At year-end, you value any work-in-progress like unfinished double glazing, unfinished furniture, half-built computers and such like. Usually, appropriate individuals within the company who have expertise in placing values on unfinished goods are responsible for arriving at a valuation, which also needs to accord to the IAS 2 principles of lower of cost or net realisable value.

You may need to make lots of estimates and judgements, and therefore calculations may get somewhat complicated. In some instances, auditors who are gathering audit evidence to support work-in-progress calculations may appoint their own experts to corroborate the company's valuation of its work-in-progress, particularly where work-in-progress is complex and significant (material) to the financial statements.

Don't confuse internal valuations and those you make for financial accounts. If you produce internal management accounts and value inventories and work-in-progress using internal valuations for planning and budgeting purposes, the year-end valuations used for the financial accounts (not management accounts) may well be different.

Here's an incredibly important point: you must account for any work-in-progress properly and you must not manipulate valuations placed on work-in-progress (and inventories for that matter) to achieve a desired outcome. Inventories and work-in-progress figures can involve a lot of estimation and are a key hotspot when it comes to profit manipulation!

Also, some countries have strict tax guidance that governs the accounting treatment for work-in-progress and it may well be you have to recognise a certain percentage of work-in-progress as revenue rather than work-in-progress; this situation is particularly the case in the UK and usually affects law firms and accountants where service revenue is subject to different rules. I look at the accounting treatment for service revenue in Chapter 8.

Intangible non-current assets

Sometimes companies create a product that becomes so well-known that the management decide that the brand is an asset in its own right. The brand is *intangible* – you can't touch it. Intangible non-current assets can be a range of things; here are some of the more common ones you may see on a company's statement of financial position:

- ✔ Brands
- ✔ Computer software
- ✔ Copyright ownerships
- ✔ Licences
- ✔ Trademarks

IAS 38 *Intangible Assets* deals with intangible non-current assets, with the exception of goodwill, which comes under IFRS 3 *Business Combinations* (see Chapters 10 and 11).

Asking when an intangible asset is an intangible asset

The first 'test' that a potential intangible asset has to pass is whether it meets the identifiability criteria. To meet this criteria, the potential intangible asset must

- ✔ Be capable of being detached from the company and sold, transferred, licensed, rented or exchanged, individually or together with a related asset or liability
- ✔ Arise from contractual or other legal rights, regardless of whether those rights are transferable or separable from the company or from other rights and obligations

After the potential intangible asset has passed this test, it needs to pass the recognition criteria, which means

- ✔ It is probable (in other words, more likely than not) that future economic benefits that are attributable to the asset will flow to the entity.

- ✔ You can measure the cost of the asset reliably.

I break down the recognition criteria of an asset earlier on in this chapter in the section 'When is an asset an asset?', so flick back if you need to refresh your memory on this area.

When the potential intangible asset has passed both tests, you can drop the word *potential* and recognise the intangible asset on the statement of financial position.

Recognising and measuring your intangible assets

When you buy or acquire an intangible asset that passes the identifiability and recognition criteria laid down in the standard, you need to make sure that the asset is carried in the statement of financial position at an appropriate value.

Make sure that you keep detailed records of how you arrive at the value of the intangible non-current asset. Your auditors will be particularly interested in seeing the values attributed to non-current intangible assets, given that sometimes they can be quite subjective.

Here's how you recognise and measure an intangible asset:

1. **Bring the asset onto the statement of financial position at cost.**

   For the purposes of IAS 38, cost includes:

   - The purchase price, including import duties and other non-refundable purchase taxes. (Cost is always net of trade and settlement discounts and rebates.)

   - Any directly attributable costs of preparing the intangible asset for its intended use. (Directly attributable costs are those costs directly incurred in bringing the intangible asset to its present location and condition.)

2. **Use the cost or revaluation model to account for the intangible asset.**

   - **The cost model:** Carry the non-current intangible asset in the statement of financial position at cost less accumulated *amortisation* (writing off the cost of an intangible non-current asset over its estimated useful life) and any accumulated *impairment losses* (where the carrying value of an asset exceeds its recoverable amount).

   The cost model is the one usually used in practice.

- **The revaluation model:** Carry the intangible asset at its fair value at each reporting date, less any subsequent amortisation and impairment losses. Credit any increases in the fair value of the intangible asset directly to a revaluation surplus in the equity section (shareholders' funds) of the statement of financial position, except to the extent that the increase reverses a loss previously recognised in profit or loss.

You can only use the revaluation model if you can determine the fair value by reference to an *active market* (one where similar goods/services are traded and from which you get reliable prices). IAS 38 recognises that such active markets are uncommon for intangible non-current assets. Fishing and taxi licences are a couple of the examples cited in IAS 38 where active markets may exist.

3. **Determine an estimated useful life for the intangible asset.**

   Intangible assets can have an indefinite or a finite life.

   - **Indefinite life:** Based on an analysis of all relevant factors, you can't see a foreseeable limit to the period over which the intangible asset is expected to generate cash flows for the organisation. In this case you don't amortise the intangible asset, but instead you test the intangible asset annually for impairment (like you do for goodwill under IFRS 3; see Chapter 5). Where there's evidence that the intangible asset is impaired, you reduce it to the intangible asset's recoverable amount.

   - **Finite life:** You amortise the asset over its estimated useful life. You calculate the *depreciable amount* (the cost less its estimated residual value) and you start to amortise the balance when the intangible asset is first available for use. Normally, the residual value of an intangible asset is assumed to be zero unless you've got a commitment from a third party to buy the intangible asset, or there's an active market from which a residual value can be obtained and it's probable that such an active market will exist at the end of the asset's useful life.

Internally generating intangible assets: The accounting rules

When a company is successful, the directors may place a value on this success. This is referred to as 'internally generated goodwill'. IAS 38 is specific on the accounting treatment for internally-generated goodwill – you don't recognise it as an intangible non-current asset because you can't separate or divide it from the company or measure it reliably at cost.

The same rule applies to internally generated brands. You can't capitalise things like mastheads and publishing titles as intangible non-current assets.

Also think carefully about research and development. Research doesn't form part of any potential intangible asset because IAS 38 is clear on the accounting treatment for any costs incurred by the company during the research stage – they're written straight off to profit or loss as and when they're incurred. After all the research is finished, the company enters into the development stage, and IAS 38 has strict criteria here. You can only recognise development expenditure as an intangible asset on the statement of financial position if, *and only if*, the company

- Shows the technical feasibility of completing the intangible asset so that it will be available for use or for resale
- Demonstrates its intention to complete the intangible asset or sell it
- Demonstrates how it will use or sell the intangible asset
- Demonstrates how the intangible asset will generate cash flows for the company and whether a market exists for the output of the intangible asset, or for the asset itself (in addition, the company must also be able to demonstrate the usefulness of the intangible asset if the asset is to be used internally)
- Has adequate technical, financial and other resources to hand in order to complete the development and to use or sell the intangible asset
- Can reliably measure the expenditure attributable to the intangible asset during the development phase

When a company can't meet any one of the criteria, then it writes such costs off to profit or loss as and when they're incurred. If a company can meet all the criteria, then it starts to recognise development costs on the statement of financial position from the date on which these development costs meet all the recognition criteria. So, if a company started developing a new drug on 1 November 2011, but only on 1 January 2012 did it meet all the six criteria, the company starts to recognise costs as capitalised development expenditure on the statement of financial position from 1 January 2012 onwards.

After you've got over all these hurdles, you then need to consider how you're going to carry the intangible asset in the statement of financial position. IAS 38 allows you to recognise your internally generated asset using the cost or revaluation model.

If you decide to use the revaluation model, revalue all assets in the same class. So, if you've various development costs that you've capitalised, revalue all those costs in that class – you can't cherry-pick certain ones.

Tangible non-current assets: Property, plant and equipment and investment property

Many non-current assets (those you can kick!) do have a physical form, and these are *tangible* non-current assets. Two types of *tangible* non-current assets exist:

- ✔ **Property, plant and equipment** (PPE – covered by IAS 16 and, when held for sale, IFRS 5): Land and buildings, machinery, computer equipment, building partitions, photocopiers and other sorts of assets that the company uses over a number of years

- ✔ **Investment property** (covered by IAS 40): Property (land or a building, or part of a building, or both) a company owns that it rents or holds to benefit from a rise in price, or both

Recognising and measuring your property, plant and equipment

IAS 16 *Property, Plant and Equipment* is consistent with other standards that recognise non-current assets (like IAS 38 *Intangible Assets*, which I examine in 'Intangible non-current assets', earlier in this chapter). The same principle applies to tangible assets: you can recognise an item of PPE (in other words, include its cost in the statement of financial position) as an asset only if you can reliably measure that its cost and future economic benefits are probable.

Remember that a number of items constitute cost – this cost isn't necessarily just the purchase price. Don't forget things like irrecoverable taxes, freight costs and such like (they're easy to miss!). Go to the earlier section 'Measuring the cost of your assets' if you want to refresh your memory about things that may form part of the cost of an item of non-current asset.

IAS 16 allows two, extremely different, alternative accounting treatments that you can use to account for PPE:

- ✔ **The depreciated historic cost model:** Put simply, you account for your PPE at its initial cost and then charge depreciation over its estimated useful life and take account of any impairment losses.

- ✔ **The revaluation model:** You carry PPE in the statement of financial position at fair value (which is how much the asset is worth at the year-end).

If you're carrying your PPE at fair value – in other words, you're getting market values each year – then you must apply this model to all the items of PPE in a particular class. For example, if a company owns six buildings that it uses for trading purposes and decides to carry these buildings at fair value, management must obtain fair values for *all* buildings at the reporting date; it can't carry some buildings at fair value and some at depreciated historic cost because it must carry all assets in that class at fair value.

Here are some further considerations for recognising and measuring your PPE:

- ✔ **Dilapidation obligations:** You need to recognise an initial estimate of the costs of dismantling and removing an item and restoring the site on which the asset is located in cost. This situation is particularly the case when you've a leasehold building that you may adapt to suit your purposes; you estimate the costs of dismantling and returning the building to its original condition at the end of the lease. These are *dilapidation obligations*, which means that the lessee is obliged to return premises to the landlord in an agreed condition.

Pete's Pantry has entered into a lease agreement to rent two adjoining premises. During negotiations, the landlord has agreed that Pete's Pantry can knock through and make the two premises into one, but a clause exists in the lease agreement that at the end of the lease Pete's Pantry should make good the party wall, thus returning the one premise back to two premises. Pete's Pantry estimates the cost of this obligation and includes it in the statement of financial position as a provision for the cost of returning the premises to their original condition. The debit entry forms part of the cost of the leasehold premises that will be amortised over the term of the lease.

- ✔ **Minor items:** In some instances, a company may buy spare parts or minor items of PPE. Lots of companies have a threshold for capitalising PPE; for example, a company may say that any item of PPE under $300 is to be immediately written off to the income statement because they may consider such expenditure to be so immaterial that it wouldn't make a lot of difference to the financial statements as a whole.

On the other hand, consider a garage. It has lots of minor items of PPE (such as spanners, tools and spare parts). Clearly, recording every single item of such assets on an asset-by-asset basis in their asset register is silly – particularly if the garage is a large, well-known garage. Not only that, but such items of small PPE are difficult to control and are inevitably lost. IAS 16 suggests that you aggregate (total) such small items of tools and apply IAS 16 to the aggregate amount.

✔ **Subsequent expenditure:** A company must also consider the question of subsequent expenditure on an item of PPE. IAS 16 itself doesn't make a distinction in principle between initial costs of acquiring an item of PPE and any subsequent expenditure on it. Basically, in both cases, any expenditure on an item of PPE including subsequent expenditure must meet the recognition and measurement criteria, and if it doesn't meet this criteria, off it goes to the income statement in full.

✔ **Repairs and maintenance:** Day-to-day servicing expenditure on an item of PPE is classed as repairs and maintenance expenditure and mustn't be capitalised. IAS 16 is particular on this issue, so don't breach the standard and then run into difficulty with your auditors. However, if the expenditure involves replacing a significant part of the asset, you can recognise this part as PPE provided that the recognition criteria are met. Don't forget to de-recognise the part that's been replaced, though! I discuss writing off the cost of PPE in the next section.

IAS 16 cites an example of aircraft engines that require regular overhaul. It suggests that these are best treated as separate assets because they've a useful life that's different from that of the asset of which they're part. Where you've major parts that clearly have a useful life that are different from the asset itself, treat them as separate items in the asset register.

Note that IAS 16 doesn't cover the following:

✔ Biological assets that are related to agricultural activity. IAS 41 is the one you need here. (See the earlier section 'Considering agricultural and biological assets'.)

✔ Mineral rights and mineral reserves, which are things like oil, gas and similar non-regenerative resources. IFRS 6 is your port of call (see the nearby sidebar).

IFRS 6

IFRS 6 *Exploration for and Evaluation of Mineral Resources* is an industry-specific standard and I'm therefore not covering it fully in this book. IFRS 6 permits a company to develop an accounting policy for exploration and evaluation assets (where a mineral reserve is discovered such as natural gas) after the company has obtained legal rights to explore in a specific area. It basically says that the company can still continue to use the accounting policy it adopted before IFRS 6 was introduced. But when circumstances change, which may give rise to the carrying amount of the exploration and evaluation asset(s) being higher than recoverable amount, IFRS 6 requires that you carry out an impairment test in accordance with IAS 36.

Writing off the cost of PPE

After you've capitalised all the associated costs of PPE (see the previous section), they can't just stay on the statement of financial position sitting pretty. If you've adopted the depreciated historic cost model to account for your PPE, you have to write off the cost of PPE over their expected useful lives. You do so by way of depreciation.

I must point out at this point that you don't depreciate the land element of land and buildings because land has an indefinite life.

Depreciation is the systematic allocation of the depreciable amount of an asset over its useful life. You review this useful life annually and revise it as necessary as per IAS 8 *Accounting Policies, Changes in Accounting Estimates and Errors* (I look at IAS 8 in Chapter 2).

Now be careful here. In a lot of instances, it may be that a company says that an asset won't be worth anything at the end of its estimated useful life. For example, a computer when bought may cost $1,000 but in three years' time it'll probably be worth zilch. However, this plummeting value doesn't apply to all items of PPE. An item of plant may be bought for $20,000, with an estimated useful life of five years, and at the end of that life the company may estimate that they can sell it for $2,000. You need to take into account this estimated amount of $2,000 (known as the *residual value*) when calculating the annual depreciation charges.

Here's a simple example of depreciation. Lucas Lighting manufactures lighting equipment for use in commercial buildings. It has a year-end of 31 December 2011 and on 31 October 2011 it obtained a new item of plant for $100,000. Lucas Lighting has a policy that all new items of PPE are charged a full year's depreciation in the year of acquisition and no depreciation in the year of disposal. The management of Lucas Lighting has estimated that at the end of the plant's useful life of ten years it will have a residual value of $5,000.

Here's how you calculate the depreciation charge:

Cost:	$100,000
Estimated residual value:	($5,000)
Depreciable amount:	$95,000
Estimated useful life:	10 years
Depreciation per annum:	($95,000/10 years)
	$9,500

So, each year Lucas recognises $9,500 as a depreciation expense by crediting PPE depreciation in the statement of financial position with $9,500 and debiting depreciation expense in the income statement with $9,500.

This illustration shows a simple way of calculating depreciation charges based on an estimated residual amount. Other methods of calculating depreciation exist, not simply the 'straight-line' basis that I explain here. Another commonly used method is the *reducing balance method* (also known as the *diminishing balance method*). This method works by charging a fixed percentage on the remaining value each year, so an asset costing $10,000 depreciated at 25 per cent each year depreciates by $2,500 in Year 1 but by 25 per cent multiplied by $7,500 ($10,000 − $2,500), to equal $1,875, in Year 2. So you charge more depreciation in earlier years and less in later years to reflect the fact that more repairs and maintenance costs will be incurred in later years.

Bookkeeping For Dummies by Paul Barrow and Lisa Epstein (Wiley) discusses the various ways of calculating depreciation, and I highly recommend getting hold of a copy of the book if you need to brush up your skills in this area.

Selling your PPE

There comes a time when a company sells off non-current assets. This sell-off can be by choice – for example, when the company no longer requires the asset or when the company owns a building that becomes too small to operate out of and wants to sell it to acquire a larger building. On the flip side, unfortunate circumstances sometimes mean that a company has no choice but to sell non-current assets to raise funds; this can occur when the company is strapped for cash and creditors are banging on the door demanding payment.

When a non-current asset is held for sale, you look to the principles contained in IFRS 5 *Non-current Assets Held for Sale and Discontinued Operations* for the appropriate treatment. IFRS 5 lays down criteria, all of which must be met to classify an asset as held for sale:

- ✔ Management must be committed to a plan to sell.
- ✔ The asset must be available for immediate sale.
- ✔ There must be an active programme in place to locate a buyer.
- ✔ The sale is highly probable – in other words, it will complete within 12 months of classification as held for sale.
- ✔ The asset is being actively marketed for sale at a sales price that is reasonable in relation to its market value.
- ✔ Actions required to complete the plan indicate that the plan to sell is unlikely to be significantly changed or withdrawn.

After you've gone through all the criteria, you need to compare:

- ✔ **The carrying amount in the statement of financial position:** This is the net book value of the asset in the statement of financial position.

- ✔ **The fair value of the building less costs to sell:** I explain fair value in the earlier section 'Understanding how net realisable value affects assets'. Take the example of a building. Chances are, to get the fair value you're going to need someone like a professional valuer to give you a market price. Costs to sell include estate agents' fees and legal fees. After you work out these, you must make sure that the building is measured in the statement of financial position at the *lower* of its carrying amount and fair value less costs to sell. In addition, cease depreciation of any items of non-current assets classified as held for sale.

Show items of non-current assets that are held for sale separately on the statement of financial position.

Knowing when a property is an investment property

If a company owns a building, then this building is a non-current asset and should be recognised as such in the statement of financial position under the provisions in IAS 16 *Property, Plant and Equipment*, right? Well, not necessarily. You see, sometimes a company buys properties and holds them purely for their investment potential. Individuals may do the same – you may know someone who buys domestic properties and rents them out, waits until house prices rise, sells them and reaps the rewards of the investment. Well, this situation is exactly the same for some companies, and IFRS has a whole accounting standard on this subject: IAS 40 *Investment Property*.

IAS 40 defines *investment property* as property (land or a building, or part of a building, or both) held by the owner, or by a lessee under a finance lease, to earn rentals, or for capital appreciation, or both.

Now you've got to be careful to make sure that you apply IAS 40 in the right situations. Table 4-1 helps you see in which circumstances you don't apply IAS 40, and which standard you turn to instead.

Table 4-1	What IAS 40 Doesn't Cover
Not Covered By IAS 40	*Standard That Applies*
Property used for the supply of goods, services, administrative purposes or in the ordinary course of business	IAS 16 (this chapter)
Property in the process of construction or development for resale	IAS 2 (this chapter)
Property being constructed for third parties	IAS 11 (Chapter 5)
Property leased to another company under a finance lease	IAS 16 (this chapter) and IAS 17 (Chapter 6)
Property held for future use as owner-occupied property or property held for future development and then subsequent use as owner-occupied property	IAS 16 (this chapter)
Property occupied by employees and owner-occupied property awaiting disposal	IAS 16 (this chapter)

So after you get your head around that lot, you can see that IAS 40 isn't easy to manipulate and companies can't just decide that they've got an investment property when, in substance, they haven't!

Accounting for and revaluing your investment property in the financial statements

When you're happy that you've got a property that meets the definition of an investment property, you then need to know how to account for it. You can only recognise investment property as an asset when

- ✔ It's probable that future economic benefits that are associated with the property will flow to the organisation.
- ✔ You can reliably measure the cost of the investment property.

You must initially recognise the investment property at its cost, which includes all transaction costs like legal fees and perhaps non-recoverable taxes like stamp duty. You can't, however, include things like start-up costs, abnormal waste or any initial operating losses that you may incur before the investment property reaches the planned occupancy levels.

After you've got the cost sussed out and you're happy that you've recognised it appropriately, you then need to consider how to measure the cost of the investment property going forward. IAS 40 allows two possible alternatives: fair value (which I touch on in the earlier section 'Understanding how net realisable value affects assets') and the cost model:

✔ **Fair value:** The fair value for investment property is the amount for which the property may be exchanged between knowledgeable and willing parties in an arm's length transaction. You've got to make sure, therefore, that the fair value accurately reflects the state of the market and the circumstances at the reporting date. Generally, you're best appointing an independent valuer who undertakes a valuation exercise to arrive at a fair value, which is normally based on active markets for similar properties in the same location and condition.

In recent years, the value of property has nosedived. Now, some countries (like the UK's Generally Accepted Accounting Practice in the equivalent to IAS 40, SSAP 19) require that you set up a revaluation reserve account in the statement of financial position within the equity and reserves section, which takes the value of all gains and losses when property prices fluctuate. Under IFRS, you don't have to set up such an account – you include all gains and losses arising from changes in the fair value of investment property in net profit or loss for the period in which the gains or losses arise.

✔ **Cost:** The cost model is simply cost less accumulated depreciation and less accumulated impairment losses.

Recognising investment property using the cost model may seem like a no brainer so you avoid having to pay a valuer to get a fair value for your investment property. But the sting in the tail comes in the form of the disclosures that IAS 40 compels preparers to make in their financial statements. Hidden in the midst of IAS 40 (specifically at paragraph 79) is a requirement where you must disclose the fair value of your investment property if you adopt the use of the cost model. The harsh reality of IAS 40 is that you can't get away from obtaining a fair value price for investment property. Under either model, you're going to have to get a market value I'm afraid.

Chapter 5

Looking at Assets You Don't See Every Day

*A*ssets are the things that belong to organisations, and they can take many different forms. You account for some assets on a regular basis, and I take you through the common assets in Chapter 4. In this chapter, I cover some of the more unfamiliar assets that you may come across during your career as an accountant, or a trainee accountant.

First, I look at constructed assets. Organisations acquire assets, but sometimes they make the assets themselves. For example, a company may build a new head office. I show you how to account for assets under construction, and any finance raised to put into the build.

Next, I look at how you account for grants. Many organisations receive grants from places like government agencies to enable them to buy or build items of assets. Some companies are also encouraged to set up in deprived areas of the community to provide employment and may receive grants to meet the initial day-to-day costs of setting up.

Financial instruments often cause an element of fear amongst accountants, whether you're a trainee, professionally qualified or qualified through experience; but fear not – in this chapter, I ease you into financial instruments by taking a look at financial assets.

Finally, I look at a fairly complicated standard (IAS 36 *Impairment of Assets*) whose aim is to make sure that companies don't carry assets in their statement of financial position at any more than what they're realistically worth.

By the end of the chapter, you can count yourself competent in some tricky asset accounting.

Constructing Your Own Assets

A company may want to move into bigger premises, and rather than buy a building that's already built, it may decide to build its own. When an organisation decides to build its own asset, the accounting for this type of project can become highly complicated. The building of a new head office takes a long time. Indeed, in many cases the construction of a company's own assets may span two (or more) accounting periods. Accounting periods usually run for 12 months and at the year-end you draw up the financial statements, including the statement of financial position – the snapshot of the company's financial position as at the close of business on the last day of the financial year. To ensure that the statement of financial position is accurate for each year, you need to know how to account for ongoing costs incurred from constructing an asset.

Placing values on your unfinished non-current assets

Assets like a building are called *non-current assets*, which means they're long-term assets that the business uses to help make money. You account for non-assets under construction under IAS 16 *Property, Plant and Equipment* (see Chapter 4).

Where an asset is self-constructed, you establish the production cost by aggregating (totalling) the price paid for material, labour and other parts used in the construction of the building. These costs can include site preparation, construction, initial delivery and handling, installation, assembly, testing and professional fees. Where an obligation exists to restore the site that the building occupies to its original condition at the end of a specified time period, you include such costs.

You can only *capitalise* costs (include within non-current assets on the statement of financial position) that you can directly attribute to the cost of the new building – in other words, those costs incurred to bring the building to the location and condition necessary for it to operate in the manner in which management intends.

Knowing when property, plant and equipment isn't a non-current asset

This section focuses on a company that's building its *own* assets, not a company that's in the business of constructing assets for others – IAS 11 *Construction Contracts* covers construction as part of your business; flick to Chapter 8 for details.

Sometimes companies are in the business of constructing buildings, such as a building firm. Consider a house builder – these types of companies often have loads of projects on the go at any one point in time and when the houses are completed the companies sell them to the customer. Where house builders are concerned, the houses they're building for resale aren't classed as a non-current asset in the builder's statement of financial position. Why? Because the houses aren't going to be used to conduct the building firm's day-to-day operations – they're available for resale. Instead, the unsold, completed and uncompleted houses are part of the house builder's inventory at the year-end.

Holmes's Homes is a builder of luxury two-, three- and four-bedroomed homes. The company has been in business for over 100 years and has a good reputation for quality and workmanship. The company's year-end is 31 July 2011. In 2010, it won several contracts to build luxury homes. Prices start from $200,000 to over $700,000. Homes can be tailored to customers' specific requirements for an extra fee and the company also operates a part-exchange system that allows customers to trade in their old home for a new one, provided the customer's old home is over a minimum part-exchange value. On 31 July 2011, Holmes's Homes had over $1.5 million worth of homes in the process of being built. How is this amount shown in the statement of financial position?

Organisations like Holmes's Homes are building the properties for resale. Like any organisation that manufactures goods for resale or buys goods to sell on, at the end of the accounting year they've a stock of unsold goods. The unsold goods in Holmes's Homes case are the unfinished and finished houses that are available for resale. Therefore, IAS 16 provisions aren't relevant in these circumstances. The standard that applies is IAS 2 *Inventories* (see Chapter 4). So, Holmes's Homes must value these unfinished and finished houses in accordance with IAS 2 principles, which state that they should be valued at the lower of *cost* (the cost price, which includes things like purchase cost, freight costs and other costs directly attributable to bringing the unfinished and finished houses to their present condition and location) or *net realisable value* (the price that an independent and unconnected third party is willing to pay in the circumstances) and be shown as current assets in the statement of financial position, not as non-current assets.

Dealing with interest on loans for non-current assets

Sometimes, a company may ask the bank for a loan to finance the construction of an asset. Assuming the company is successful in its loan application, the bank wants a return on the money lent to the company, and this return is in the form of interest.

The production cost of assets under construction is essentially the total price paid for material, labour and other directly attributable costs. You capitalise all such costs, which then form part of the overall cost of the new asset (a building, say) in the statement of financial position. When a company takes out a loan to construct an asset, you need to capitalise the interest charged by the bank (known as *borrowing costs*) as well.

Now, you have to be careful here because this kind of capitalisation can be a problem child. Borrowing costs aren't just limited to property, plant and equipment (PPE); in fact, they can include stuff like inventories that require a *substantial period of time* to bring them to a saleable condition. I emphasise *substantial period of time* because these words are absolutely crucial in determining whether or not you capitalise borrowing costs along with other costs that form part of the non-current asset.

The standard that deals with borrowing costs is IAS 23 *Borrowing Costs*. Granted, it seems a bit of a pain having to look to another IAS when such a standard can quite easily sit comfortably in IAS 16, but hey ho! IAS 23 doesn't define what a *substantial period of time* equates to, and so management make this judgement (because IFRS is principles-driven). However, common sense indicates that an asset that takes more than a year to be built and be ready for use (a *qualifying* asset) qualifies as an asset that takes a substantial period of time.

IAS 23 gives guidance on how you determine borrowing costs that are going to be capitalised. Some companies may borrow money specifically for the purpose of obtaining a qualifying asset, and in such instances identifying the borrowing costs is dead easy. However, sometimes matters aren't quite so simple and the company uses a range of debt instruments to finance the project, all of which may carry different rates of interest – some may even be interest-free (though interest-free rates are like gold dust!). If the organisation uses a range of debt instruments to finance the construction of an asset, to calculate the finance costs to capitalise it uses a *weighted average borrowing rate* (sometimes known as the *capitalisation rate*), which means it takes all the interest rates charged on all the debt instruments and works out an average rate. The following example demonstrates this:

Janet's Jumpers has three sources of borrowings in the period as shown in Table 5-1.

Table 5-1	Summary of Borrowings and Interest	
	Outstanding Liability $,000	*Interest Charge $,000*
5-year loan	8,000	1,000
25-year loan	12,000	1,000
Bank overdraft	4,000	600

If all the borrowings relate to a specific qualifying asset under IAS 23, you can calculate a weighted average borrowing rate as follows: total outstanding liability divided by total interest charges; so (1,000,000 + 1,000,000 + 600,000) ÷ (8,000,000 + 12,000,000 + 4,000,000) = 10.833 per cent.

Capitalisation of borrowing costs must cease when the asset is ready for use. Also, if a company suspends active development of a qualifying asset, it must also suspend capitalisation of borrowings.

Smyth Supermarket Inc commenced building work on a new store on 1 January 2010 that met the definition of a qualifying asset in IAS 23. On 1 April 2011, it obtained a loan from the bank of $25 million that carries interest at a rate of 10 per cent per annum specifically for the project. The store was ready for use on 1 January 2012. The company's year-end is 31 March 2012.

In the year to 31 March 2012, Smyth Supermarket Inc has incurred borrowing costs on the loan of $2.5 million ($25 million x 10 per cent). However, the store was ready for use on 1 January 2012 so it can only recognise ⁹⁄₁₂ of the borrowing costs ($1,875,000) because IAS 23 says that capitalisation of borrowing must end when the asset is ready for use. Smyth Supermarket could recognise the full year's borrowing costs had the asset not been ready for use at its year-end.

Writing off the cost of self-constructed non-current assets

When the asset has been constructed and is ready for use, you account for it in accordance with IAS 16 *Property, Plant and Equipment* (I introduce this standard in Chapter 4). You write the cost of the asset off over its estimated useful life by way of *depreciation* charges (the method of writing off the cost of the self-constructed asset over its estimated useful life). For example, if the self-constructed building had an estimated useful life of 50 years and cost $200,000 to construct, you write off $4,000 ($200,000 ÷ 50 years) as depreciation each year.

Land has an indefinite life (with some exceptions, such as quarries and sites used for landfill), but generally you can't depreciate it. You do, however, depreciate buildings because they don't have an indefinite life.

IAS 16 allows you to use the depreciated historic cost model or the revaluation model to write off the self-constructed asset over its estimated useful life (see Chapter 4 for an explanation of each model).

If you use the revaluation model subsequent to initial recognition, you need to apply this model to all assets in that class; in other words, if one building is subject to revaluation then you subject all buildings in that asset class to the revaluation model. The revaluation model requires that you carry assets at fair (market) value at the date of the revaluation, less any subsequent accumulated depreciation and any subsequent accumulated impairment losses.

Because each class of asset has a different useful life, you account for them separately for depreciation purposes. Generally speaking, a building is an asset in its own right, as is the land it stands on. Other assets are within the building, such as fixtures and fittings, escalators and/or lifts. In this case, you split the property into elements, as follows:

- ✔ Land (non-depreciating)
- ✔ Buildings
- ✔ Fixtures and fittings
- ✔ Escalators/lifts

This type of accounting is often referred to as *component depreciation*. IAS 16 doesn't explicitly refer to component depreciation, but instead says that you depreciate separately each part of an item of PPE whose cost is significant in relation to the item's total cost. So, because land doesn't depreciate, you have to separate out the value of the land from the value of the buildings.

Receiving Grants for Assets

Some companies may be eligible for grants from various government bodies. Grants can be for all sorts of things and usually involve setting up a business in a deprived area to create employment and get people in those deprived areas working, or helping new companies obtain plant and machinery. Bodies also give grants for other reasons such as enabling a business to meet running costs before it becomes firmly established. Whatever the circumstances of a grant, you have to account for it properly.

IAS 20 *Accounting for Government Grants and Disclosure of Government Assistance* prescribes the accounting treatment for government grants and the disclosure of government-related assistance. The standard itself is simple to apply; IAS 20 is not a difficult standard (phew!) and basically applies the principles within IFRS and IAS to the area of grants.

Accounting for a grant

Without a standard prescribing the appropriate treatment in given situations, companies that receive grants may just treat them all as income, which in many cases is incorrect. So, the principal aim of IAS 20 is to achieve consistency.

You can only recognise a grant in the financial statements when the company receiving the grant has complied with the conditions for its receipt. In addition, if any, or all, of the grant is to be repaid (in the future or because of a breach of the conditions), you provide for the amount that's due to be paid back if this situation is likely to happen.

Three ways of accounting for grants exist, depending on the nature and terms of the grant:

- ✔ **Recognise the grant entirely in income.** In the books, you debit cash at bank and then credit income.

- ✔ **Defer the income over a period of time.** In the books, you debit cash at bank and then credit liability (deferred income).

- ✔ **Offset.** In the books, you debit cash at bank and then credit the cost of the non-current asset in the statement of financial position.

Offsetting a liability against an asset

Offsetting assets against liabilities and vice versa is essentially prohibited under IFRS because such a practice distorts the financial statements and misleads the user (for more explanation, head to Chapter 4). Well, IAS 20 actually allows you to offset a liability against an asset, and I show you how in the following section 'Getting the right accounting treatment for grants'. But you need to be careful to make sure that you offset a liability against an asset lawfully.

Offsetting grants against assets in the UK

An example of a country that prohibits grants being offset against non-current assets is the UK. Schedule 1 to SI 2008/410 Companies Act 2006 requires that organisations state non-current (fixed) assets, under the historical cost accounting rules, at their purchase price or production cost. The statutory definitions of these prices don't make any provision for any deduction from those amounts in respect of grants. This situation illustrates the general rule that you can't offset amounts in respect of items representing assets or income against amounts in respect of items that represent liabilities.

SSAP 4 *Accounting for Government Grants*, which governs the accounting treatment for government grants in the UK, does allow you to offset grants against the cost of an asset. But the standard also recognises that the opinion of those setting companies legislation on this action is that offsetting amounts in respect of items that represent liabilities is unlawful and can't be used by organisations that apply Schedule 1 to SI 2008/410. This opinion would suggest, however, that the offset option is permissible for unincorporated entities such as sole traders.

In some countries, the practice of offsetting assets and liabilities isn't only prohibited in Generally Accepted Accounting Practice (GAAP), but is also forbidden in legislation. Remember, legislation always prevails over an accounting standard and therefore you need to make sure that you double-check your country's legislation before you go about offsetting assets against liabilities and vice versa.

Getting the right accounting treatment for grants

Significantly different ways of accounting for grants exist. So you need to scrutinise the terms and conditions attached to the grant – not only to see whether any of it is repayable (see the later section 'Repaying the grant – what to show in the financial statements'), but also to see what the grant is for. Generally, a company can receive two types of grant:

- ✔ Revenue-based grants
- ✔ Capital-based grants

Organisations usually receive revenue-based grants to meet day-to-day running costs. Some of the grant may become repayable, and therefore you need to recognise some element of the grant as a liability. But you recognise the balance in the income statement when the expenditure to which the grant applies is incurred (this recognition is to enable the income from the grant to be matched to the expenditure it relates to). Alternatively, organisations receive grants to reimburse costs that have already been incurred (again, the grant simply goes straight into the income statement). This situation is straightforward.

The complexities arise through capital-based grants, which are usually given to organisations so that they can invest in non-current assets, such as items of plant and machinery or computer equipment to enable them to become more efficient and more profitable.

First, you need to apply IAS 16 (see Chapter 4) in respect of the new machine by recognising in the statement of financial position the machine at cost (the purchase price), plus all other costs that are directly attributable to bringing the machine to its location and condition, such as freight and irrecoverable taxes. Then you deal with the grant. Under IAS 20, you've two options:

- ✔ **Treat the grant as deferred income.** You debit the bank account with the amount of the grant and credit deferred income (liability) with the amount of the grant. Then you release the grant to the income statement over the life of the equipment to which it relates. So, each year you debit deferred income (liability) with the amount of the grant and credit the income statement with the amount of the grant.

- ✔ **Offset the grant against the cost of the new machine.** You debit the bank account as normal (because the bank account is where the money has gone to in the first place), but instead of crediting deferred income, you credit the cost of the asset in non-current assets. Then you charge depreciation on the asset over its useful life on the net cost.

Charlotte's Champagne Co manufactures expensive bottles of champagne for distribution to luxury hotels. On 1 January 2012, it received a government grant for $40,000 towards the cost of a new item of machinery worth $100,000. The expected useful life of the new item of machinery is ten years and it was delivered on 1 January 2012. The year-end of Charlotte's Champagne Co is 31 March 2012 and the depreciation policy is to charge a full year's depreciation in the year of acquisition and none in the year of disposal.

First, you apply IAS 16 (see Chapter 4) in respect of the new machine and its initial cost, which is $100,000 – so you debit PPE (non-current assets) in the statement of financial position with $100,000 and credit cash at bank with $100,000. That's the easy bit done!

Now you deal with the grant:

- ✔ If you **treat the grant as deferred income,** you debit the bank account with $40,000 and credit deferred income (liability) with $40,000. Then, over the ten-year life of the equipment, each year you debit deferred income (liability) with $4,000 and credit the income statement with $4,000.

- ✔ If you **offset the grant against the cost of the new machine,** you debit the bank account with $40,000 and credit the cost of the machine in non-current assets with $40,000, so the cost price of the machine in the statement of financial position shows:

Cost	$100,000
Grant received	($40,000)
Net cost	**$60,000**

Then you charge depreciation over ten years on the net cost: so each year you charge $6,000 ($60,000 ÷ 10 years) worth of depreciation.

In the first option, where you recognise a deferred income account, you charge depreciation on the full $100,000 over ten years; in other words, $10,000 worth of depreciation. The grant is recognised by reversing a year out of deferred income each year and putting it in the income statement. In the second option, you recognise the grant in the income statement by way of a reduced depreciation charge. Do you see? In the first option, you charge $10,000 worth of depreciation; in the second, you only charge $6,000.

Disclosing grants and government assistance

As with most things in the financial statements, you need to make additional disclosures about government grants and related assistance to ensure that the user has all the available information when looking at the financial statements.

The good news is that the disclosure requirements under IAS 20 are relatively straightforward, and merely require that you disclose the following in the notes to the financial statements:

- ✔ The accounting policy the company has adopted for grants, which should also include the method of presentation in the statement of financial position (in other words, whether the grant is offset against the cost of non-current asset(s) or whether the grant is recognised as a liability)

✔ The nature and extent of grants recognised within the financial statements

✔ Any unfulfilled conditions and contingencies that relate to grants that have been recognised in the financial statements

Some countries may tailor IAS 20 to their own specific reporting requirements and require disclosure of the effect that grants have had on the financial statements for the accounting period.

A reputable disclosure checklist helps you make sure that you get the disclosures spot on. Keep in mind that many countries have additional disclosure requirements over and above those contained in IFRS.

Repaying the grant – what to show in the financial statements

There may well be conditions in the terms of the grant that the company receiving the grant has to repay some (or all) of the grant back at some point in time. Alternatively, the terms of the grant may be that the company doesn't have to repay any of the grant back *provided* that the company complies with certain conditions. If the company doesn't comply with those conditions (in other words, the company is in breach of the grant terms), some (or all) of the grant may become repayable.

Always scrutinise, carefully, the terms and conditions attached to a grant. A sneaky condition may be buried deep within the small print that means that some of the grant is repayable, and you need to take this condition into consideration when preparing the financial statements.

If all, or part, of the grant is repayable at a later date, you need to work out whether it's payable within or after 12 months from the date of the statement of financial position. In some cases, part of the grant may be payable within 12 months and part may be payable after more than 12 months, and therefore you need to split the repayments in the statement of financial position accordingly to ensure that the company reports the correct amount of current and non-current liabilities.

IAS 1 *Presentation of Financial Statements* (see Chapter 1) requires that you show liabilities on the statement of financial position between those falling due within 12 months from the reporting date (current liabilities) and those falling due after more than 12 months from the reporting date (non-current liabilities).

Accounting for Financial Assets

So what are financial instruments all about then? Well, companies often need to raise finance for various things, such as expansion projects or building new assets and such like. For every company that obtains finance, another party has to provide it. So, basically, a *financial instrument* is any contract that gives rise to both a financial asset of one company and a financial liability (or *equity instrument* – a form of shares recognised in the equity section of the statement of financial position) of another company. Here, I show you how to account for the various different types of financial asset.

The accounting standard that deals with the recognition and measurement of a financial asset is IAS 39 *Financial Instruments: Recognition and Measurement.* IAS 39 is a companion standard to IAS 32 *Financial Instruments: Presentation* and IFRS 7 *Financial Instruments: Disclosures* (see 'Dicing with derivatives' later in this chapter).

Pinning down the definition of a financial asset

IAS 39 is a humungous standard and contains all sorts of complexities – in fact Sir David Tweedie, the guy who wrote the standard, once said that if you understand IAS 39, you haven't read it properly! IAS 32 gives a detailed and complex definition of a financial asset; if you're feeling brave, have a butchers at it on the International Accounting Standards Board (IASB) website at www.iasb.org (go to the IFRS tab and bring up IAS 32). But the best way to understand what a financial asset is to know what it may include, which is:

- ✔ Cash
- ✔ Contractual rights to cash or shares
- ✔ Deposits in other companies
- ✔ Investments in bonds
- ✔ Loans to other companies
- ✔ Receivables (third parties that owe the company money)

You also come across some more complex financial assets, such as derivatives (which I look at in the later section 'Dicing with derivatives').

Financial instruments: the mud never clears!

The accounting standards on financial instruments, particularly IAS 39, go back as far as 1984. Over the decades, the accounting for financial instruments has become more and more complicated, and in a lot of cases firms of accountants have specialists that deal with the accounting for financial instruments. Lots of books relating to IFRS and IAS cover the area of financial instruments in a separate publication because they've become so complicated that even the most experienced and qualified of accountants can glaze over at the mere thought of accounting for financial instruments. In this section of the book, and in Chapter 7 when I cover financial liabilities, I merely gloss over the area with the intention of equipping you with basic knowledge of financial instruments.

Financial instruments are renowned for being incredibly complicated. In fact, many people say that the accounting standards on financial instruments are *the* most complex of all the standards. In a nutshell, if you keep in mind that a financial instrument can be a financial asset (such as a receivable), or a financial liability (such as a loan) or an equity instrument (such as shares), you're not wrong!

Looking at the different sorts of financial assets

After you establish that you've a financial asset (the previous section explains the criteria), you need to know how to classify it. Now IAS 39 isn't exactly the most user-friendly of accounting standards. (Its successor, IFRS 9, proposed to take effect for accounting periods commencing on or after 1 January 2015, will hopefully be somewhat more user-friendly.)

Under IAS 39, four possible classifications of financial instruments exist within a set of financial statements:

- ✔ **Available-for-sale financial assets:** *Non-derivative* financial assets (which means they don't derive their value from an underlying transaction) that aren't classified as any of the other three items in this list; in other words, this category is a default for those that you can't classify as financial assets at fair value through profit or loss, held-to-maturity investments and loans and receivables.

- ✔ **Financial assets at fair value through profit or loss:** When you've a financial asset at fair value through profit or loss, you must carry it at *fair value* (carry the financial instrument at its market value with any changes in the instrument's fair value being recognised in profit or loss). You also recognise any changes in this fair value in profit or loss for the period. In order to be able to recognise a financial asset at fair value through profit or loss, it has to meet one of the following conditions:

- The financial asset is classed as held-for-trading; in other words, you intend to sell it within a short period of time (usually within one year).

- Upon initial recognition, the financial asset was designated at fair value through profit or loss.

✔ **Held-to-maturity investments:** Non-derivative fixed-term investments that the company intends to hold on to until they mature and must be quoted in an active market. Strict 'tainting' rules in IAS 39 say that if a company sells or reclassifies a 'significant' amount of held-to-maturity investments, it must reclassify the entire portfolio of held-to-maturity investments to the available-for-sale category.

✔ **Loans and receivables:** Non-derivative financial assets that have fixed or determinable payments, aren't quoted in an active market, aren't held-for-trading and, upon initial recognition, haven't been recognised as assets at fair value through profit or loss. Something like a bog standard loan to another company is a good example, but if a substantial risk of non-recovery of the loan exists, you can't classify it as a loan or receivable.

IAS 39 requires the subsequent measurement of financial assets (and financial liabilities, which I cover in Chapter 7) in the financial statements as laid out in Table 5-2.

Table 5-2	Financial Assets in the Financial Statements	
	In Statement of Financial Position	*Gains or Losses Recognised In*
Fair value through profit or loss	Fair value	Statement of comprehensive income
Available-for-sale	Fair value	In equity until de-recognition, then recycled via the statement of comprehensive income
Held-to-maturity	At amortised cost	Not applicable
Loans and receivables	At amortised cost	Not applicable

In drafting the new IFRS 9 *Financial Instruments*, the IASB has tried to make the standard more user-friendly and has got rid of held-to-maturity assets and available-for-sale financial assets. Phew! But you still need to know what *at amortised cost* means in Table 5-1.

The term *at amortised cost* means the amount at which you state a financial asset (or financial liability, which I look at in Chapter 7) in the financial statements on initial recognition. You then:

- ✔ Deduct any *principal* (also known as *capital*) payments – these are payments against the original loan and not interest payments.

- ✔ Add, or subtract, any amounts of *cumulative amortisation* (the difference between the amount initially recognised and the amount that will eventually be paid).

- ✔ Deduct any write-down due to uncollectability (*write-downs* are amounts you write off because you don't think that you'll get them, also known as *allowances*).

When you recognise financial assets at amortised cost, you calculate the interest on that financial asset using the *effective interest method*: you allocate interest income or expense over a relevant period, usually over the life of the financial instrument, and you include all fees, transactions costs and premiums and discounts in the calculation. This gets you to the *effective interest rate*, which exactly discounts (brings to present-day values) the estimated future cash receipts or payments over the expected life of the instrument.

Getting rid of financial assets in the financial statements

The problem with de-recognising a financial asset in the financial statements is that doing so is complicated! The first thing you need to consider is what you're actually getting rid of, so ask yourself whether the financial asset is a financial asset in its entirety, or is it

- ✔ Specifically identified cash flows from an asset
- ✔ A full proportionate share of the cash flows from an asset
- ✔ A full proportionate share of 'specifically identified' cash flows from a financial asset

After you identify what you're (potentially) getting rid of, you then need to consider whether the asset has actually been transferred to the third party and thus is eligible for de-recognition.

An asset is essentially transferred, and thus eligible for de-recognition, when the contractual rights to receive the cash flows connected with the financial asset have passed to the new owner. The key factor is establishing whether all the risks and rewards of ownership of the financial asset have been transferred. If, *substantially*, all the risks and rewards of ownership have been passed, you can de-recognise the financial asset. If, *substantially*, all the risks and rewards haven't been passed, you can't de-recognise it.

IAS 39 has a particularly useful flowchart when it comes to deciding whether or not you de-recognise a financial asset. On the IASB website (www.iasb.org) go to the tab IFRS and select IAS 39. You have to register on the site first, but it's free! Bonus!

Dicing with derivatives

Derivatives, eh? How cool does that word sound in the right circles? Well, *cool* isn't a word that a lot of accountants would use to describe derivatives – *a minefield* may be more apt!

A *derivative* financial instrument derives its value from an underlying transaction; for example, changes in foreign exchange rates or interest rates. The thing to consider with derivatives is that at the reporting date, the derivative may be in a favourable position (an asset), or it may be in an adverse position (a liability). IAS 39 says that when you've a derivative financial instrument, you must classify it as 'fair value through profit or loss'.

IAS 39 defines a derivative as a financial instrument that

✔ Has a value that changes in response to a change in underlying variables such as interest rates

✔ Requires no initial investment, or one that is smaller than would be required for a contract with a similar response to changes in market factors

✔ Is settled at a future date

The following are examples of derivative financial instruments:

✔ **Forward contracts:** A contract between two parties to buy or sell an asset at a specified future time at a price agreed at the outset.

✔ **Futures contracts:** A contract between two parties to exchange a specified asset for a price agreed at the outset with delivery occurring at a future date.

✔ **Options:** A contract between two parties for a future transaction on an asset at a specified price. The buyer of the option gains the right (but not the obligation) to engage in that transaction. The seller incurs the obligation to fulfil the transaction.

✔ **Swaps:** The parties involved exchange cash flows of one party's financial instrument for those of the other party's financial instrument.

The accounting for financial instruments, particularly derivatives, can be complicated. If you don't feel comfortable with the accounting treatment, liaise with a specialist in this field.

IFRS 7 *Financial Instruments: Disclosures* deals specifically with the disclosures that a company has to make in connection with its financial instruments (both financial assets and financial liabilities). IFRS 7 also applies to companies that have few financial instruments (for example, simply receivables and payables – money you're owed and money you owe).

In essence, IFRS 7 requires disclosure of the following:

✔ The significance of financial instruments in respect of the company's financial position and performance.

✔ The nature and extent of risks that arise from financial instruments to which the company is exposed during the period as well as at the end of the accounting period. The company also needs to disclose how it manages those risks.

The company must also make qualitative and quantitative disclosures about the organisation's exposures to risk. The *qualitative* disclosures describe management's objectives, policies and processes for managing identified risks. *Quantitative* disclosures provide the information needed about the extent to which the organisation is exposed to risk based on information that's provided internally to the organisation's key management personnel. The disclosures should also include information about credit risk, liquidity risk and market risk.

If you have complex financial instruments, look to the provisions in IFRS 7 further to make sure that you disclose everything you should. And because the disclosures can become extremely vast and complex, use a reputable disclosure checklist that describes the info you need to include.

Dealing with an Impaired Asset

Sometimes the value of your assets may fall unintentionally. I don't mean through normal wear and tear or consumption of the asset by way of depreciation or amortisation; what I'm referring to is a drop in the value of an asset because of external circumstances or because the asset is damaged.

When an asset falls in value and this fall in value isn't because of normal consumption (in other words, depreciation or amortisation), this reduction is referred to as *impairment* – basically, a situation where the carrying value of an asset exceeds its recoverable amount. IAS 36 *Impairment of Assets* considers impairment.

You can't state the assets you own in the financial statements at any more than their recoverable amount. So, if you've an asset stated at more than its recoverable amount, you're going to have to do something about it to reduce this value accordingly so that the user isn't misled and the financial statements convey the right information (in other words, they present fairly the financial affairs of the organisation).

When I talk about impairment, I refer to *recoverable amount*. Generally, a company can recover the amount it invested in an asset by selling the asset to a third party or using the asset in the business to generate cash flows. For example, if you consider a firm of printers, it has printing machines to make stuff it sells on to customers, which generates sales, which then generates cash.

Assessing the company's assets for impairment

At the end of each reporting period, a company must assess the assets it owns and consider whether any indicators of impairment exist that may mean that the assets are stated in the statement of financial position at a higher amount than what would be recoverable. Management must consider some basic factors when assessing the company's assets for impairment:

- ✔ Has the asset become idle or is it about to be discontinued?
- ✔ Has the asset been damaged?
- ✔ Have profits in a subsidiary or jointly controlled entity diminished to the point that dividends received by the parent exceed total comprehensive income?
- ✔ Have there been changes in the legal, economic, technological or market environment that would give rise to assets no longer being worth as much as originally thought?

✔ Has the asset gone from having an indefinite life to a finite life?

✔ Is the asset obsolete?

✔ Has the economic performance of the asset(s) been worse than expected?

Where the answer to any of the questions is 'yes', the chances are that the related asset is impaired.

Finding out about fair value

People use the term *fair value* an awful lot in the world of financial reporting. Fair value is the same as market value.

Think about what may happen when you change your car. You go looking for a new car, spot the car of your dreams and then you find out that the dealer is willing to give you part exchange for your old car. The dealer comes along and gives you a price for your old car, to be offset against the price of the new car. The price the dealer gives you for your old car is the fair value.

Determining whether you've an impairment loss (or reversal of a prior period impairment loss, for that matter) on your hands is a little trickier than simply comparing the net selling price of an asset and comparing it to the value you've carried in the statement of financial position. IAS 36 says that an asset is impaired if its carrying amount in the financial statements exceeds the amount to be recovered through use or sale of the asset (the asset's recoverable amount).

Now, you sub-divide *recoverable amount* into two component parts:

✔ **Fair value less costs to sell:** The amount obtainable from the sale of an asset in an arm's length transaction between knowledgeable, willing parties less the estimated costs involved in the sale.

✔ **Value in use:** The present-day value of the future cash flows expected to be derived from the asset (I cover this component in the following section).

Recoverable amount is the *higher* of the above two sub-divisions.

Considering value in use

Value in use is the net present value (or present-day value) of a cash flow, or other economic benefits, that an asset generates for its owner. Included in the calculation of these cash flows are the sales proceeds that arise through the asset's disposal at the end of its useful life. In a nutshell, to obtain a value in use you have to estimate how much dosh (or other economic benefit) an asset is going to generate for you over the asset's life. You then discount all this revenue that you expect the asset to generate (including any estimated proceeds you may receive when you come to sell the asset) to present-day values to take into account the time value of money, because what's worth $10,000 now won't be worth $10,000 in, say, five years.

Getting a value in use figure for an asset in real life is often pretty difficult and in many cases can be a bit like walking around a maze blindfolded. Whichever method you adopt in an attempt to get a value in use, make sure that your method is justifiable.

To calculate a value in use you follow these steps:

1. **Multiply the *cash inflow* (all the monies you're going to get in from the asset) for each year of the expected life of the asset by the present *value factor* (the appropriate discount rate at which you restate the cash inflows to today's values – so, present values).**

   You can freely download present value tables to get your present value factor by doing a 'Google search' for *present value tables*. Some reputable financial management text books often have these tables in them also.

2. **Add up all the results of Step 1 for each year.**

   The total present value of the cash inflows is the value in use.

Daniel's Days Out is in the travel industry. It organises days out to various seaside resorts for senior citizens. It has a fleet of coaches, which it considers to be the main income-generating unit. The company's internal rate of return is 5 per cent. Table 5-3 shows the estimated cash inflows as at 31 December 2011 for the next four years from the fleet of coaches that it has arrived at based on historic trends.

Table 5-3	Calculating Value in Use		
Year	*Cash Inflows*	*Present Value Factor (5%)*	*Present Value of Cash Flows*
2012	$47,000	0.95238	$44,761.86
2013	$38,000	0.90703	$34,467.14
2014	$10,000	0.86384	$8,638.40
2015	$5,000	0.8220	$4,110.00
			$91,977.40

Now you want to calculate an impairment loss. Here's how:

1. **Compare the value in use of the asset (or assets) with the asset's fair value less costs to sell.**

2. **If the value in use is higher than fair value less costs to sell, value in use becomes the asset's recoverable amount (or vice versa because recoverable amount is the higher of the two).**

3. **If the recoverable amount is *lower* than the carrying amount (the amount stated in the statement of financial position) then the asset is impaired and you write if off down to its recoverable amount.**

Daniel's Days Out has got the group of coaches carried in the statement of financial position at a net book value of $123,000. On 31 December 2011, it commissioned a prominent dealer to attend its premises to place a fair value on the coaches. The dealer said that the coaches were worth $84,500.

So, to recap, you've the following information to hand:

  ✔ Value in use of $91,977.40 (round this amount down to $91,977)

  ✔ Net book value in the financial statements of $123,000

  ✔ Fair value from the dealer of $84,500

You can see that value in use ($91,977) exceeds the fair value, the net selling price, ($84,500), so because value in use is *higher*, you use value in use as the recoverable amount. Therefore, you compare the recoverable amount ($91,977) to the amount stated in the statement of financial ($123,000). The value in the statement of financial position is overstated by $31,023 ($123,000 less $91,977). Daniel's Days Out writes off $31,023 to the income statement as an operating expense (for example, additional depreciation).

Accounting for goodwill impairment

In Chapter 11, I talk about accounting for goodwill under the provisions in IFRS 3 *Business Combinations.* When a company buys the net assets of another company (or a share of the net assets) and pays more than the net assets are actually worth, *goodwill* is essentially a balancing figure between the purchase proceeds and what the company buys.

Goodwill is an intangible non-current asset (*intangible* means that it doesn't have a physical form). However, unlike other intangible non-current assets, you *don't* amortise goodwill over its estimated useful life. IFRS 3 requires that you test annually for impairment instead. In situations when goodwill is impaired, you reduce the goodwill by the amount the goodwill is impaired by. If you've any remaining impairment left, then you write the remaining impairment off against the rest of the assets that you bought when you acquired your subsidiary, using a reasonable basis.

On 1 October 2011, Bill's Builders (Bill) acquired 100 per cent of the net assets of Tim's Trucks (Tim). In the transaction, Bill acquired machinery of $2,000 and the goodwill recognised was $1,000. On 31 March 2012, the company was sued because of defective vehicles, which gave rise to a significant amount of bad press attention. On that date, the directors estimated that the value in use of Tim's Trucks was $500.

In this example, the total assets that were acquired on acquisition of the subsidiary (Tim) were $3,000 (machinery $2,000 and goodwill $1,000). However, the directors have estimated that the value in use is only $500, which gives rise to an impairment of $2,500 ($3,000 carrying amount of assets less $500 value in use) so the first thing you do is to write off the whole of the goodwill of $1,000, therefore goodwill will be $nil and the remaining $1,500 will be charged against the machinery, which will result in machinery having a value of $500 ($2,000 minus $1,500 remaining impairment).

Recognising and reversing impairment losses

You write off impairment losses to the statement of comprehensive income (income statement) as an operating expense (apart from when the asset is subject to revaluation, when you recognise such impairments directly in equity). You can include impairments recognised as operating expenses within depreciation charges, or if they're material (significant), show them as a separate line item in the income statement so that the user is aware of them.

You can reverse a previously recognised impairment loss only if you've a change in the estimates used to determine the asset's recoverable amount. When the estimates used to determine the asset's recoverable amount have changed, you increase the carrying value of the asset to its recoverable amount. But be careful! The amount of the reversal can't exceed the asset's carrying amount (net of depreciation charges) had no impairment originally been recognised.

Chapter 6

Accounting for Liabilities

*E*very organisation incurs some form of liability on a daily basis. If you buy goods from a supplier on credit, you owe them money – that's a liability; if your organisation has a bank loan, that's a liability. You can't get away from liabilities! The problem with liabilities is that, like everything else in the world of financial reporting, you get easy bits and then you get not so easy bits. But with a little help from this chapter, you can soon be handling liabilities expertly.

Here, you get a good grounding in what liabilities are, and how you classify them and recognise them in the financial statements under IFRS. And you discover how to account for the liabilities that you come across almost on a daily basis: trade payables, operating and finance lease commitments and income taxes that you owe. (For less familiar liabilities, take a look at Chapter 7.)

Defining a Liability

For some people, the word *liability* has negative connotations: something unfavourable, a clumsy person, something or someone that infuriates you. To accountants, a liability is something less disparaging (perhaps). If you owe money to a friend or family member, you've a liability; similarly, if you've a mortgage on your house then you've a liability to the bank or building society. In a nutshell, a *liability* is simply something that a company owes to another person or another company. The 'something' that a company owes can take the form of cash, or the company may settle the liability in goods, services or even shares in the company.

The International Accounting Standards Board (IASB) has quite a technical definition of what a liability is:

> *A liability is a present obligation of the enterprise arising from past events, the settlement of which is expected to result in an outflow from the entity of resources embodying economic benefits.*

This definition is not the easiest one in the world to get your head around, but you can break it down into easier chunks. Put the definition into the context of when you borrow money from a friend (call him Fred) to pay for your car to be recovered when it breaks down on the motorway:

> *A liability is a present obligation of the enterprise (the money you owe to Fred) arising from past events (the car breaking down), the settlement of which is expected to result in an outflow from the enterprise of resources embodying economic benefits (when you cough up the cash to repay Fred).*

So, you can see that all the definition is saying is that you've obtained something from a third party and the third party is going to expect payment for it (in one form or another).

Deciding when a liability is a liability

In a nutshell, a liability becomes such when an organisation has an obligation to another party, and the only way to discharge this obligation is to part with cash or other asset(s). You must also be able to reliably measure the cost of the liability and it must also be probable (more likely than not) that cash, or another asset belonging to the company incurring the liability, will be used to settle the obligation.

Liabilities (and assets) are characterised as rights and obligations. *Rights* are the rights to receive future economic benefits in the form of cash *inflows* (resources coming into the business). *Obligations* are transfers of economic benefits in the form of cash *outflows* (resources going out of the business). So for something to be a liability, a right or obligation must exist. So, to determine whether a liability exists, you determine whether a right or obligation exists.

Here's an example. Gabriella Gardening Equipment Ltd has been looking to expand its range of goods from traditional gardening tools and equipment to selling products such as barbeques and gazebos. It has sourced a supplier for the barbeques, who seem to be competitive against other prominent suppliers. Gabriella Gardening Equipment Ltd has received a quotation to be supplied with 20 barbeques as an initial order. The directors of Gabriella Gardening Equipment Limited have had a meeting and have decided to go ahead with the order of 20 barbeques to see how they sell; if they're successful, the company will place future orders for more. The question arises as to whether Gabriella Gardening Equipment Ltd should now recognise a liability to the supplier for the 20 barbeques.

The answer, in short, is 'no'. Just because the directors have had a meeting and have resolved to go ahead with the order doesn't result in an obligation resulting in an outflow of cash for Gabriella Gardening Equipment Ltd. The obligation arises when the company places the order and accepts the delivery of goods.

Looking to the future: Future liabilities

You can only recognise a liability when you've a *present obligation* as a result of past events. Something has to have happened in the past to give rise to an obligation (a liability).

Many companies prepare budgets at the start of their financial accounting period and these budgets can span many years. The idea behind these budgets is that companies, particularly those that see seasonal peaks and troughs in their profitability, know exactly when profits are likely to be high (which means that cash flow may be good) and when profits are likely to be low (which means that the company tightens the purse strings). This practice is fairly common and the chances are that your company (or some of your clients) prepare budgets to assist with planning.

Budgets and forecasts look to the future. They therefore include an estimate of future costs and expenditure, because otherwise how can management determine periods when profits may not be as high or when profits may peak?

In the world of accountancy, the *matching concept* says that all expenditure must match the income to which it relates. If you don't match costs with the income to which they relate, the financial statements are distorted and they mislead the users of such statements. General purpose financial statements are all about the users and their needs. But the matching concept *doesn't* mean that you can bring costs that relate to future periods into the current year's financial statements, because doing so also disproportionately reduces profitability and again misleads the users. So you can only recognise liabilities in the period(s) in which they relate.

Here's an example of what *not* to do . . . Dodgy Dealings is in the process of preparing its financial statements for the year ended 31 December 2011. The financial statements currently show pre-tax profits amounting to $90,000 and the company's accountant has nearly keeled over at the thought of the potential tax bill. 'Oh heavens, I'm not having that!' screams the accountant. 'Dave, the managing director, is going on a month's cruise around the Mediterranean right at the time the tax bill is going to be paid so we need to get it down! Go and stick a large accrual in the accounts for $40,000 – I know that we're going to have repairs to the building done next summer so we'll bring forward some of those costs into this year's accounts.' What Dodgy Dealings essentially wants to do here is to recognise future liabilities in the accounts in order to manipulate the tax bill. Now, not only is this practice grossly inappropriate, but the practice is also illegal.

It's worth pointing out that present obligations aren't necessarily the same as something you owe *now*. For example, a company that has an obligation to decommission an oil rig at the end of its life would have a present obligation for the decommissioning costs even though it may not be paid for a significant amount of time.

Recognising a Liability in the Financial Statements

Recognising a liability in the financial statements has an impact on the financial results for the accounting period. If you recognise a liability inappropriately, you disproportionately increase your costs (or inflate your assets depending on where the corresponding debit entry has gone to) and this increase misleads users into thinking that costs, or assets, are higher than they actually should be. So, understanding exactly when to recognise a liability (the previous section helps you here) and how to account for it correctly is vital.

Knowing how much to account for

After you establish that the recognition criteria for a liability have been met (in other words, that the organisation has an obligation that will result in an outflow of cash; see the earlier section 'Defining a Liability'), you need to know how to account for it.

In many cases, accounting for liabilities is dead straightforward, but in some cases you need to do some nifty calculations to ensure that you account for liabilities correctly.

You must recognise the liability in the financial period in which the obligation arises, which is not necessarily the same period in which an invoice arrives.

Irene Tablets Inc purchases a batch of computer tablets from one of its suppliers for resale onto the general public. Irene Tablets' year-end is 31 December 2011. It placed the order on 28 December 2011, the goods were delivered on 29 December 2011 and the invoice was received on 4 January 2012. Because Irene Tablets Inc placed the order on 28 December 2011 and the goods were received on 29 December 2011, it recognises the liability in the 2011 year despite the invoice being received in the next financial year. It needs to do so because the obligation to the supplier arose in the December 2011 financial year.

Here's another example: Amanda's Attics Ltd has a year-end of 31 December 2011. On 30 December 2011, it received an invoice from its trade body for the 2012 membership fees. The invoice was dated 20 December 2011 and the membership that's been invoiced runs from 1 January 2012 to 31 December 2012. Amanda's Attics can put the invoice into its purchase ledger dated 20 December 2011 (the invoice date), but it must immediately prepay the entire invoice and carry it over to the next accounting period to make sure that the costs are included in the correct period (2012). The professional body will require payment by the due date, but the accounts for the year-end 31 December 2011 won't show the cost hitting the income statement because the cost has been debited to prepayments as a current asset (because Amanda's Attics has paid upfront for next year's subscription). In the 2012 accounts, Amanda's Attics reverses the prepayment out of prepayments (credited) and debits it to subscription costs in the income statement to ensure that the expenditure is included in the correct period.

You need to be careful with things like subscriptions and other expenditure that you may pay for in full when the invoice arrives. Say that you've a year-end of 31 March 2012 and you receive an invoice dated 1 March 2012 for services for the period 1 April 2012 to 31 March 2013. The income statement can't take the full hit of the invoice in the 31 March 2012 accounts because doing so would disproportionately increase the company's costs. Instead, you drop the portion of the costs into the income statement in the periods to which the invoice relates.

Eddie the electrician's year-end is 31 March 2012. On 1 January 2012, he received an invoice from his trade body for $200 membership fees that cover the period 1 January 2012 to 31 December 2012. In this situation, the membership fees cover a calendar year; however, part-way through this calendar year is Eddie's year-end of 31 March 2012. Eddie apportions the fees over the two accounting periods. In the 31 March 2012 financial statements, Eddie recognises subscription fees of $50 ($200 x 3 months ÷ 12 months), and the remaining 9 months of $150

($200 x 9 months ÷ 12 months) is prepaid (as a current asset) in the 31 March 2012 accounts and carried over into the next accounting period.

So, as you can see, sometimes you need to ponder over the calculations a little in order to make sure that the financial statements contain the correct amount of liabilities and costs.

Classifying current and non-current liabilities

The earlier sections of this chapter examine the recognition and measurement criteria of a liability. In this section, I take you one step further. You've recognised all your liabilities in the financial statements and you're happy that you've recognised any costs that cover more than one accounting period in the right period, but you need to consider another fundamental issue: at which point the liability is going to be settled.

IAS 1 *Presentation of Financial Statements* prescribes how organisations' must show their liabilities, both current and non-current, in the financial statements. The standard requires that you classify liabilities as follows (when the company's normal operating cycle isn't clearly identifiable then its cycle is deemed to be 12 months):

✔ **Current liabilities:**

- The liability is expected to be settled in the company's normal *operating cycle* – the time between the acquisition of assets for processing and the realisation of these assets into cash or cash equivalents.

- The liability is held primarily for the purpose of trading.

- The liability is due to be settled within 12 months after the year-end (or period-end as the case may be).

- The organisation does not have an unconditional right to defer settlement of the liability for at least 12 months after the year-end (or period-end).

✔ **Non-current liabilities:** A liability that falls due after more than 12 months from the date of the statement of financial position (this date is referred to as the *reporting date*). For example, a company may enter into an agreement with a third party whereby the third party provides an asset, or loan, to the company and the company pays back the third party over time. This situation is particularly the case with things like bank loans and hire purchase agreements.

You show liabilities on the face of the statement of financial position between those that fall due within 12 months of the reporting date (current) and those that fall due after more than 12 months of the reporting date (non-current).

So how do you classify liabilities correctly? Well, you have to split up what's current and what's non-current. Find the boundary between the two – the point at which a current liability becomes non-current, and work out the sums for the two parts of the liability.

A loan is a liability, and it includes an interest cost. For the purposes of calculating the portion of current and non-current, you can ignore all interest payments because these payments can simply be charged to the income statement as finance costs when they're incurred. The statement of financial position should only show the *capital* element of the loan outstanding at the year-end.

Here's an example of how you work out what's current and what's non-current for a liability. Ben has a chain of pubs that have just undergone a programme of refurbishment. In order to undertake the refurbishment, Ben obtained a loan for $60,000 on 1 January 2011. The terms of the loan are that repayments be made monthly over five years starting one month after the loan has been made. Ben has a year-end of 31 December 2011. You're trying to establish the portion of the loan that's current and the portion that's non-current as at 31 December 2011.

You know that the initial amount of the loan was $60,000 and this amount is payable over five years, so repayments are $1,000 per month ($60,000 ÷ 60 months). The loan repayments commenced one month after the loan was made, so repayments started in February 2011. At the end of the financial year, Ben will have made 11 monthly repayments, so the capital amount outstanding as at 31 December 2011 is going to be $49,000 ($60,000 less (11 x $1,000)).

You can now work out the element that is to fall due within one year and more than one year by determining how many instalments are left at 31 December 2011. The initial term of the loan was 60 months and Ben has repaid 11 months so 49 instalments are left as at 31 December 2011. You work out the current liability portion as follows:

12 months x $1,000 per month = $12,000

And you work out the values for non-current liabilities as follows:

(49 – 12) = 37 x $1,000 per month = $37,000

Can you see why correct classification of current and non-current liabilities is vital? If Ben was to get the classification wrong, or forget to do it, he would either overstate or understate his current or non-current liabilities, which would have an effect on ratios like the current ratio (calculated as current assets divided by current liabilities), which investors are particularly interested in.

Liability classification can have a significant influence on stakeholders such as potential investors and financiers because any errors in the classification of current and non-current liabilities affect financial ratios such as the *current ratio* (a ratio used to measure a company's ability to pay short-term liabilities) and *gearing ratios* (a measure of a company's borrowings in relation to its equity). Financiers are interested in the relationship between current assets (things like inventories, trade receivables and cash at bank) and current liabilities (liabilities due within 12 months of the reporting date). If the current liabilities are in excess of current assets, the company may not have sufficient current assets (in other words, assets expected to turn into cash within 12 months) in order to meet its obligations to creditors due within 12 months, which may also be an indicator that the company may not be a *going concern* (have the ability to continue in business for the foreseeable future). In this case, the company may be forced to sell non-current assets to raise funds should the company's current creditors all demand payment at once – particularly when a bank overdraft is called in unexpectedly, especially in times of economic difficulties, which some companies have unfortunately faced in recent times.

Dealing with the disclosures

IAS 1 *Presentation of Financial Statements* prescribes that you disclose the following on the statement of financial position in respect of liabilities:

- ✔ Trade and other payables
- ✔ Provisions
- ✔ Financial liabilities (excluding trade and other payables and provisions)
- ✔ Liabilities for current tax
- ✔ Liabilities for deferred tax
- ✔ Liabilities included in disposal groups classified as held for sale

Figure 6-1 shows a typical example of how you illustrate current and non-current liabilities.

	2011	2010
	$000	$000
Non-current liabilities		
Long-term borrowings	X	X
Deferred tax	X	X
Long-term provisions	X	X
Total non-current liabilities	X	X
Current liabilities		
Trade and other payables	X	X
Short-term borrowings	X	X
Current portion of long-term borrowings	X	X
Income tax	X	X
Short-term provisions	X	X
Total current liabilities	X	X

Figure 6-1:
Illustration of current and non-current liabilities.

Chapter 18 explains other disclosures you may need to make in the notes to the financial statements concerning liabilities that are secured and provisions.

To make sure that you're complying with all relevant requirements in IFRS and legislation relating to the disclosure of liabilities, keep a reliable and up-to-date disclosure checklist to hand. Remember, standards frequently change so the checklists need to be up-to-date!

Taking a Close Look at Trade Payables

A type of liability that most (if not all) companies incur during their everyday business dealings is trade payables. When a company sells goods to the general public, it gets those goods from a supplier. The company doesn't usually pay for the goods at the moment it receives them from the supplier: the company owes the supplier money. The amount owed is called a *trade payable*.

Defining a trade payable

In a nutshell, a *trade payable* is *an amount you owe* to someone you buy goods from on a frequent basis for resale in your business. Trade payables can also be amounts owed to service organisations, such as your accountancy firm, law firm, telephone service provider and other such suppliers that supply your business.

Ordinarily, a trade payable is *not* a sum of money owed to, or in respect of

- A finance company that has supplied some sort of finance, for example a loan or hire purchase
- The tax authority
- Provisions you may make under IAS 37 *Provisions, Contingent Liabilities and Contingent Assets* (see Chapter 7)

IAS 1 considers all trade payables to be classified as current, regardless of the fact that you may agree to settle some, or all, trade payables after more than 12 months. Why? Well, it all boils down to the nature of the transaction. IAS 1 recognises that trade payables are part of the working capital used in the company's normal operating cycle (usually 12 months) and therefore are classified as current. In real life, not many suppliers offer payments terms that exceed 12 months, but in rare cases you may come across such a situation. Still, the trade payable is current.

Refer to the minimum disclosure rules if you're unsure whether a certain item is a trade payable or not. In many situations, whether or not an issue falls to be treated as a trade payable is fairly obvious.

Accounting for trade payables

Accounting for trade payables can be easy: you get an invoice from a supplier, you enter the invoice and you pay it when it falls due – simples! But accounting is more complex when you enter into transactions with companies located overseas.

When a trade payable located in another country sends in an invoice that's denoted in a foreign currency, you must translate the invoice into your domestic currency using the rate of exchange on the date of the transaction. When you pay the transaction, the chances are that the amount of money you pay the trade payable may be more or less than the amount you translated the invoice at, because of fluctuations in the exchange rate; you recognise this variation, known as an *exchange gain or loss*, in the income statement.

Foreign currencies

IAS 21 *The Effects of Changes in Foreign Exchange Rates* deals specifically with foreign exchange currencies. The history of this standard goes back as far as December 1977 and prescribes the way that transactions that are denoted in a foreign currency should be translated and how the financial statements of a company (usually a subsidiary) located overseas should be translated when their financial statements are presented in a foreign currency. Among other things, the main thrust of IAS 21 requires a company to determine its *functional currency*: the currency of the primary economic environment (the environment in which the company generates and spends cash) – for example, in the UK the functional currency is Great British pounds (GBP); in other countries, such as Germany and Spain, the functional currency is the euro.

IAS 21 states that a transaction undertaken with a foreign company should be translated to the functional currency of the reporting organisation at the rate of exchange at the date of the transaction. You translate monetary items in the statement of financial position (for example, cash) at the *closing rate* (the exchange rate at the reporting date), and translate non-monetary items (for example, inventories) using the *historic rate* (the rate of exchange at the date the transaction was entered into).

When a company (for example, a foreign subsidiary) prepares financial statements in a foreign currency, you have to translate assets and liabilities (including comparatives) at the closing rate at the date of the statement of financial position. You translate income and expenses for each income statement (including comparatives) at exchange rates at the dates of the transactions and all exchange differences are recognised in other comprehensive income. You can also use an average rate if no great fluctuations in exchange rates occurred.

Kai's Kayaks supplies kayaks and canoe equipment for sale to the general public and to outdoor sports companies. The company has recently sourced a new supplier, Chris's Canoes, whose currency is the euro. Kai's Kayaks has a year-end of 31 December 2011. On 30 September 2011, it placed an order with Chris's Canoes to supply 10 canoes. The goods were delivered on 15 October 2011 and the invoice for €5,000 was received on 23 October 2011. The exchange rate on 23 October 2011 for €1 into $1 was 1.187.

Kai's Kayaks enter the invoice received from Chris's Canoes at a value of $4,212.30 (€5,000 ÷ 1.187).

Assume that Kai's Kayaks pays Chris's Canoes Inc on 4 January 2012, when the exchange rate has moved from 1.187 to 1.180. This movement means that Kai's Kayaks doesn't actually pay Chris's Canoes $4,212.30 because the rate of exchange applied at the date of the transaction (1.187) isn't the same as the rate of exchange at the date of payment (which is 1.180). Therefore, Kai's

Kayaks actually pays Chris's Canoes $4,237.29 (€5,000 ÷ 1.180). The invoice entered was at an amount of $4,212.30, but Kai's Kayaks pays $4,237.29, so this difference means that a loss on exchange of $24.99 exists, which the accountant must recognise in the income statement.

So, there's more to accounting for trade payables than meets the eye and IAS 21, which I explain in the sidebar 'Foreign currencies', comes into the mix. If accounting were straightforward, it would be boring!

Recognising a supplier who hasn't invoiced in time

Occasionally, a supplier may either forget to invoice you for goods, or the invoice may get lost en route to your company. Now just because the invoice hasn't arrived, for whatever reason, doesn't mean that you can simply ignore it for the purposes of the financial statements. You have to exercise prudence when you prepare the financial statements and this prudence also includes correctly recognising any liabilities that may not have been invoiced so that the financial statements give a true picture as to the state of the company's affairs at the year-end.

The statement of financial position is a snapshot of the company's affairs at the close of business on the last day of the accounting period and must take into consideration all relevant transactions and events.

When a company won't receive an invoice in time due to circumstances beyond the control of the supplier, the company must *make an accrual* (recognise an amount in the financial statements for goods or services received at the year-end but for which no invoice has yet been received) for the late invoice. This accrual is needed to comply with the provisions in the *Conceptual Framework*, which state that you must recognise liabilities when an obligation exists to another party.

Here's an example: Sheila's Chamois Co provides cleaning services to various organisations. It buys its bleaches and other biocide products from Sparkling Shiny Products. The accounts manager at Sheila's Chamois Co, Lynn, has heard on the grapevine that Sparkling Shiny Products had a major virus infect their computer equipment during the month of December that resulted in the sales invoices for the month of December failing to go out. Lynn rang the financial director of Sparkling Shiny Products on 27 December 2011 and informed them that as the year-end of Sheila's Chamois Co is 31 December 2011, she could really do with the invoice being sent. Alex, the managing director of Sparkling Shiny Products, said he couldn't guarantee that he would be able to. So Lynn must estimate the value of the invoice that Sheila's Chamois Co hasn't yet received and include it in the books at the year-end.

Exploring Operating and Finance Leases

IAS 17 *Leases* covers leasing. Leases are a common form of liability. Lots of companies enter into lease agreements in some form or another. For example, a company may purchase a fleet of vehicles on *hire purchase* (a form of finance that allows the lessee to use the vehicles by making monthly payments of capital and interest), or it may rent its building from a landlord. When a company enters into a lease transaction, it absolutely must ensure that the substance, not the legal form of the lease, is accounted for. You may have heard the phrase 'substance over form': you account for the commercial reality of the transaction, not the legal form, of the transaction.

After you enter into a leasing agreement, the next vital step is to correctly classify the lease in the accounting records. Leasing classification is one of the most controversial subjects in accounting at present because some companies deliberately engineer lease transactions to achieve a desired outcome (see the sidebar 'Leasing – it's all kicking off!'). You have to look at every leasing agreement in isolation and you need to determine whether the agreement is a finance lease or an operating lease.

Classifying and accounting for operating leases

Operating leases are deemed as such when the risks and rewards of ownership of the asset subject to the lease arrangement remain with the *lessor* (the person who owns the asset).

Stuart runs an outdoor sports company. In the office, he has a photocopier, which he leases from Jamie. When the photocopier breaks down, or requires routine service, Jamie has to attend Stuart's premises and undertake this work at Jamie's cost. In addition, Stuart can also cancel the photocopier lease at any time without recourse, and if the machine completely breaks down, Jamie has to supply another one without any additional costs.

This lease is indicative of an operating lease because all the risks and rewards of ownership remain with Jamie such as servicing the machine at his own cost, supplying an additional machine in the event the photocopier breaks down and not being able to charge an early termination fee if Stuart cancels the lease agreement.

The good news about operating leases is that they're incredibly easy to account for (feel free to cheer!). Basically, when the lease is entered into, the lessor (the person leasing the equipment to you) sends you invoices periodically (usually every month). You then enter these invoices onto your purchase ledger and pay them in accordance with the terms (usually the lessor collects payments using Direct Debit).

Leasing – it's all kicking off!

The area of leasing has long since been a controversial subject. Some companies have been known to deliberately understate liabilities in the statement of financial position by not correctly classifying finance leases. Pre IAS 17, companies would use lease accounting as a means of 'off balance sheet finance'. Instead of taking out a bank loan to purchase an asset (for example, a van), the company leased the van and simply charged the payments to the income statement as and when they were incurred. Companies followed this procedure in the belief that, because they were not the legal owner of the asset, they could do it; in other words, companies had no regard to the substance over form concept.

You don't need to make entries on the statement of financial position for an asset or liability because IAS 17 says that payments for operating leases are simply charged to the income statement on a straight-line basis over the lease term, unless another systematic basis is more appropriate. (The term *straight line* simply means that if you sign up to a lease for three years at $12,000 per year, you can charge monthly payments of $1,000 per month.)

 Don't forget to carefully scrutinise the lease agreement to check that the substance of the arrangement is an operating lease! Don't default to the legal form of the transaction; this error is a common one that results in 'off balance sheet finance'. There are also requirements as to what you disclose in the notes to the accounts for leases – a reputable disclosure checklist can help you out with these.

Classifying and accounting for finance leases

A *finance lease* is when the vast majority of the risks and rewards of ownership of the asset subject to the lease have passed to the lessee. You bring the asset onto the statement of financial position at the asset's *fair value* (an unbiased estimate of the market value), or the present value of the guaranteed minimum lease payments if this value is lower than fair value, and you then set up a lease creditor (a liability) in the statement of financial position. IAS 17 says that risks and rewards of ownership are passed to the lessee if any of the following criteria are met:

- The lease transfers ownership to the lessee at the end of the lease term.
- The lease contains a bargain purchase option at the end of the term.
- The lease is for the major part of the asset's useful economic life.

   ✔ The present value of the minimum lease payments at the start of the lease is at least equal to substantially all the fair value of the leased asset.

   ✔ The leased asset is of such a specialised nature that only the lessee can use it.

   ✔ If the lessee can cancel the lease, the lessor's costs associated with cancellation are paid by the lessee.

   ✔ Gains or losses from fluctuations in the asset's fair value accrue to the lessee.

   ✔ The lessee can continue to rent the asset at the end of the term for a rental value that's substantially lower than market value (a 'peppercorn' rent).

So, if the terms of the lease include any of these criteria, you're dealing with a finance lease.

Hill Haulage Company enters into a lease agreement to lease five trucks from Lisa's Leasing Company for use in their business. Hill Haulage has done its sums and figured out that to buy the trucks outright would cost $100,000 and that the *present value* (the value today of the payments to be made in the future) of the minimum lease payments is about $95,000. Hill Haulage has to insure and pay for the maintenance of the trucks, and if it cancels the lease agreement early, it has to pay an early termination fee.

In this example, it's clear that the risks and rewards of ownership of the asset have passed from Lisa's Leasing Company to Hill Haulage because

   ✔ The present value of the lease payments is more or less the same as the cost to purchase them outright.

   ✔ Hill Haulage has to pay for the maintenance and upkeep of the trucks.

   ✔ If Hill Haulage cancels the lease early, it has to pay an early termination fee.

The substance of the transaction – the commercial reality – is that Hill Haulage has acquired assets using leasing as a way of financing it. This lease is a typical finance lease, so Hill Haulage recognises a non-current asset and a lease creditor in the statement of financial position.

Unfortunately, accounting for finance leases is a little more complicated than for operating leases (deep sigh). The fact is that a lot of leases exist that are really finance leases but that companies are reluctant to recognise them as finance leases because they have to bring liabilities onto the statement of financial position.

Leasing: More kicking off

Because the issue of leasing is so controversial, the International Accounting Standards Board (IASB) and the American standard-setters (the Financial Accounting Standards Board (FASB)) have got together and have come up with proposals to completely change the way leases are accounted for. In a nutshell, what they're proposing is that they remove the classification of an operating lease, so that all leases, regardless of whether they fall to be treated as an operating lease, are classed as finance leases. They think that when a lessee enters into a lease agreement, they enter into a transaction that meets the definition of an asset and a liability as defined in the *Conceptual Framework*. The lessee has the rights to the asset (so here is an asset that should be treated as such in the financial statements) and also has obligations to the lessor (the payments they're required to make under the terms of the leasing arrangement), thus a liability.

The IASB have introduced a concept known as the 'right-of-use model' into the proposals. This concept has caused uproar because many organisations, like supermarkets, lease their vehicles using genuine operating leases. If the proposals get the go-ahead, they have to bring these vehicles onto their statements of financial position and also recognise liabilities in respect of the lease creditors. Critics are saying that these proposals will distort the financial statements and distort profitability for those companies that are a casualty of the proposals. Critics also express concern that smaller companies that have loans and other borrowings that contain loan covenants may breach those covenants if the proposals go ahead. Given the controversial aspect of these proposals, the IASB and FASB re-exposed their proposals in the fourth quarter of 2011 with a target IFRS due out in 2012, but they hadn't decided an 'effective from' date at the time this book went to print.

When you've a finance lease, you must bring the asset subject to the finance lease onto the statement of financial position at its fair value, or the present value of the guaranteed minimum lease payments if these payments are lower than fair value. You also recognise a lease liability for the same amount.

John enters into a finance lease agreement with Janet to lease a machine. The fair value of the machine is $50,000 and John has worked out that the present value of the guaranteed minimum lease payments is $55,000.

John records an asset in the statement of financial position for $50,000 and a corresponding lease liability in the statement of financial position for $50,000 by:

Debit non-current assets	$50,000
Credit lease liability	$50,000

John also uses the provisions in IAS 16 *Property, Plant and Equipment* (refer to Chapters 4 and 5 for more) and *depreciates* (writes-off) the machine over the *shorter* of the useful economic life of the asset and the lease term.

Of course, because this lease is a finance lease, Janet charges interest over the term of the lease. Interest is allocated to the lease liability and charged to the income statement using either the interest rate implicit in the lease or sometimes the sum-of-digits method. (The *sum-of-digits method* involves working out the number of lease rentals that are payable and calculating the sum-of-digits, so if John makes five annual payments, the sum of digits is 1 + 2 + 3 + 4 + 5 = 15; if the total interest charge for the year is $5,000, Year 1 will be (5/15) x $5,000 = $1,667, in Year 2 it will be (4/15) x $5,000 = $1,333 and so on.) Whichever way interest is calculated, John should charge the interest as a finance cost in the income statement by crediting the lease liability account and debiting finance costs in the income statement.

As with all liabilities, you present finance leases on the statement of financial position split between the portion of the capital (not capital and interest) that falls due within 12 months from the reporting date and the portion that falls due after more than 12 months from the reporting date. If you don't present finance leases in this way and you include all the payments as a current liability, your net current assets may be substantially reduced, or may even turn into net current liabilities!

Looking from the other side of the fence: Lessor accounting

In the previous sections, I consider leasing transactions from the perspective of those entering into lease agreements – lessees. But what about the lessor, the person leasing out the asset? Here's how the lessor accounts for operating and finance leases:

- ✔ **Operating leases:** When a lease is classified as an operating lease, the lessor needs to record a non-current asset at the fair value of the asset. The lessor recognises rental income in the income statement on a straight-line basis over the term of the lease (unless another systematic basis is more appropriate in the circumstances). An operating lease is as easy as that.

- ✔ **Finance leases:** The lessor records a receivable at the amount of the net investment in the lease. The net investment in the lease is the total future income less future finance costs. The lessor allocates income received under the lease to give a constant rate of return. When income is received, the lessor debits cash at bank and credits the portion that relates to the receivable that the lessor recognised initially and credits finance income for the amount of the interest charged under the lease.

All this accounting requires lots of disclosures in the notes to the financial statements.

Getting to Grips with Income Taxes

Most people agree that tax is a liability. Well, in accounting terms, if you make a profit you have to pay tax on that profit, and the tax you have to pay to the tax authority leads to liability to the tax authority. So you need to know how to account for the tax on your profit in the financial statements, how to handle deferred tax and how to deal with the disclosures of taxes in the financial statements.

Taxable profit is, in almost all cases, different from the profit before tax you see on the income statement. This difference is because pre-tax profit in the financial statements is often made up of some expenditure (or income), which the tax authority doesn't recognise for the purposes of calculating taxable profit.

The standard that deals with income taxes is IAS 12 *Income Taxes.*

Dealing with tax on your profits in the financial statements

When you (or your accountant) is preparing the tax computation (usually termed the *tax comp*), you take the pre-tax profit per the income statement and add back any items of expenditure that make up pre-tax profit in the financial statements but that aren't allowable for the purposes of tax. The most common item of expenditure that's involved in arriving at a financial statement pre-tax profit but that's not allowable for tax purposes is *depreciation* (writing off the cost of a tangible non-current asset over its estimated useful life). In the tax computation, you add back depreciation to accounting profit (thus essentially increasing the profit for tax purposes) but then the tax authority usually grants its version of depreciation, sometimes called *capital allowances*. You don't include capital allowances in the financial statements, so you deduct these allowances to reduce the adjusted profit. After all this adding back and deducting, you arrive at a taxable profit.

The tax computation usually looks something like the following:

Profit per financial statements	X
Add back:	
Depreciation	X
Entertaining	X̲

Less:
Capital allowances   (X)
Profit chargeable to tax   X

In simplistic terms, you then apply the rates of tax to the profit chargeable to tax to arrive at a tax liability.

The illustration I use here is simplistic to demonstrate how taxable profit is different to accounting profit. In many cases, you've other, more complex, issues to consider in tax that are outside the scope of this book.

When you arrive at a tax liability, you need to get this liability into the financial statements. You do so by debiting the income tax expense in the income statement and crediting income tax payable in the statement of financial position.

Income tax payable is always a current liability, even if an arrangement has been put in place with the tax authority to repay tax using instalments over a period of time that may span more than 12 months (though repayment over such a lengthy period of time is rare!).

Getting into the nitty gritty of deferred tax accounting

One of the most critical points to understand where deferred tax is concerned is that this tax is not a real type of tax that you pay over to the tax authority. It's all about making an accounting adjustment to deal with the future tax consequences on *current* period transactions. Many accountants glaze over at the mention of deferred tax because it can become problematic, so I'm going to keep the explanation simple.

The starting point in understanding deferred tax is to get to grips with some of the terminology that you come across when deferred tax kicks in. Here are some of the most common terms, together with definitions:

- ✔ **Accounting profit:** The profit before income tax expense (pre-tax profit), which is shown in the income statement.

- ✔ **Tax base:** The amount of an asset that is deductible for tax purposes against any taxable economic benefits (for example, sales) generated by that asset. If the economic benefits aren't taxable, the asset's *tax base* (the value for tax purposes) is equal to its *carrying amount* (the amount stated at in the financial statements).

✔ **Temporary difference:** The difference between the *carrying amount* of an asset or liability in the statement of financial position and its *tax base* (the value of the asset or liability for tax purposes). A temporary difference can be *deductible*, which means that the difference can be deducted in the future to determine taxable profit or loss. A temporary difference can also be *taxable*, which means that the difference gives rise to an amount you use to determine future taxable profit or loss.

So, what's deferred tax all about then? Well, accounting profit (profit before tax expense) is often, if not always, different to taxable profit (the profit on which a company pays tax). This difference is because some stuff that makes up accounting profit isn't allowable for tax purposes so gets added back. And events in the current year can have a tax consequence in future periods. Many occurrences can give rise to deferred tax, but the most frequent example of a transaction that's recorded in the current year but that has a future tax consequence is the acquisition of a new *non-current asset* (an asset used in the business that can't be easily turned into cash and isn't expected to be turned into cash within 12 months).

Considering depreciation

The most common item of expense recognised in the financial statements but not recognised for tax purposes is depreciation. You depreciate a non-current asset (other than land) to conform with IAS 16 *Property, Plant and Equipment* (more on this in Chapter 4).

Tax authorities often disallow depreciation because depreciation is a 'man-made' policy (in other words the management of a company chooses the rate at which to depreciate non-current assets). However, tax authorities do recognise that non-current assets depreciate in value, so instead they grant *capital allowances*, which allow you to write off the value of the non-current asset for tax purposes. You account for depreciation in the financial statements, but not capital allowances.

Some tax authorities allow companies to write off as much as 100 per cent of the value against current year's taxable profit in capital allowances, providing the item of non-current asset(s) meets qualifying criteria; but in many instances, the rate of capital allowances granted by a tax authority is different to the rate at which the same non-current assets are being depreciated, resulting in a difference between the net book value of some non-current assets for accounting purposes and the tax base of the same assets for tax purposes. These differences are known as *temporary* differences, and IAS 12 requires a company to recognise the tax effects of those differences in the current year's financial statements by way of a deferred tax charge or credit.

Working through an example calculation

When you buy a new item of non-current asset (such as a van or a machine), you write off the cost of that non-current asset over its estimated useful life by way of *depreciation*. The organisation determines the depreciation policy – so it may depreciate the asset over anything between 12 months and 50 years. For example, if you've a machine that costs $20,000 and its estimated useful live is five years, the annual amount of depreciation is ($20,000 ÷ 5 years) $4,000 (flick to Chapter 4 for more calculating depreciation).

Even though depreciation is an expense you include in arriving at profit, the tax authorities don't like it because depreciation is 'man-made', hence the tax authority has its own version of depreciation called *capital allowances*. Capital allowances work in the same way as depreciation (by writing off the cost of the asset) but are given at prescribed rates determined by the tax authority. Because the rates of depreciation are often different than the rates of capital allowances given by the tax authority, this gives rise to a difference in the value the machine is worth at the end of the accounting period for tax purposes and the value the same machine is worth in the financial statements (the *net book value*). This difference may give rise to *deferred tax*.

To work out and deal with deferred tax liability, you need to:

1. **Find out how much the non-current asset(s) is worth in the financial statements (the *net book value*).**

2. **Work out the value of the non-current asset(s) for tax purposes.**

   No tricky maths here; just get these details from the capital allowances computation prepared when the company works out its tax expense on its profit. Ask your tax guy or gal for this information.

3. **If the value in Step 1 is higher than the value in Step 2, work out the difference and then multiply this difference by the tax rate at which the company pays tax.**

   The figure you arrive at in Step 3 is the deferred tax liability.

4. **Include the deferred tax liability in the financial statements by debiting deferred tax expense in the income statement and crediting deferred tax liability (a non-current liability) in the statement of financial position.**

Aidan buys an item of machinery for $30,000, which is expected to last for five years and will have nil residual value at the end of its life. Aidan charges a full year's depreciation in the year of acquisition and none in the year of disposal and he depreciates the machine on a straight-line basis over five years. The net book value at the end of the Aidan's financial year is therefore $24,000 ($30,000 – $6,000 ($30,000 ÷ 5)). Aidan is located in a country where the tax authority allows companies to write off 100 per cent of the value of new and qualifying assets. Aidan's new machine is eligible for this allowance and he takes advantage of it.

You can see that Aidan's new machine in the financial statements has a net book value of $24,000 at the end of his financial year, but the same item of machinery has a value (the tax base) of nil dollars for tax purposes because he's chosen to take advantage of the allowance to write off the cost in full. Taking advantage of this concession by the tax authority has given him additional capital allowances in the current year (which he wouldn't have otherwise got if he hadn't bought the new machine) that reduces his profit chargeable to tax.

The difference between the net book value of the machine for accounting purposes and for tax purposes of $24,000 is the temporary difference, which gives rise to a deferred tax liability because next year Aidan won't get the same allowance on the same machine and his tax bill will therefore be higher. So Aidan needs to account for this future 'refund' of a temporary cash flow advantage by way of deferred tax. As you can see, deferred tax irons out these tax/accounting inequalities.

To calculate the deferred tax, you simply take the temporary difference of $24,000 and multiply it by the tax rate applicable in Aidan's country. If you assume that this tax rate is 25 per cent, then Aidan recognises a deferred tax liability of $6,000. Aidan then debits income tax expense in the income statement and credits deferred tax in the statement of financial position.

Deferred tax is *always* a non-current liability, so don't include it in current liabilities! Also, IAS 12 prohibits you from discounting deferred tax balances to present day values.

Every year, Aidan needs to go back to the deferred tax calculation and recalculate it as the temporary differences start to unwind.

If Aidan ignored the deferred tax implications of this transaction, in future years the tax charge would be disproportionately high. Remember, Aidan has achieved a cash flow saving in the year when he bought the qualifying non-current asset. In the next year, he won't get the same saving on the same asset and, assuming that he doesn't buy any more qualifying non-current assets in the next year, his tax charge in the income statement would be too high if he doesn't recognise the deferred tax charge in the year he bought the non-current asset.

Assume that in the following year Aidan makes a pre-tax profit of $100,000. He hasn't bought any non-current assets in the year. The $100,000 includes another $6,000 worth of depreciation. Aidan's tax computation looks as follows:

	$
Profit before tax	100,000
Add back depreciation	6,000
	106,000
Less capital allowances	$nil
Profit chargeable to tax	$106,000
Tax rate	25%
Tax charge	**$26,500**

Aidan needs to make an adjustment, in the current year, to the deferred tax charged last year because the asset is worth less this year. The tax base of the machine is still nil dollars because it was all written off last year for tax purposes, and the net book value of the machine this year is $18,000. The temporary difference is therefore $18,000 multiplied by the tax rate of 25 per cent, so $4,500. The deferred tax position is now as follows:

Opening deferred tax balance	$6,000
Closing deferred tax balance	<u>$4,500</u>
Reduction in deferred tax	**$1,500**

To get the reduction in the financial statements, Aidan debits deferred tax provision in the statement of financial position and credits income tax expense in the income statement. After this adjustment, the income statement shows:

Profit before tax	$100,000
Income tax expense*	<u>$25,000</u>
Profit after tax	**$75,000**

* Income tax per computation $26,500 less the reduction in the deferred tax charge of $1,500

On occasion, a deferred tax *asset* may be eligible for recognition. The most common transaction giving rise to a deferred tax asset is a company's unused tax losses. A company can offset tax losses against taxable profit in subsequent years when it makes a profit after making a taxable loss and these tax losses are a tax reducer. The company can only recognise a deferred tax asset when it's probable that there will be future taxable profits against which it can use the unused tax losses (in other words, that the deferred tax asset will be recovered). Be careful here: the mere existence of tax losses may well be an indicator that the company may not return to profitability, so the management should consider whether the company is a going concern carefully.

Dealing with the disclosures in the financial statements

You need to disclose the income tax expense as a separate line item in the income statements. Then you disclose the following in the notes to the financial statement:

- ✔ Tax expense for the current period
- ✔ Any adjustments to the tax expense in respect of prior periods
- ✔ The deferred tax expense or income for the period

✔ Any amounts used to reduce the current period's tax charge in respect of unutilised tax losses, credits or other temporary differences that haven't been recognised previously

✔ Any tax expense that has arisen because of a change in accounting policy or prior period error

✔ The deferred tax expense or income that arises because of a write-down, or reversal, of a prior period deferred tax asset

The list isn't exhaustive, so use a reputable disclosure checklist to make sure that any additional disclosures you need are included in the notes to the financial statements correctly.

Accounting for income taxes: the future unfolded

Nothing stands still for long in the world of IFRS. The IASB have proposed changes to IAS 12 *Income Taxes*. In March 2009, the IASB issued an exposure draft 'Income Tax' that essentially retains the basic approach to accounting for deferred tax. The changes apply to accounting periods commencing on or after 1 January 2012. The IASB want to change the methodology used to calculate deferred tax as well as changing a couple of the definitions and eliminating some of the recognition exceptions.

The draft proposes to only recognise deferred tax in respect of assets and liabilities when the company expects the recovery, or settlement, of the carrying amount of those assets and liabilities, to affect taxable profit. The IASB are also proposing a slight change to the definition

of tax base (the amount at which an asset or liability is carried in the tax comp).

Quite a lot of detailed changes are in the proposal, but the important thing to remember is that the fundamental principle of comparing the book values of assets and liabilities with their associated tax bases to calculate deferred tax is still the same.

The IASB's website at www.iasb.org.uk has details of these changes and the work plan for the standard-setters (click on the 'Standards development' tab). Nothing stands still for long in the world of financial reporting, so make sure that you keep an eye on this site. Doing so can count towards your continuing professional development as well – bonus!

Chapter 7

Examining Liabilities You Don't See Every Day

Companies incur liabilities on a daily basis. For example, buying goods from a supplier may incur a liability on the part of the company to the supplier, which is only settled when the company pays the supplier (known as a *trade payable*). Another example is a bank loan that a company takes out. These are liabilities that you come across during your life as an accountant (for more on common liabilities, see Chapter 6).

In this chapter, I look at liabilities that may not crop up in every company. Some companies can undertake extremely complex transactions, which may give rise to issues that need careful thought and consideration.

To kick off, I look at provisions and contingencies. Say a company has a disagreement with a third party. The company may have to look at making a provision for a liability or make additional disclosures concerning the issue. I examine why you must only recognise provisions when certain criteria are met, and show you how to go about handling disclosures on the financial statements.

Another type of liability you may not encounter on a daily basis is the financial liability. This liability can be a tricky, but I take you through the basics you need to know so you can tame the beast. And finally, you may work for a company that operates a pension plan, which is another form of liability. I take a butchers at the two types of pension plan and how you account for each correctly.

Considering Provisions and Contingencies

IAS 37 *Provisions, Contingent Liabilities and Contingent Assets* deals with provisions and contingencies, one of the most subjective areas in the world of accountancy and one that can also be sensitive in terms of what a company wants and doesn't want to disclose. So what are provisions and contingencies all about then? Well, a *provision* is an amount that's recognised in the financial statements that's not subject to a certain timing of settlement or amount (a bit like an estimate of legal fees when you're involved in a legal dispute). A *contingency* is a possible asset or liability whose existence will only be confirmed by uncertain future events.

In this section, I examine why a standard is necessary in the area of provisions and contingencies, when you can and can't make a provision and what disclosures you need to make in the financial statements relating to provisions and contingencies.

Understanding the necessity for a standard for provisioning

Back in the days before the world of accountancy had a standard on provisions, accountants made some pretty dubious entries in the books of certain companies. Before IAS 37 rocked up, you could manipulate the financial statements to achieve a desired outcome. Many companies cottoned on to the concept of *big bath accounting*, which enabled companies to foresee future costs in the belief that the company was being prudent.

In years when profits were higher than anticipated, companies would recognise extra costs as a *provision* on the statement of financial position to bring profits down. Accountants called these extra costs *big bath provisions*, hence the term 'big bath accounting'. The idea is that you know what your profit needs to be so you use big bath accounting to achieve your need. If the next year's results showed lower than anticipated profit, companies would then release part (or all) of the previous year's big bath provision, which would, again, achieve a desired profit.

Such a practice resulted in companies reporting some pretty dubious figures, so in came IAS 37, which stopped this fudging. Some companies were pretty cheesed off by IAS 37 changing the rules of the game, but let's face it: big bath accounting was dodgy!

It's as true today as it was back in the days before IAS 37 that the tax authorities don't look favourably on inappropriate provisions or excessive provisions. So make sure that any provisions you make in the financial statements are credible.

Knowing when to make a provision and when not to

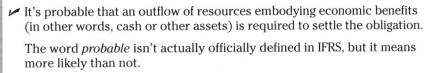

IAS 37 lays down three strict criteria that have to be met before you can recognise a provision in the financial statements:

✔ The company has a present obligation (legal or constructive) as a result of a past event(s).

   A *legal* obligation is fairly easy to comprehend; this obligation is essentially when the solicitor or a court says that you're going to have to cough up dosh, or give up another form of asset, to settle the liability. A *constructive* obligation is an obligation that arises because of the company's actions such as a pattern of past practice (for example, a long history of paying bonuses based on pre-tax profits using a specified formula), or because it creates a valid expectation in the minds of those parties (for example, announcing a programme of redundancies due to a division closing down or ceasing to trade).

✔ It's probable that an outflow of resources embodying economic benefits (in other words, cash or other assets) is required to settle the obligation.

   The word *probable* isn't actually officially defined in IFRS, but it means more likely than not.

✔ A reliable estimate of the obligation can be made.

If a company can't meet the three criteria, it must not make a provision. Instead, it must disclose a contingent liability (see the following section).

Demystifying the complexities of contingent liabilities

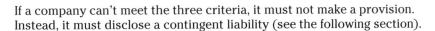

A *contingent liability* is only a *possible* obligation that arises from a past event. The obligation itself is subject to uncertain future events; for example, in legal proceedings uncertainty may exist as to whether the court will find in favour of the company or not. Also, a contingent liability may only be such because you can't make a reliable monetary estimate of any obligation.

IAS 37 defines a contingent liability as one of the following:

✔ A possible obligation that arises from past events and whose existence will be confirmed only by the occurrence or non-occurrence of one or more uncertain future events not wholly within the control of the entity

✔ A present obligation that arises from past events but isn't recognised because it's not probable that an outflow of resources embodying economic benefits will be required to settle the obligation, or the amount of the obligation cannot be measured with sufficient reliability

You never recognise a contingent liability as a liability in the financial statements (in other words, you don't include the liability within the statement of financial position nor in the corresponding cost in the income statement).

Isabelle Interiors has received a letter from a customer's lawyers, who are claiming for damages to their property. Isabelle Interiors is disputing the claim on the grounds that it believes that the damage was done after it had completed the interior design work. The claim is for $10,000 and the accountant at Isabelle Interiors is currently preparing the annual financial statements. The legal letter has been passed to the lawyers representing Isabelle Interiors, who have confirmed that they can't establish whether or not Isabelle Interiors is liable at the moment.

This is an example of a contingent liability. Out of the three criteria that have to be met before you can recognise a provision, only one is valid. A reliable estimate of the claim ($10,000) exists but the company can't be certain that a legal obligation will arise (because the lawyers representing Isabelle Interiors can't say whether or not Isabelle Interiors will be successful in defending the claim). In addition, because of the uncertainty surrounding the outcome of the claim, it won't be possible to identify whether an outflow of resources (hard cash) will be paid to settle the claim. The upshot is that Isabelle Interiors can't recognise the $10,000 as a liability in its statement of financial position. Instead, it must disclose the contingent liability in the notes to the financial statements.

Dealing with the disclosures in the financial statements

The notes to the financial statements contain a lot of detailed information regarding the amounts recognised in the financial statements and other issues that have affected the company during the year. These notes are to enable the user to fully understand what's gone on in the year. So when you've a *material* issue (one whose omission or mis-statement would influence the decisions of the users of the financial statements) that's given rise to the recognition of a provision, or the disclosure of a contingency, you need to make additional disclosures that explain the issue and the reasons for recognising the provision or disclosing the contingency.

In respect of provisions and contingencies, I cover some of the disclosures in Chapter 18, but for each class of provision you should disclose

- The carrying amount of provision(s) at the beginning and end of the accounting period including:
  - Any changes during the period
  - Unused amounts that have been reversed during the period
  - Any increases that have been caused by any amounts that have been discounted for the time value of money arising from passage of time or changes in discount rates
- A description of the obligation
- When payments are going to be made
- Details of any uncertainties concerning payment timing
- Any amounts that are expected to be reimbursed
- Any major assumptions that have been made concerning future events

For contingent liabilities, you must disclose

- The nature of the contingent liability
- An estimate of the contingency's financial effect
- Details of any possible reimbursements
- Details of uncertainties relating to the amount or timing of payments

Sometimes, a company may be reluctant to make detailed disclosures concerning contingent liabilities because it may consider such disclosures to be seriously prejudicial to its position in a dispute with another party. In such cases, don't disclose all the information; instead, simply disclose the general nature of the dispute and the reason you haven't disclosed additional information.

Because IFRS and IAS often interact with one another, IAS 37 may not apply when provisions or contingent liabilities are *specifically* covered by another standard. For example, IAS 12 *Income Taxes* (see Chapter 6) requires you to provide an amount for the current tax on the profit for the period, so IAS 37 doesn't apply in this respect.

Exploring Financial Liabilities

Financial liabilities can be complex to deal with. The key to breaking the ice is to understand what gives rise to a financial liability. When a company wants to raise finance for whatever reason, it goes to a third party to provide that finance (for example, the bank). If the third party agrees to the loan, a *financial liability* arises on the part of the company because it then owes the third party the loan, plus any interest on that loan. (The third party, meanwhile, recognises the loan as an asset, not a liability; Chapter 5 explains assets.)

This section focuses on some pretty hard-to-understand standards: IAS 32 *Financial Instruments: Presentation*, IAS 39: *Financial Instruments: Recognition and Measurement* and IFRS 7: *Financial Instruments: Disclosures*. Many accountants who work in accountancy practice find that IAS 39 is probably *the* most difficult standard to understand and to apply in real life. In some cases, you may need specialist assistance to ensure that you account for financial liabilities correctly. If you're not sure then get help, because asking for help is much better (and easier) than getting it wrong and financial instruments can lend themselves to a whole host of misdemeanours.

Understanding what financial liabilities are all about

A *financial liability* arises when a company owes money to third party. The key concept to get your head around where financial instruments are concerned is that when a company raises finance, a third party provides it – and the company receiving the money has a liability to that third party. Of course, financial instruments get much meatier than my simple outline here, but you have to start somewhere.

IAS 39 contains a rather complicated definition of a financial liability. It says that a financial liability is a contractual obligation to one of the following:

- ✔ Deliver cash or another financial asset to another company
- ✔ Exchange financial instruments with another company under conditions that are potentially unfavourable

After you've figured out that you've a financial liability, the next step is figuring out how to classify it in the financial statements.

The standards that govern financial instruments are changing – the International Accounting Standards Board (IASB) is composing a new accounting standard (IFRS 9: *Financial Instruments*). They will take a while to get it ready to be issued as a standard; the IASB has recently said that the plan is to have it effective in 2015 (it was previously estimated to be operational in 2013).

Looking at the classifications of financial liabilities

You must correctly classify a financial liability in the financial statements. IAS 32 *Financial Instruments: Presentation* outlines the two options:

- ✔ Recognise the financial liability as *debt* (in other words as a liability).

- ✔ Recognise the financial liability as *equity* (in other words, like ordinary shares). Equity is also known as *shareholders' funds*.

Consider shares in a company, which may be *ordinary shares* (entitle the holder to a share in profits and to vote at annual general meetings) or *preference shares* (may entitle the holder to a fixed rate of dividend that ranks higher than dividends paid to ordinary shareholders and may also have a redemption feature so that the holder cashes in the value of their preference shares at a later date). These kind of financial instruments entitle the holder to receive a fixed amount of cash (the *dividend*).

When a financial instrument (say, preference shares) entitles the holder to receive cash, or contains a redemption feature, IAS 32 states that you class these instruments as debt instruments. You do so because the substance, not the legal form, is reflected in the financial statements. A contractual obligation exists to deliver cash and this obligation gives rise to a liability (debt).

When a financial instrument (say, ordinary shares) doesn't entitle the holder to receive cash or doesn't contain a redemption feature, you recognise these types of instruments in equity (shareholders' funds).

The correct classification between debt and equity is important. Getting the classification wrong impacts *gearing*, which is the relationship between the amount of a company's borrowings and its equity (a company with high gearing is over-reliant on borrowings for a large proportion of its amounts needed to continue in business, or capital, requirements) in other words the company is using borrowings to pay for it to continue in business. Mistakes also influence reported earnings, which is significant to investors and other users of the financial statements.

Placing values on financial liabilities

After you determine that you need to recognise a financial liability as debt, not equity, in the financial statements, then the accounting for it can sometimes be as simple as debiting cash at bank (because the bank is where the money has been paid into) and crediting liability (because after you receive the money you owe an obligation to the third party providing the finance, hence a liability).

At other times, though, life isn't simple. The following sections lead you though some of the more complex ways of handling financial liabilities.

Compound financial instruments

Some financial instruments can contain a mix of both debt and equity (these are *compound financial instruments*). In such cases, you need to split the proceeds between those that relate to the debt portion and those that relate to the equity portion. You calculate the debt portion by taking the cash flows associated with the instrument (for example, interest payments and redemption of the principal amount at the end of the term) and discounting these cash flows to present-day values. Then you deduct the value of the proceeds and recognise the balance as equity.

Convertible financial instruments

With financial instruments that are *convertible*, you've an option to convert the capital amount of the loan into equity shares at a specified time rather than pay out a chunk of cash to redeem the capital amount (if the instrument holder(s) want to take up the option, of course).

When you've a convertible financial instrument, you need split the instrument (sometimes known as the loan note) into its debt component (the liability) and its equity component (the amount that you recognise in the equity section of the statement of financial position). Convertible financial instruments also attract interest payments to the owner of the instrument, and you need to deal with two lots of interest: the interest paid to the owner of the convertible financial instrument (the *coupon rate*) and the interest that would be charged at the company's interest rate (the company's *cost of capital*). You include the difference between the coupon rate paid to the owner of the convertible financial instrument and the interest that would be charged at the company's cost of capital rate in the financial statements (the difference between the two rates is the *effective* interest). Here are the five steps you follow:

Step 1: Discount the cash flows to present-day values

The owner of the convertible financial instrument will be entitled to receive cash from you in respect of the interest payments and the repayments of the *capital element* (the original sum borrowed) over the life of the instrument. (It works in the same way as your mortgage – the bank charges you interest on the sum you borrowed, and the sum you borrowed is the capital that you have to repay.) The capital and interest payments are the instrument's *cash flows.* You need to work out the value of these cash flows at today's values (present value) because what's worth $1,000 now won't be worth $1,000 in, say, five years' time.

You work out today's values using present value tables and the company's cost of capital. To find out the present value rates to discount the cash flows to present-day values, type 'present value tables' into a search engine and download a copy of the tables. To find out the cost of capital, ask your company's finance director or chief accountant. (If you're a student tackling a convertible financial instruments question, you should be given this info in the question.)

To discount the cash flows to present-day values, you simply take the cash flow for each year and multiply it by the present value factor. You get the present value factor by taking the present value tables and finding your company's cost of capital (the cost of capital rates usually run across the top row heading of the present value tables and are expressed in percentage terms). You then look at the number of periods for which payments are made to the owner of the convertible financial instrument (the number of periods of payment are usually down the left-hand side of the present value tables expressed in periods). The present value factor is the number (usually expressed to three decimal places, such as 0.909) that's under the cost of capital percentage for the number of years the convertible financial instrument has to run.

A company takes out a convertible loan on 1 April 2012 for $600,000, which is repayable in Year 4. The loan note holders require the company to pay interest to them at 8 per cent per annum. The company's cost of capital and the rate of interest that would be charged on a similar loan *without* the option to convert into shares is 10 per cent. Present value rates for a 10 per cent loan note are:

Year 1	0.909
Year 2	0.826
Year 3	0.751
Year 4	0.683

You have to pay $48,000 interest each year to the loan note holders ($600,000 x 8 per cent) in Years 1 to 3. In Year 4, you pay the final $48,000 interest *plus* the capital amount of $600,000. Table 7-1 shows how you discount these cash flows to present-day values:

Table 7-1	Present Value Calculation	
	Cash Flow Multiplied by Present Value Factor	*Discounted Value of the Cash Flows*
Year 1 (2012)	$48,000 x 0.909	$43,632
Year 2 (2013)	$48,000 x 0.826	$39,648
Year 3 (2014)	$48,000 x 0.751	$36,048
Year 4 (2015)	$648,000 ($48,000 interest plus $600,000 capital) x 0.683	$442,584
		$561,912

Step 2: Calculate the debt and equity portions

When you're dealing with a convertible financial instrument, you have to work out both

- ✔ The **debt portion** (liability), which you recognise as a liability in the statement of financial position. The debt portion is the present value of all the cash flows associated with the instrument – the figure you come up with in Step 1.

- ✔ The **equity portion**, which you recognise in the equity section of the statement of financial position (because a convertible financial instrument contains an option for the instrument holder to convert the capital element of a convertible financial instrument into shares at a later date, so the option has a value attached to it and the equity portion represents the value). To work out the equity portion, deduct the debt portion of the instrument (see Step 1) from the original money received from the third party when the third party entered into the convertible financial instrument (the money that physically came to you).

In the Step 1 example, the present value of all the cash flows associated with this instrument is $561,912. So the liability portion of the financial instrument is $561,912. You recognise this amount in liabilities in the statement of financial position.

The difference between the initial proceeds you received from the loan ($600,000) and the liability portion ($561,912) is the equity portion of the financial instrument. So $38,088 ($600,000 minus $561,912) is the value of the option available to the holder of the convertible financial instrument to convert the capital element into shares at a later date. You recognise this amount in the equity section of the statement of financial position.

Step 3: Work out how much interest the company has paid

If the company has already paid interest to the owners of the financial instrument, you need to know how much has been paid (the coupon rate). You can get this information from the accounting records or the signed agreement.

In Step 1, the coupon rate was 8 per cent and the amount of interest paid to the loan note holders in Year 1 was $48,000 ($600,000 x 8 per cent).

Step 4: Work out the interest rate that would be charged if no option exists to convert the loan into shares at a later date

When a company enters into a loan where no option exists to convert the capital amount into shares at a future date, the risk to the third party making the loan is greater because the company may not have the cash available to pay the instrument holder when the capital amount is due for repayment. So the interest rate charged by the third party making the loan is often higher. With a convertible financial instrument, you need to work out the interest rate that would be charged if the option to convert the capital element of the instrument into shares wasn't present and this rate is the company's cost of capital – the rate you use to discount the cash flows to present value (see Step 1). All you do is multiply the cost of capital (which you found in Step 1) by the liability portion (see Step 2).

In the example, the company's cost of capital is 10 per cent. Multiplied by the liability portion, you get $56,191 ($561,912 x 10 per cent).

Step 5: Find the effective interest

The *effective interest* (sometimes referred to as *rolled-up interest*) is the difference between the rate of interest that is paid to the owner of a convertible financial instrument and the rate of interest that would otherwise be paid at the company's cost of capital rate. You include the effective interest in the financial statements by debiting finance costs in the income statement with the effective interest and crediting the loan note liability in the statement of financial position with the effective interest.

In the example, you take the interest you calculated in Step 4 ($56,191) and deduct it from the coupon rate of interest paid to the owners of the financial instrument in Step 3 ($48,000). The result is the effective interest: $8,191. In the financial statements, you debit finance costs in the income statement with $8,191 and credit the financial instrument liability in the statement of financial position with $8,191.

You include the effective interest in the financial statements because the financial statements interest charge needs to reflect the company's cost of capital. In the example, you discounted the cash flows at 10 per cent (see Step 1), but you only paid interest to the loan note holder at 8 per cent so you have to increase the interest charge to take account of the difference in the interest rates.

Amortised cost

Financial instruments can get fairly complicated – particularly when you've both debt and equity portions to consider in one financial instrument. Table 7-2 shows you how to recognise financial liabilities after initial recognition.

Table 7-2	Classification of Financial Liabilities	
Classification	*In Statement of Financial Position*	*Gains or Losses*
Fair value through profit or loss	Fair value	Statement of comprehensive income
Available-for-sale	Fair value	In equity until de-recognition, then recycled via the statement of comprehensive income
Held-to-maturity	At amortised cost	Not applicable
Loans and receivables	At amortised cost	Not applicable

Keep in mind that the forthcoming IFRS 9 removes the available-for-sale and held-to-maturity classifications.

Fair value means that you carry the financial instrument in the statement of financial position at its market value on the reporting date. Any changes in fair values go in the statement of comprehensive income (if classified as fair value through profit or loss) or in equity until de-recognition and then recycled via the statement of comprehensive income (if classified as available-for-sale).

When you recognise financial instruments at *amortised cost*, you need to calculate the interest using the *effective interest method*. This method is a technique that allocates interest income or expense over a relevant period, usually over the life of the financial instrument. You must include all fees, transaction costs and premiums and discounts in the calculation. This calculation gets you to the effective interest rate, which you use in the calculation and which exactly discounts the estimated future cash payments or receipts over the expected life of the instrument.

With amortised cost, you charge the income statement with the effective rate of interest. You charge the difference between the interest paid and the effective interest (the *debt discount amortisation*) to the income statement as a finance cost and then add on to the loan amount in the company's financial statements.

Cash Strapped Co enters into a financial instrument with a financier. The principal amount of the instrument is $90,000 but the financier agrees to enter into the contract at a discount of $10,000 so actually receives $100,000 back by the end of the term of the contract. Cash Strapped Co must pay three interest payments amounting to $5,000 each. The company receives $90,000 and records it as a liability. The financier records the instrument as held-to-maturity because it holds the instrument until it matures.

From the financier's perspective, based on a cash outflow of $90,000 to acquire the investment, three interest payments of $5,000 each and a principal amount of $100,000 at maturity, the financier calculates that the effective interest rate is 8.95 per cent. The financier can summarise the financial instrument using Table 7-3 (the effective rate of interest is 8.95 per cent).

Table 7-3	**Amortised Cost Table**				
	(A)	*(B)*	*(C)*		
Year	*Opening Amortised Cost*	*Interest and Principal Payments*	*Interest Income (A x 8.95 per cent)*	*Debt Discount Amortisation (C – B)*	*Closing Amortised Cost*
1	90,000	5,000	8,055	3,055	93,055
2	93,055	5,000	8,328	3,328	96,383
3	96,383	105,000	8,617	3,617	100,000

Getting rid of financial liabilities in the financial statements

At some stage, a financial liability may no longer be a liability of the company. At this point the company *de-recognises* the liability, which means that it removes the liability from the financial statements – because it doesn't want to keep a liability in the statement of financial position if it has no more contractual obligations to the third party. De-recognition takes place *only* when the company no longer has any further obligations to the third party that originally supplied the financial instrument.

You absolutely must get the timing of de-recognition of financial instruments in the financial statements correct. You can de-recognise a financial liability from the financial statements only when the obligation that is specified within the contract itself is discharged, cancelled or expires. When you've a gain or loss upon de-recognition of a financial liability, you must recognise this figure in the statement of comprehensive income (income statement).

In situations when one financial liability becomes extinguished and the company enters into another, you must recognise the new one in the financial statements at its fair value.

Handling Employee Benefits

This section looks at the area of employee benefits and how such benefits give rise to liabilities within the financial statements. A company that employs people pays the staff wages or salaries. In addition, the company may provide other benefits such as medical care, pension plans, holiday entitlement and other such perks. We needed an accounting standard in this area to make sure that the financial statements of companies clearly reflect their obligations to employees, and the standard that takes care of all this area is IAS 19 *Employee Benefits*. The basic principle in IAS 19 is that you only recognise the cost of benefits when those benefits have been earned by the employee as opposed to when they become payable.

The standard itself is complex and in some cases you need specialist information such as actuarial information (info from an *actuary* – a person who comes up with the numbers to put into the financial statements), in order to ensure that the company correctly applies the provisions in IAS 19 within the financial statements.

IAS 19 aims to be a catch-all in relation to employee benefits. In particular, the standard covers things like:

- Compensated absences
- Housing benefits
- Medical care
- Performance-related remuneration such as profit-sharing and bonuses
- Provision of company cars
- Wages, salaries and social security contributions

You often hear the term *post-employment benefits* when you're dealing with IAS 19-related issues. All this term means is that a pension plan is in operation.

IAS 19 compared to UK FRS 17

IAS 19 was first introduced as an exposure draft by the IASB in April 1980. It became effective for accounting periods commencing on or after 1 January 1983 and throughout its lifecycle it has been subjected to many amendments. The latest amendment to IAS 19 has been proposed by the IASB with an effective date for accounting periods commencing on or after 1 January 2013. IAS 19 covers all types of employee benefits, but in the UK the equivalent standard (FRS 17 *Retirement Benefits*) only covers post-employment benefits – in other words, retirement benefits. IAS 19 is therefore a much bigger standard than some countries' domestic equivalents.

IAS 26 *Accounting and Reporting by Retirement Benefit Plans*

People often get confused between IAS 19 and IAS 26 merely because they both consider retirement benefit plans. IAS 26 looks at retirement benefit plans purely from the perspective of those providing the plans (like a pensions company or a government providing pensions). IAS 26 was introduced in July 1985 as an exposure draft and is highly industry-specific, which is why this book won't go into a lot of detail about it. IAS 26 hasn't been amended much – in fact, it was last reformatted in 1994. This standard is a (sort of) companion standard to that of IAS 19 but deals with the accounting and disclosures needed by a company that's involved in retirement benefit plans.

A retirement benefit plan is an arrangement where an organisation provides benefits for employees on, or after, termination of employment in the form of annual income or as a lump sum – a bit like the government (which provides state pensions), but instead it's a pension company. IAS 26 basically says that these companies must provide a statement of net assets that are available for the payment of benefits as well as providing a description in the financial statements relating to the company's funding policy. In addition to the statement of net assets, the company must also provide:

- ✔ A statement of changes in net assets available for benefits

- ✔ A summary of their significant accounting policies

- ✔ A description of the pension plan and the effect of any changes in the plan during the accounting period

Dealing with short-term employee benefits

IAS 19 outlines the accounting treatment for *short-term employee benefits* – stuff like compensated absences, wages and salaries. You must recognise the cost of short-term employee benefits in the period they're incurred. In addition, you can't discount any of these types of benefits to present-day values, and you wouldn't want to do this anyway because to do so would be quite time-consuming and fiddly.

The accounting for short-term employee benefits is dead easy. All you do is record a short-term employee benefit as an accrued expense and deduct any amount that has already been paid.

When you've worked out the amount to be accrued less any payments made, if the amount paid exceeds the benefit cost then it results in a prepaid asset (not a liability) to the extent that it reduces the amount of a future payment or triggers a refund.

Judith Jewellery Co has five members of staff. The members of staff are paid a profit-related bonus, and in 2011 Judith Jewellery Co paid a bonus of $1,000 per each staff member based on the estimated profit at the year-end. When the company finalised the financial statements, it found that the profit wasn't as high as originally anticipated and the bonus should only have been $900 per employee. The staff members have all agreed that the $100 excess can be repaid back to the company in the next payroll run. The directors have requested that the finalised financial statements be corrected to reflect the adjustments to the bonus.

Judith Jewellery Co recognises a prepayment at the year-end of $500 (five members of staff multiplied by the $100 over-payment per staff member) because this amount will be recovered in the next payroll run.

Had it been the other way around and the bonuses should have been $100 more for each member of staff, Judith Jewellery Co would have recognised a $500 accrued expense (a liability).

Taking a look at defined benefit and defined contribution plans

IAS 19 provides the relevant accounting treatment for two types of pension plan that you probably come across during your working life: the defined contribution pension plan and the defined benefit pension plan.

Defined contribution pension plan

The company pays a fixed amount of contributions into the pension plan on a regular basis (for instance, each month); hence the pension is defined by the amounts paid into the plan plus any investment income. The employee may also pay into the same pension plan by way of deductions from his monthly (or weekly) salary/wages. Under a defined contribution pension plan, an employer has no further legal or constructive obligation to pay any further contributions – even if the fund doesn't have sufficient assets to pay all the employee benefits.

Defined benefit pension plan

Often referred to as a *final salary pension scheme* or *final salary scheme*, this type of plan is significantly different to a defined contribution pension plan and is defined by a pre-determined formula usually based on an employee's salary and years of service. In addition to being different in substance, the defined benefit plan is also more difficult to account for than the defined contribution plan. (I show you why in the later section 'Accounting for defined benefit pension plans'.)

Final salary pension plans

Final salary pension plans are a hugely attractive benefit for employees because they provide a pension following retirement based on the final salary of the employee at retirement. However, recent years have seen the value of such pension plans fall dramatically and this fall has had a shocking effect on the value of some companies' defined benefit pension plans to the extent that the deficit on some defined benefit plans runs into millions. Companies then have to pump more and more money into their pension plans in an attempt to reduce the deficit. So although a defined benefit pension plan may still be an attractive option to employees who have one, for the company providing the plan they're an extremely expensive monster to fund. That's why some companies have closed their defined benefit pension plans to new members.

When a company enters into a defined benefit pension plan, the employer (the company) has an obligation to pay further contributions, over and above those that it may already pay on a periodic basis, if the plan doesn't have sufficient assets to pay all the employee benefits. This obligation can have catastrophic consequences on the company's cash flow because, legally, the company is obliged to make additional payments when a defined benefit pension plan has a deficit. If the company doesn't make additional payments, regulatory bodies may have the power to enforce the company to do so. Under a defined benefit pension plan, *actuarial risk* (the risk that benefits cost more than expected) and investment risk fall, in substance, on the company providing the pension plan.

It's worth pointing out that IAS 19 doesn't cover share-based payment transactions under IFRS 2 *Share-based Payment*. I discuss such issues in Chapter 9.

Accounting for defined contribution pension plans

Defined contribution pension plans are really easy to deal with. What happens is that, say, each month a company pays money into a defined contribution pension plan for their employee(s). These payments usually consist of two elements:

- ✔ The employee has a deduction from their weekly wages or monthly salary for their share of the contribution.
- ✔ The employer pays a set percentage into the employee's pension.

Companies that pay into a defined contribution pension plan can also get tax relief on these payments. *Tax For Dummies* by Sarah Laing (Wiley) gives a good insight as to how tax relief is granted by not 'adding back' the cost of defined contribution pension contributions to accounting profit when adjusting accounting profit to arrive at a profit for tax purposes.

To account for a defined contribution pension plan, you simply credit the bank account by the cost of the pension contribution and debit the pension cost.

Lynn Linen Co operates a successful chain of dry cleaning businesses. It employs 120 staff throughout each of its 10 branches and over the years has become the market leader in dry cleaning. It operates a defined contribution pension plan for all its staff where some employees pay into the plan (others have chosen not to) but Lynn Linen Co pay into the pension plan for all 120 staff. The monthly cost of the pension contribution is $10,000.

Every month, Lynn Linen Co makes an entry in its books as follows:

Credit bank account	$10,000
Debit pension cost (income statement)	$10,000

Accounting for defined benefit pension plans

Many people like a challenge, and if you're one of these types of people then you're going to love accounting for a defined benefit pension plan! In this section, I examine what you need before you can even think about getting the numbers into the financial statements and why many companies throw their toys out of the pram when it comes to accounting for such schemes.

The first thing you need before you can begin to account for a defined benefit pension plan is information from the actuaries, who come up with the figures for the financial statements by using variables such as estimates as to how long employees may live as well as other various mathematical conundrums and assumptions.

Many companies have a major gripe about getting the accounting information from the actuaries because the cost of obtaining this information from actuarial companies can often be quite high. In some cases, companies have even refused to spend the money to obtain the information and the result of this refusal is that the auditors can't see that the company's financial statements contain all the accounting input and relevant disclosures that they should contain under IAS 19. Companies that choose not to obtain the relevant actuarial information may well end up facing the consequences of an *unclean* audit opinion (the auditors disagree with the way in which a company has applied IAS 19), which doesn't exactly bode well with external stakeholders such as credit-rating agencies, suppliers, customers and possibly the bank!

When you're accounting for a defined benefit pension scheme, the charges to the statement of comprehensive income usually comprise the following:

✔ **Current service cost:** The increase in the present-day value of the plan's liabilities. This cost is an increase in the accounting period because the employees have completed another year's service and are therefore another year closer to retiring.

✔ **Interest cost:** The imputed cost that arises because of the unwinding of the discounted values as the plan's liabilities are a year closer to settlement.

✔ **Past service cost:** An increase in the present-day value of the plan's liabilities that also relate to service in prior periods because of new retirement benefits or improvements to existing retirement benefits.

✔ **Expected return on plan assets:** The increase in the market value of the plan's assets.

✔ **Actuarial gains and losses:** Changes in the actuaries' assumptions that can be recognised in the statement of comprehensive income if they exceed *the 10 per cent corridor* – that is, a company can defer, until the next accounting period, recognising actuarial gains and losses that fall outside the greater of 10 per cent of the defined benefit obligation or 10 per cent of the fair value of plan assets. The changes in the actuaries' assumptions usually involve changes in estimated mortality rates and other assumptions made.

✔ **Ten per cent corridor:** A materiality level. The corridor rule requires that a company makes disclosure in the financial statements if the actuarial gains or losses exceed 10 per cent of the pension benefit obligation or the fair value of the plan assets. In this case, the company can allow the actuarial gain or loss to be amortised gradually over time in the income statement.

✔ **Costs of settlement or curtailment:** *Settlements* are transactions that relieve the company, or the pension plan itself, of the responsibility for a pension benefit obligation or eliminate the risks to the employer or the plan, and are usually lump sum cash payments. A *curtailment* is an event that significantly reduces the expected years of future service of present employees or eradicates (for a substantial number of employees) the accrual of defined benefits for some, or all, of their future services. Curtailments usually arise because of termination of contracts for services.

To sum up, the defined benefit pension plan liability is the net total of the present value of the benefit obligation plus any unrecognised actuarial gains, less:

✔ Any unrecognised actuarial losses

✔ Any unrecognised past service costs

✔ The fair value of any plan assets from which obligations are to be directly settled

The IASB has revised IAS 19. Actuarial gains and losses are renamed *remeasurements* and the *corridor approach* is no longer used – instead, you're to recognise remeasurements directly in 'other comprehensive income' (the bit at the end of the income statement; flick to Chapter 1 for details).

As you can see, accounting for defined benefit pension plans is hugely complicated and is usually undertaken by someone within an accounting firm or organisation who has experience in accounting for these types of plans.

Chapter 8

Accounting for Revenue

*R*evenue is usually the biggest number in the financial statements of a company and revenue is also defined differently around the world. Sales and turnover are often the more familiar terms used for *revenue*, but they all boil down to the same thing – revenue is the lifeblood of a company. Without revenue, a company won't generate cash, and the phrase 'cash is king' is as relevant in business today as it was 100 years ago.

Be careful not to confuse what constitutes revenue and what gives rise to a gain. *Revenue* arises from a company's ordinary activities. *Gains* are one-time events that don't relate to the company's core business. Gains include things like profits that you may make when you sell off non-current assets (long-term assets that the business uses to help make money, such as machinery) or gains from foreign exchange transactions.

The accounting standard on revenue is IAS 18 *Revenue*. IAS 18 is one of the most important standards because revenue recognition is an area that accountants can easily manipulate. Indeed, over the years, investigators into well-publicised corporate disasters have frequently cited the area of revenue recognition as one of the most commonly used methods to deliberately mislead users of financial statements in attempts to achieve a desired outcome. Some companies deliberately delayed the recognition of revenue to reduce tax liabilities; others deliberately accelerated revenue recognition to achieve bonuses and to satisfy shareholders' expectations. So the aim of IAS 18 is to prescribe strict accounting treatments in the area of revenue recognition.

Revenue can encompass a range of things. You'd be correct to say that many companies buy and sell goods and the sales of these goods generates revenue. Other companies (like firms of accountants) offer services and sell time to generate revenue. Other companies receive royalties, interest and other forms of income that constitute revenue. IAS 18 covers all these sorts of transactions, and this chapter explains how IAS 18 requires you to account for such transactions in the financial statements.

Timing of Revenue

One of the most crucial things to get right in preparing financial statements is correctly recognising revenue. You need to make sure that the timing is spot on and you don't *accelerate* revenue (you don't recognise revenue too soon). And on the flip side, you must make sure that you don't *disproportionately delay* revenue (you recognise revenue in the right period). Tax authorities are particularly keen to ensure that companies don't delay revenue too much because if companies do so, the tax authority doesn't get its slice of the profit (the tax) at the right time.

The timing of revenue recognition is critical because if you recognise revenue at the wrong time you can seriously mislead the user of the financial statements and the company can also run into difficulty with the tax authorities. So where revenue spans two accounting period, you apportion the revenue accordingly.

Computers R Us sell software products to its customer base. When a customer purchases the software, she can subscribe to a 12-month technical support service that can resolve queries relating to the product and also advise on what to do when things go wrong. Many customers take up this subscription, which runs from 1 January to 31 December each year. Computers R Us has a year-end of 31 March.

In this example, you can see that subscriptions run from 1 January to 31 December each year but slap bang during part of this period is the company's year-end! So, on 1 January 2012 the company invoices its customers for a year's subscription, which runs up to 31 December 2012. On 31 March 2012, the company won't be able to recognise the full value of these subscriptions because they span two accounting periods. In the 31 March 2012 financial statements, they can only recognise the period 1 January 2012 to 31 March 2012 (in other words, three-twelfths) of the subscription. Computers R Us recognises the remaining nine-twelfths in the 31 March 2013 financial statements.

Revenue recognition: The controversy

Urgent Issues Task Force (UITF) is a department of the UK's Accounting Standards Board that issues interpretations and guidance when conflicting or confusing issues arise in an accounting standard or companies legislation (it acts in the same way as the International Financial Reporting Interpretations Committee (IFRIC), which I cover in Chapter 1).

In March 2005, UTIF issued UITF 40. Firms of accountants and solicitors in the UK were among the most high-profile casualties of UITF 40 and it caused uproar within the accountancy profession. Why? Well, UITF 40 was designed to recognise partially completed work as revenue earlier than was done pre-UITF 40. The effect of UITF 40 is that a company under its scope has to report higher profits, which then increases the tax charge. If you consider that many companies may not actually get paid from their customer/client until such time the work was completed, you can understand why many organisations were furious about the impact UITF 40 now has on their financial statements.

Coming up with reliable estimates

Sometimes you have to estimate revenue. This estimation is particularly the case for construction contracts that fall under the scope of IAS 11 *Construction Contracts*.

You must ensure that when you need to exercise professional judgement to estimate revenue, you do so with extreme care. The value of revenue has a significant impact on the company's overall results for the period. And the tax authority will be particularly interested to see that revenue is neither disproportionately understated or overstated. So make sure that estimates are credible and can stand up to scrutiny.

When a company is involved in the construction of assets (see Chapter 4 for more about assets) for its customer, it usually relies on a specialist, such as a surveyor, to visit the construction site and make an assessment as to how complete the construction contract is so that the company can recognise the correct levels of revenue in the financial statements. The company then recognises the part of the work estimated to be complete in its year-end financial statements.

Kapoor Construction is building a new head office complex for Vadher Enterprises. The contract price has been agreed at $70 million and at Kapoor Construction's year-end, Simon the surveyor said that the contract was 40 per cent complete. Kapoor Construction needs to recognise $28 million (40 per cent x $70 million) as contract revenue in its financial statements.

Calculating a reliable estimate of costs

The general rule in the world of accountancy is that costs must match the income that such costs generate (this rule is *the matching concept*). Consider electricity bills, which may span two accounting periods at the year-end. It wouldn't be appropriate to charge the income statement with the portion of the electricity bill that relates to the next financial year because doing so disproportionately increases costs and also reduces profitability. So you carry the excess over to the next financial year by way of a prepayment.

Prepayments are a fairly well-established practice and have been drummed into the heads of student accountants from early on in the days of studying for accountancy exams. Bookkeepers are also familiar with the concept of *accruals* (goods and services received by the company that haven't yet been billed) and prepayments. And prepayments and accruals are also built into any reputable off-the-shelf accounting package you may use.

If you're a little rough around the edges when it comes to accruals and prepayments, I recommend you get hold of a copy of *Bookkeeping For Dummies* by Paul Barrow and Lita Epstein (Wiley), which looks at this area in a lot of detail.

Anyhow, back to measuring estimates for costs. In the previous section, I implore you to be careful when estimating revenue, and the same message applies to estimating costs. Over- or under-estimating costs disproportionately has a significant influence over the levels of profits (or losses) that the company reports. And investors (and the tax authorities) want to see that any levels of costs that require an element of judgement have been calculated correctly.

After you recognise the appropriate amount of revenue (see the previous section), the story doesn't end there. You need to match that revenue with the appropriate amount of costs.

Barney the Builder (Barney) is in the middle of building a new office complex. The contract price has been agreed at $100 million and contract costs have been calculated to be $80 million. On 31 March 2012 (Barney's year-end), Stan the surveyor calculates that the contract is 30 per cent complete. Barney recognises $30 million worth of revenue (30 per cent x $100 million) and $24 million worth of costs (30 per cent x $80 million). This gives Barney a gross profit of $6 million ($30 million less $24 million).

Losing money on a contract

Not all construction contracts make a profit. The accounting treatment for loss-making contracts is different from those that are *expected* to make a profit (but keep in mind that a construction contract that's expected to make a profit could well turn out to make a loss).

IAS 11 requires that you include losses in the financial statements *as soon as you foresee them*. You recognising the relevant percentage of revenue (see the earlier section 'Coming up with reliable estimates') as normal, but the cost you recognise isn't the percentage of completion multiplied by the contract costs, but instead the balancing figure to generate the required loss (the revenue minus the costs).

Brian the builder has commenced work on a construction contract. The contract price was agreed at $50 million and contract costs to date amount to $65 million. Seema the surveyor has calculated the contract is 40 per cent complete. Brian recognises $20 million in revenue (40 per cent x $50 million). However, contract costs to date amount to $65 million, and because the contract price was agreed at $50 million this now means that the contract is anticipated to make a loss of $15 million ($50 million − $65 million). Brian recognises this loss *immediately* even though the contract is only 40 per cent complete. Brain recognises costs amounting to $35 million in order to generate a $15 million loss ($20 million revenue − $35 million costs).

Deciding on the probability that a sale will occur

To avoid recognising revenue inappropriately, you can only recognise a sale, whether it be the sales of goods or services, as such when it meets certain criteria. Clearly, if no criteria existed, companies would be free to come up with all sorts of nonsense that wouldn't make sense to the user of the financial statements and the tax authorities would be pulling their hair out trying to establish whether the correct levels of revenue have been recognised so they get their fair share of the profits.

IAS 18 contains criteria in respect of revenue recognition for:

- Dividends
- Interest
- Rendering of services
- Royalties
- Sales of goods

A company can only recognise revenue in respect of sales of goods when it meets the following criteria:

- ✔ The company has transferred to the buyer the significant risks and rewards of ownership of the goods.

- ✔ The company retains neither the continuing managerial involvement to the degree normally associated with ownership nor effective control over the goods.

- ✔ The amount of revenue can be measured reliably.

- ✔ It's probable that the economic benefits associated with the transaction will flow to the company.

- ✔ The costs incurred, or to be incurred, in respect of the transaction can be measured reliably.

For a company that renders services, the company can only recognise revenue in respect of these services when it meets the following criteria:

- ✔ The amount of revenue can be measured reliably.

- ✔ It's probable that economic benefits associated with the transaction will flow to the company.

- ✔ The stage of completion of the transaction at the reporting period can be measured reliably.

- ✔ The costs incurred for the transaction and the costs to complete the transaction can be measured reliably.

Taking a Close Look at Revenue Recognition Rules

IAS 18 *Revenue* is the accounting standard that dictates how and when you recognise revenue from various sources. Rules exist for a range of revenue, from supplying goods to selling services, and from dividend income to royalty revenue. You need to know all the rules, so that you account for the types of revenue correctly.

Supplying goods

Lots of companies buy and sell goods. For example, a supermarket buys food and sells it to the general public; a car dealership buys vehicles and sells them on to individuals and other companies. Whatever business a company is in, you recognise the sales of goods as revenue within the company's financial statements only when the strict criteria I list in the section 'Deciding on the probability that a sale will occur', earlier in this chapter, have been met.

The following sections cover some issues that you may come across, covering when the risks and rewards of ownership of goods passes to your customer and what to do when you receive payments upfront from your customer for goods you don't yet have in stock, as well as what happens when you sell goods to customers that they may return. I also take a look at software and warranties, and what happens if you get involved in bartering transactions.

Transferring risks and rewards of ownership

The general rule in IAS 18 is that all the risks and rewards of ownership of the goods must have passed to the buyer before the selling company can recognise a sale in its financial statements. If the selling company retains any of the risks and rewards of ownership, it can't recognise a sale in the financial statements.

The transfer of *significant* risks and rewards is vital. Consider a transaction where a company sells goods to its customer, but the company only receives payment if its customer is able to sell the goods on. The significant risks and rewards still remain with the company and it can't recognise the sale.

Bart Baling Equipment Ltd, a company located in the UK, has entered into a contract to ship three items of waste balers to a company located in South East Asia. The terms of the sale contract is that Bart Baling Equipment Limited also install the equipment at a later date to the point where the baling equipment is in full working order. Bart Baling Equipment Ltd can't recognise the sale of the waste balers on the date of delivery to the customer. Because the risks and rewards of ownership haven't transferred to the customer located in South East Asia, a substantial part of the transaction (the installation) has yet to be completed.

Michelle's Motor Homes Inc sells motor homes to the general public and has entered into a contract with a holiday company to sell it 40 motor homes at a cost of $150,000. The holiday company has the right to cancel the purchase in accordance with agreed terms in the contract. The risk and rewards of ownership of the motor homes remains with Michelle's Motor Homes Inc because of the uncertainty arising from the terms of the contract. Michelle's Motor Homes Inc can't recognise a sale until such time as it becomes clear that the holiday company won't cancel the sale.

You don't just consider the risks and rewards. IAS 18 also requires that the probability that the company will receive payment must be present in the sale arrangement. In situations where the receipt of payment is in doubt, you can't recognise a sale until this uncertainty is removed.

Receiving payments in advance from the customer

Lots of companies operate schemes whereby a customer must pay, say, a deposit upfront beforehand. Companies such as tour operators often require the customer to pay so much up front when they book a holiday and the balance becomes payable so many weeks before departure. The issue with these sorts of arrangements is when to recognise the payments made in advance as revenue.

The simple answer is that you can't recognise payments made in advance as a sale. You treat any advance payments received from a customer, whether they be for goods or services, within the financial statements as a liability until such time as the contractual obligations to the customer by the company have been fulfilled.

Fancy Funky Furniture sells a range of domestic furniture to the general public including sofas, beds, tables and chairs and a range of soft furnishings. The customer discusses her requirements with a sales representative, who then designs the furniture on a computer to show the customer how it would look. When the customer is happy with the design, a consultant then goes to the customer's house to measure the room to make sure that the furniture will actually fit into the customer's home. After all this preparatory work, the customer signs an agreement for the supply of the furniture and makes a 50 per cent deposit. The customer pays the remaining 50 per cent when the furniture is delivered and the customer then signs to say that she's happy with it.

In this instance, the 50 per cent deposit that is paid by the customer is recognised as a current liability in Fancy Funky Furniture's financial statements at the year-end (provided, of course, the sale hasn't completed at the year-end). Only when the customer is happy that the goods are in accordance with their requirements and she's signed to that effect can Fancy Funky Furniture recognise the 50 per cent deposit as a sale, together with the remaining 50 per cent. Fancy Funky Furniture recognises the 50 per cent deposit as a liability to represent the work the company is required to perform for the customer. (Chapters 6 and 7 cover liabilities.)

Thinking about sale and return issues

Organisations such as those in the retail industry have to expect a certain level of returns. Think about a real-life scenario. You've seen an item of clothing and you think 'wow, that would look great on me' only to get it home and find that, in fact, purple trousers are a fashion faux-pas. What do you do? You take the trousers back and ask for either a refund or a credit note.

Many companies, therefore, have a returns policy, which is usually a set number of days from the date of sale. For example, a clothing retailer may say that you can return goods within 28 days from the date of purchase.

In this case, IAS 18 requires the clothing retailer to recognise revenue only when the window of opportunity to return the goods has closed.

Eddie's Electricals sells electrical equipment. It buys a batch of ten top-of-the-range televisions for $10,000 from the wholesaler and sells one of them to a customer for $2,000. Eddie's Electricals has a policy enabling the customer to return the goods within 14 days but doesn't estimate the value of future returns.

In this example, Eddie's Electricals can't recognise the $2,000 sale until the 14-day return period has elapsed because Eddie's Electricals can't estimate the value of future returns. In the meantime, the televisions remain in Eddie Electrical's inventory at a value of $1,000 until the 14 days have passed. After this time period has passed, Eddie Electrical can recognise a sale.

Where customers have a right to return goods, provided that the retention of risks and rewards isn't considered significant, the seller can recognise revenue at the time of sale *provided* that the seller can estimate future returns and recognise such as a provision under IAS 37 *Provisions, Contingent Liabilities and Contingent Assets* (which I cover in Chapter 7).

Looking at sales of software and warranties

Some companies require such bespoke and complex information technology (IT) systems that designing and implementing the software can take a significant amount of time. Even though designing and implementing a bespoke software package may take months or years to complete, the IT company needs paying during the designing and implementation phase to continue working on the project.

In real life, what normally happens with these types of projects is that the IT company draws up a contract with its customer that contains stages at which payments will be expected: for example, 10 per cent of the fee when the contract is 25 per cent complete, 40 per cent when the contract is 50 per cent complete and such like, with a remaining balance at the end that is payable when the project is up and running and all teething problems have been resolved.

New Technology Co designs bespoke software for the manufacturing industry. Depending on the customer's actual requirements, development and subsequent completion of the software can take anything between three months and one year. Usually, smaller companies can expect to have a fully functional software package in place within the three-month window, whereas larger organisations that have much more complicated systems in place may expect to wait a year until their specially made system is up and running.

In this example, IAS 18 requires New Technology Co to recognise fees from development of customised software in the financial statements by reference to the stage of completion at the reporting date. The company must also include any post-delivery support it may offer as well, such as a warranty.

Warranties are offered by companies in the event that something goes wrong with the product they supplied. Companies often offer you a warranty with electrical goods such as TVs, computer equipment, washing machines and such like. Usually, warranties are included with the price at which you purchase and they last, typically, between one to three years. You can also buy extended warranties separately when the original warranty has expired.

You set up a provision for warranty costs to meet the requirements in IAS 37 *Provisions, Contingent Liabilities and Contingent Assets* (see Chapter 7). Then you release the additional sale of warranty costs to the income statement as revenue over the life of the warranty itself.

Bartering? What's all that then?

One of the criteria for recognising revenue is that you can reliably measure the revenue (in other words, you can place a reliable monetary estimate on the sale). If you can't place a reliable estimate on the sale, as per IAS 18, you can't recognise a sale.

Bartering, where no cash changes hands, is therefore tricky. Bartering usually concerns advertising services and the IASB has issued an interpretation specifically on this area: SIC-31 *Revenue – Barter Transactions Involving Advertising Services.* In some arrangements, a seller may enter into a barter transaction to provide advertising services in exchange for receiving advertising services from its customer.

The problem is that you can't measure the *fair value* (market value) of the advertising services, so you can't recognise revenue. SIC-31 applies to the measurement of fair value of revenue from these barter transactions. Basically, the thrust of the SIC states that you can measure revenue only by reference to non-barter transactions that

- Involve advertising similar to the advertising in the barter transaction
- Occur frequently
- Represent a predominant number of transactions and amount when compared to non-barter transactions to provide advertising that is similar to advertising in barter transactions
- Involve cash and/or another form of consideration that has a reliably measurable fair value
- Don't involve the same third party as the one in the barter transaction

SIC-31 applies to an exchange of dissimilar advertising services. If an exchange of *similar* advertising services takes place, such an exchange *doesn't* give rise to revenue on the part of either party.

Selling services

The previous section 'Supplying goods' concentrates mainly on companies that buy and sell goods. But other organisations, such as firms of accountants and lawyers sell services. Many people carry out work related to the service sector, so this area is a vast one.

In this section, I take a look at the way firms that sell services must recognise revenue for those services. I also take another look at the area of construction contract accounting under IAS 11 (I touched on IAS 11 issues in the earlier sections 'Coming up with a reliable estimate' and 'Calculating a reliable measurement of costs') and what happens when you pass certain milestones. Finally, I examine companies such as gyms and other sorts of companies where members of the public pay membership and subscription fees and how to recognise revenue in relation to these types of revenue streams.

Performing work over time

Many companies do work for their customer/client over a long period of time. Consider, for example, a firm of lawyers who are acting on behalf of a client in a conveyancing transaction. Buying a house can be a lengthy process and clearly the firm of lawyers acts for the client over a lengthy period of time.

When an organisation performs work over a period of time for its customer/client, it must be able to reliably determine the stage of completion of the transaction. The company can then measure revenue up to the stage of completion of the transaction, provided that the company can demonstrate the following:

✔ The amount of revenue can be measured reliably.

✔ The stage of completion can be measured reliably.

✔ The costs incurred for the transaction and the costs to complete the transaction can be measured reliably.

✔ It's probable that economic benefits associated with the transaction will flow to the entity.

The golden rule for recognising service revenue is to make sure that it meets the four criteria within IAS 18. If you can't meet one of the criteria, you can't recognise revenue.

Passing a milestone – contracts with milestone payments

In the section 'Timing of Revenue', earlier in this chapter, I cover revenue and costs that you recognise in respect of a construction contract. Well, I'm going to go into more detail where construction contracts are concerned because these contracts are quite complex things to account for.

During the life of a construction contract, the contractor makes what are known as *progress payments*: in other words, as the contract progresses the contractor gives the sub-contractor (the builder) stage payments. Progress payments themselves are *not* revenue; they're merely 'on account' payments that you credit to a contract account in the nominal ledger.

To recognise the appropriate amount of revenue and costs during the life of a contract, you follow these steps:

1. **Work out how much of the contract is complete.**

2. **Decipher whether the contract is profit- or loss-making.**

3. **Recognise the loss or profit.**

   If the contract is loss-making, immediately recognise the loss (see the example in the earlier section 'Losing money on a contract').

   If the contract is profit-making, recognise a percentage of the contract price as revenue and a percentage of the contract costs as costs depending on how complete the contract is in Step 1.

4. **Gather all the costs together (not forgetting things like depreciation of any machinery used in the construction contract) and add on the profit estimated to be achieved on the contract.**

   This tells you how much dosh is still due from your customer that you include in the statement of financial position as an asset, taking into account any progress payments you've already received.

On 1 October 2011, Leah Inc commenced work on a contract. The price agreed for the contract was $50 million. Leah purchased plant at a cost of $15 million exclusively for use on the contract. The directors of Leah Inc estimate that the plant will have no value at the end of the contract, which is due to finish on 30 September 2012. Costs incurred on the contract, plus estimated costs to complete, amount to $44 million made up as follows:

	$,000
Purchase of plant	$15,000
Materials purchased	$9,000
Labour and overheads	$7,000
Estimated costs to complete	$13,000

The valuation agency has said that, as at 31 March 2012, the contract was 40 per cent complete. On 31 March 2012, the contractor made a progress payment to Leah Inc amounting to $15 million.

The contract is 40 per cent complete. Leah Inc recognises 40 per cent of the contract price of $50 million, which is $20 million as revenue, and on the flip side recognises 40 per cent of the costs of $44 million, which amount to $17.6 million. That's the easy bit out of the way (Steps 1, 2 and 3), and the resulting gross profit as at 31 March 2012 is $2.4 million ($20 million less $17.6 million).

Now on to Step 4, to deal with the information that needs to go into the statement of financial position, which represents the rest of the monies due from the contractor. Leah Inc gathers together all the costs, which are as follows:

	$,000
Purchases of materials	$9,000
Labour and overheads	$7,000
Plant depreciation ($15 m x 6/12)	$7,500
Total costs to date	**$23,500**

You can't forget about IAS 16 *Property, Plant and Equipment* provisions (I cover IAS 16 in Chapter 4). Leah Inc has to depreciate the plant bought for $15 million over the life of the contract. Depreciation is a cost, and that's why I include the $7.5 million plant depreciation in the costs in the previous table.

To work out the profit the contract is expected to make, Leah Inc takes the contract price $50 million and deducts from this figure the estimate of costs to complete of $44 million. The overall profit on the contract is $6 million. Leah Inc adds this profit onto the total costs to date as follows:

	$,000
Total costs to date	$23,500
Contract profit	$6,000
	$29,500

Leah Inc considers the progress payment that the contractor paid on 31 March 2012, which amounted to $15 million. Leah Inc deducts this figure because the progress payment is simply an 'on account' payment. This calculation leaves a gross amount due from the contractor of $14.5 million ($29.5 million less $15 million).

Any advances and progress payments are based on contract terms that don't necessarily measure contract performance.

So, as you can see, receiving payments when you pass a milestone can involve a lot of complex work – you mainly find such payments in construction contracts.

Receiving membership and subscription fees

If you're a member of a gym or other sort of leisure centre, the chances are that you have to pay a subscription. Similarly, if you're a member of a professional body, you have to pay annual membership fees to retain your membership of such an organisation.

Such organisations have to comply with the provisions in IAS 18 to recognise such membership and subscription fees as revenue in their financial statements. Many organisations like gyms offer members the facility to pay their annual membership fees monthly by direct debit so that they don't pay a chunk of money all at once. When this happens, IAS 18 requires the organisation to recognise the membership fees as revenue over the life of the membership. The organisation can recognise as revenue only those memberships where the organisation has fulfilled its contractual obligations. You treat part of a membership fee for which the organisation hasn't yet fulfilled its contractual obligations as a liability (as deferred income) in the financial statements.

Be careful with the timing of revenue recognition. An annual membership may run a calendar year (1 January to 31 December) but the financial year may end part way through the calendar year. You may have to *defer income* (carry it over to the next accounting period). Make sure that you do so correctly because the tax authorities are particularly hot on deferred income.

Gillian's Gymnasium provides fitness and leisure facilities for paying members. Annual membership fees run from 1 January to 31 December and fees vary depending on the level of gym memberships. To entice customers, the gym offers the facility to members to pay their memberships monthly by direct debit. Gillian's Gymnasium has a year-end of 31 October each year. Gillian's Gymnasium recognises memberships from 1 January to 31 October as revenue, and treats memberships in November and December as a liability in the financial statements.

Subscription fees are sometimes a bit different. Consider the publisher of a magazine where customers enter into a subscription agreement to receive the magazine periodically. Basically, the publisher recognises subscription revenue on a *straight-line basis* (included in the income statement in equal instalments) over the period when the magazines are issued. However, if the publisher publishes several magazines, all with varying prices or publications where prices vary by period, the publisher must recognise revenue based on the sales value of each item in proportion to the total estimated sales value of all the items included in the subscription.

Looking at admission fees

Have you ever been to an event where you pay on the door? A good example is when you go to the horse races. You pay at the turnstile and gain admission. Sometimes attendees pay some dosh up front and the balance is due either on the day of the event, or close to the event. The event organiser must recognise revenue at the correct time.

IAS 18 says that you recognise admission fees as revenue in the financial statements only after the event has taken place. You do so because after the event, the event organiser has fulfilled all contractual obligations to the customer. Where a customer is required to pay any money up front (a bit like a deposit for the annual Christmas party), then the organiser recognises such monies as a liability because it still has customer obligations to fulfil.

Crazy Christmas Parties Ltd organises Christmas parties for companies. It organises a marquee to be situated at a venue where several companies attend over a week-long period. Entertainment is provided and the companies can expect a three-course meal in with the total cost. Drinks, however, are paid for by the customers at the event. To secure bookings, companies must pay the balance owed to Crazy Christmas Parties Ltd by 31 October and the parties run during the second week of December. IAS 18 says that you need to recognise admission fees when the event occurs. So Crazy Christmas Parties Ltd recognises revenue when the parties take place. Any payments received from customers before the parties take place are recognised as a liability.

Under the provisions in IAS 18, if a company has organised several events, it allocates fees received to each event when the event occurs.

Dealing with dividend income

In this section, I show you what exactly constitutes dividend income and at what point you recognise such income in the financial statements. IAS 18 deals with situations when a company may receive a dividend as a form of income.

Understanding what constitutes dividend income

Some of you may own shares in large companies or even own shares in the company you work for. Whatever the situation, the primary reason people, and even companies, buy shares in a company is to make a return on this investment. When you, or a company, receives a return on this investment, this return is a *dividend*. Dividends are always paid out of post-tax profits.

A company sometimes uses another company's assets for use in its own business, and IAS 18 deals with dividend income that arises due to the use by others of the company's assets, which in turn gives rise to revenue.

Note: IAS 18 itself doesn't deal with dividends arising from investments, which you account for under the *equity method* and IAS 28 *Investments in Associates* (see Chapter 12).

Receiving and accounting for dividend income

Normally, the Board of Directors approves dividends in a meeting (usually the Annual General Meeting (AGM)) when the financial results for the period/year are known. A company may declare a dividend, say, on 31 March 2012, but may not actually pay that dividend out until 10 April 2012. You must get the timing of this right and recognise the dividend in the correct period. If you've a year-end of 31 March 2012, do you recognise the dividend in the 31 March 2012 accounts, or do you wait until you physically receive the dividend and recognise it on 10 April 2012 (in the next accounting period)?

You recognise dividends in the financial statements at the time the shareholders *receive the right to payment.* Establishing the correct time to recognise the dividend is particularly important because the timing of the dividend receipt has an influence on the financial statements for that particular period. So in the example, you recognise the dividend as a receivable (an asset) in the 31 March 2012 accounting period. (For more on timing, see the earlier section 'Timing of Revenue'.)

This distinction ensures that the recognition of the dividend is in accordance with the *accruals concept,* which means that you recognise transactions and events in the financial statements when they arise rather than on a paid (or cash) basis. The entries for the dividend receipt are as follows:

On initial recognition:

Debit dividend receivable	X
Credit income statement	X

When payment of the dividend is received:

Debit bank account	X
Credit dividend receivable	X

Handling royalty revenue

Royalties are fairly straightforward things to understand. Basically, a company creates work for another company to use (for example, an accounting firm writes books for a publisher). In return for the services, the publisher (or third party) pays the creator of the work a *royalty*. Royalties are usually agreed percentages of gross or net revenues that arise from the use of an asset or a fixed price per unit sold (for example, a book). Royalty revenue can arise in other situations; for example, when a third party wishes to use the work of someone else, the third party may pay the originator of the work a royalty.

In other circumstances, an organisation may make charges for the use by others of its long-term assets such as patents, trademarks and computer software. Such charges constitute royalty revenue and as such you account for them under the provisions in IAS 18.

IAS 18 also prescribes the accounting treatment when companies receive revenue from royalties. Royalties are much less common than other major revenue streams such as sales of goods and rendering of services, and therefore the accounting for royalty revenue under IAS 18 is fairly basic. Royalties essentially accrue to the company that owns the asset, giving rise to the royalties in accordance with the terms of the relevant agreement. You recognise royalty revenue in the financial statements on an accruals basis in accordance with the terms of the agreement.

Accruals basis in the context of royalty revenue means when the right to receive payment of the royalty arises, which may differ from the date of actual payment.

Recognising interest income

Interest income is any interest that the company receives because of an investment it has undertaken. For example, the company may have made a loan to another company or supplied goods under deferred settlement terms which attracts interest. You account for the interest income generated from such investments under the provisions in IAS 18.

If a company receives interest and also pays interest, IAS 1 *Presentation of Financial Statements* (see Chapter 1 for more on IAS 1) prohibits interest received and interest paid being offset (see Chapter 5 for more on offsetting). What you can do, however, is recognise gross interest payments and gross interest receipts and then strike a sub-total that shows net interest.

You account for interest income using the *effective interest method* – the gross amount of interest due under a loan. The interest rate a company pays (known as the *coupon rate*) to another organisation that has provided the loan may not be the *effective* interest it actually pays. Using the effective interest method gives an additional amount of interest and this *additional* interest turns the interest paid into *gross* interest. (I illustrate the effective interest method in Chapter 7 using the effective interest calculation table.)

Chapter 9

Accounting for Equity

· ·

· ·

*E*quity is the residual value left over when you take all other costs into consideration (a bit like what's left after you work out your bills for the month and take them off your monthly salary). Equity, in the context of companies, works on exactly the same principle: from the viewpoint of a company, equity is the shareholders' funds.

Under IFRS, the statement of financial position has a section dedicated to equity, also known as *shareholders' funds*. In this chapter, I examine the various components of the equity section. The equity section of a company's statement of financial position often comprises:

✔ Share capital

✔ Share premium account

✔ Revaluation reserve

✔ Retained earnings

I take a look at each of these components in this chapter. First, I explore what happens when a company issues shares to its shareholders, as well as what to do when a company issues shares to shareholders at a *premium* (for a price over and above what the shares are actually worth). Then I explore share-based payment transactions, which arise when companies offer share options to their employees, and I show you how deferred tax interacts with a share-based payment transaction.

I move on to explain how you handle revaluing non-current assets like buildings, because when an asset goes up in value, you reflect this uplift in the equity section as the revaluation reserve. Then I round off by taking you through retained earnings, which are the profits kept in the business (reinvested) that shareholders can receive in the form of a dividend (which is why they fall under the equity or shareholders' funds section of the statement of financial position).

Issuing and Accounting for Share Capital: The Basics

A company is owned by its shareholders (sometimes called *members*). After the company is formed, the shareholders buy their shares in the company by pumping cash into the company in return for the shares. The cash that the shareholders give the company represents the shareholders' investment in the company and is classed as *equity* (also known as *shareholders' funds*). The company uses this money from the shareholders to invest in the business.

Accounting for share issues is fairly easy. When the company receives the money for the shares it has issued to the shareholders, it debits cash at bank with the money the company has received for the share issue, and credits issued share capital in the equity section of the statement of financial position.

Joyce decides to open a cafe, to commence trading on 1 January 2012. After seeking advice from her accountant, she decides that the best way to operate the cafe is through a company and subscribes to $100 worth of $1 ordinary shares. The entries in the books of Joyce's Cafe are debit bank account with $100 and credit share capital with $100.

Joyce's statement of financial position as at 1 January 2012 is as follows:

	$
Current assets:	
Cash at bank	100
Total assets	**100**
Equity:	
Issued share capital	100
Total equity	**100**

When a company issues its shares, often the value of the share capital in the equity section of the statement of financial position remains at the same amount for a long time (sometimes for the life of the company). On occasion, a shareholder may decide to transfer some of his shares to another person.

This situation can happen for various reasons – for example, a wife may transfer some shares to her husband by choice. But you need to understand that such transfers have no effect whatsoever on the company's equity section of the statement of financial position. When a shareholder transfers some of his shares to another person, this transaction is between the two shareholders, not a transaction between the company and the shareholders, because the company still has the same number of shares in issue.

The only time that shares in the equity section of the statement of financial position change is when the company issues more shares (the shares increase) or when the company reduces its share capital (the shares reduce).

Sunita's Salon started in business with 50 $1 shares in issue. During the year, Sunita decides to transfer 25 of these shares to her husband. The transfer of 25 shares from Sunita to her husband makes no difference to the statement of financial position. The company still has $50 worth of shares issued; this transaction is merely one between Sunita and her husband. On the other hand, if Sunita decides to issue her husband with 25 shares for cash, rather than transfer 25 of her shares, this is a different story. The company debits cash at bank with the $25 money received from Sunita's husband for his shares and credits ordinary share capital in the equity section of the statement of financial position with $25. The result is an increase in the bank balance of $25 and an increase in issued share capital from $50 to $75 ($50 shares plus the additional $25 to Sunita's husband).

Issuing Shares at a Premium

A business can raise finance (sometimes known as *raising capital*) in many ways, and issuing shares is just one of them. In today's modern world of business, banks and other finance houses often want companies to ask their own shareholders to stump up cash to raise finance – for example, if the company is undergoing an expansion project and it needs funds in place to finance its working capital requirements. Usually, the company offers to sell more shares to investors in order to raise money.

When a company issues shares for more than they're actually worth, this act is known as issuing shares at a *premium*. Because shares are a component of the equity section of the statement of financial position (shares belong to the shareholders so are shareholders' funds, and shareholders' funds are equity, which you show in the equity section of the statement of financial position), you record any further issues of shares in the equity section of the statement of financial position. If the company makes a further issue of shares at a price that's higher than the shares are actually worth, a *share premium account* takes the excess of the price paid over the price the share is worth.

Understanding why and how companies issue shares at more than their par value

When a company issues shares to a shareholder, it does so on the basis of the share price. In smaller companies, the price of a share is often $1. In much larger companies that sell shares on a stock market, the stock market determines the share price (hence it may go up or down on a daily basis). To keep this section simple, I concentrate on a smaller company whose shares are valued at $1 each. The value of a share is also known as the share's *par value* or *face value*.

One of the common reasons a company undertakes a share issue is to raise finance. For example, the company may need to raise capital in order to fund its expansion plans. Sometimes banks and other finance houses want the company's shareholders to invest more of their money into the company before the bank or finance house is prepared to lend the company any money. This situation is when a share issue more than likely takes place.

A company may not be able to raise enough money by issuing more shares at the shares' par value because the par value is usually the minimum value of the shares. So the company issues more shares at a price that's higher than the share's par value – it issues shares at a premium (the premium is the difference between the par value and the price paid for the shares).

An inherent disadvantage of sourcing money by issuing shares at a premium is that the offer of further shares to other investors reduces existing shareholders' shareholding, because more shareholders have come on board after the company issues additional shares. So if a shareholder held 5 per cent of the shares before the additional share issue, he may find that he only holds 3 per cent when the company issues more shares to outside investors (this is *dilution* of existing shareholdings).

Don Dining Co operates a chain of restaurants throughout the UK and is planning to expand its chain quite quickly within the next two years. It has approached its bank, which has agreed to fund 75 per cent of the expansion plans, and the management of Don Dining Co has agreed that, in order to finance the remaining 25 per cent, it will issue shares to outside investors. Each share in Don Dining Co is worth $1, but in order to gain the necessary funding it has to issue shares at a price of $1.50. Don Dining Co issues shares at a premium: the premium is the difference between the par value and the price paid of $0.50 ($1.00 minus $1.50).

Accounting for shares issued at more than their par value

When a company issues shares at more than the par value of the shares, the accounting side of things is fairly simple:

1. **Record the proceeds of the share issue by debiting the bank account.**

   This action increases the bank balance (or reduces an overdrawn balance) by the total amount of money you've received from issuing the shares.

2. **Credit the ordinary share capital account in the equity section of the statement of financial position with the par value only of the share issue.**

3. **Credit the remaining balance (the premium at which you issued the shares) to the share premium account in the equity section of the statement of financial position.**

   The share premium is usually directly underneath 'Share capital'.

The issued share capital of Weavers Wedding Cars on 31 March 2012 was 10,000 $1 ordinary shares and the company has a year-end of 30 April 2012. In order to fund current expansion plans, Weavers Wedding Cars has issued a further 5,000 shares at $2 per share. You can see the par value of the shares is $1 each, but Weavers Wedding Cars have issued further shares at a premium of $1. The total raised from the share issue amounts to $10,000 ($5,000 x $2) so the entries into the books of the company are as follows:

Debit cash at bank	$10,000
Credit ordinary share capital	$5,000
Credit share premium	$5,000

Extracts from the statement of financial position as at 30 April 2012 show:

	2012	*2011*
Equity	*$*	*$*
Ordinary share capital	15,000	10,000
Share premium	5,000	–

This situation has no effect at all on the income statement – any issues of share capital, whether rights issues or general issues, purely affect the items within the statement of financial position. I deal with rights issues in Chapter 16.

Dealing with Share-Based Payments

A *share-based payment transaction* is an agreement between a company and a third party that entitles the third party to receive equity instruments (shares or share options) of the company, or cash (or other assets) for amounts based on the price or value of the equity instruments of the company making the offer, providing certain conditions are met. For example, a company may offer its employees such a share-based transaction or pay a supplier in shares rather than hard cash (known as offering *share options*).

Share options have always been somewhat problematic for the accountancy profession, because no cash flow is associated with the transactions. In the past, accountants often didn't recognise an expense in the income statement. So what changed? Along came IFRS 2 *Share-based Payment*, which completely overhauled the way companies deal with share-based payment transactions.

The objective of IFRS 2 is to show the effects of share-based payments on the company's income statement and statement of financial position. IFRS 2 specifies when to recognise the charge for share-based payments and how much to recognise in the financial statements.

In this section, I take a look at how the accounting for such share-based payment transactions works as well as looking at how deferred tax comes into the equation.

Understanding a share-based payment

Accounting for a share-based payment depends on how the transaction is settled. In a lot of cases, the main way of settling the transaction is through issuing equity shares or paying cash where the third party has the option of receiving equity or cash.

IFRS 2 requires that you recognise an expense in the income statement that represents the goods or services received by the company. The corresponding credit entry in the books is a liability or an increase in the equity of a company, depending on whether the transaction is settled in cash or shares.

IFRS 2 covers three types of share-based payment transaction:

✔ **Equity-settled** share-based payment transactions, where the company receives goods or services as consideration for equity instruments in the company.

✔ **Cash-settled** share-based payment transactions, where the company acquires goods or services by incurring liabilities to the supplier. The amount of the liability is based on the price, or value, of the company's shares or other equity instruments.

✔ **Transactions that involve a choice of cash or shares**, in which the company acquires or receives goods or services and the terms of the arrangement say that the company, or the supplier, has a choice of whether to settle the transaction in cash or shares.

When a company receives goods to be settled in shares, you can easily recognise when the goods will be received and therefore when the entries into the books must take place.

Share-based payments get a bit more complicated when services are involved. You often hear the term *vesting conditions* – conditions that the third party must satisfy in order to become entitled to receive cash, other assets or shares under a share-based payment arrangement.

Now, in the case of goods the vesting date isn't particularly relevant because the date on which the goods are received essentially becomes the vesting date; but the vesting date becomes relevant for employee services. When a company issues shares that vest immediately, the general presumption is that these shares are a consideration of past employee services. So the company must immediately recognise the expense for the employee services, because they're received in full on the date on which the shares or share options are granted.

In contrast to shares and share options that vest immediately, some exist that may not vest for a period of time. For example, the conditions may say that employees granted share options have to remain in employment with the company on a certain date in the future. Then, the equity instruments relate to services that are to be provided over a period of time, known as the vesting period.

Conquering the calculations in a share-based payment

In this section, I show you how to calculate the value of share options that you include in a company's financial statements at the year-end. The calculations are fairly simplistic, but in real life they can get complex because the bigger the company, the more share options granted.

Some companies offer share options that contain a condition that says the shares only vest if the share price reaches a certain price. You must ignore any increases in the market price of a company's shares for the purposes of calculating the value of share options to be included in the annual financial statements of a company.

When a company offers share options to its employees, those employees are then benefiting from a form of remuneration for their services. You have to use fair values to calculate the value of the share options, and to do so you need to use a share-option pricing model (for example, the Black-Scholes Pricing Model). These pricing models can be quite tricky, so if you're not comfortable with them, get someone who's quite savvy to do the calculations for you.

Going through the basic calculation

When a company enters into a share-based payment with its employees (or other third parties), here's how you deal with the transaction:

1. **Find out how many share options have been granted.** You can get this figure from the share options agreement, or from your finance director or chief accountant.

2. **Find out how many people are receiving shares.** You can get this figure from the minutes of the meeting approving the share option or the share options agreement (or by asking your finance director or chief accountant).

3. **Find out how many people are expected to remain in the employment of the company at the date the shares are given.** You can get this figure from your finance director or chief accountant.

4. **Find out the vesting conditions.** You can get these details from the agreement or by asking your finance director or chief accountant. The share options agreement may stipulate that the shares only vest if the share price reaches a certain price, or other conditions in the agreement may have to be met before the shares can vest.

5. **Find out the fair value (the market value) of each option at the date the share options are given to the employees (or third parties).** You can get these details from the agreement or by looking on the stock market (if your company trades its shares on one).

6. **Work out the time-fraction.** If your company grants share options that will vest in five years and you're recognising the expense in the first year, the time fraction is one year over five years ($\frac{1}{5}$).

7. **Multiply the number of options (Step 1) by the number of people receiving shares (the number of people expected to be employed by the company when the shares vest) (Steps 2 and 3) by the fair value of each option (Step 5) by the time-fraction (Step 6).** The result is the value of the expense.

8. **Debit the income statement with the value of the expense.**

9. **Credit equity in the statement of financial position with the value of the expense.**

Lucas grants 2,000 share options to each of its three directors on 1 January 2011. The terms of the option are that the directors must still be employed by the company on 31 December 2013 when the options vest. The fair value of each option as at 1 January 2011 is $10 and all the options are expected to vest. The options vest only if the Lucas share price reaches $16 per share. As at 31 December 2011, the share price was only $7 per share and this share price isn't expected to rise in the next two years. Further, the company expects that only two directors will be employed as at 31 December 2013. Your job is to account for the share options in the financial statements as at 31 December 2011.

Remember, you must ignore the increase in the share price for the purposes of calculating the value of the share options as at 31 December 2011. However, you must take into account the fact that only two directors will be employed as at 31 December 2013 (see Step 3).

The calculation (as in Step 7) is as follows:

2,000 options $\times$ 2 directors $\times$ $10 $\times$ 1 year $\div$ 3 years = $13,333

You debit the income statement with the value of the expense ($13,333) and credit equity in the statement of financial position with $13,333.

Stepping up to a more complex calculation

In the last section I go through a fairly simplistic example of how you calculate the share options in the first year, but obviously you have the future years to deal with. I want to go one step further now and look at what happens each year-end until the options vest, taking into account staff who leave.

It's a well-known fact that an organisation's employees come and go. Just because they have share options in the company doesn't mean that employees stay until the options vest. The management of the company has to make a best-estimate of how many employees may leave during the period until the share options vest. Obviously, these estimates are a bit hit and miss, but sometimes management is spot on. The following is an example to illustrate what happens over the life of a share option when management is within a ballpark when estimating leavers.

Lucas grants 120 share options to each of its 400 employees. The terms of the grant are that each employee must stay in the employment of Lucas over the next three years. The fair value of each share option is $11 and Lucas has estimated that 25 per cent of employees leave during the three-year period, and in doing so forfeit their rights to the share options. The estimates on how many employees would leave turns out to be accurate.

Table 9-1 shows the amounts Lucas recognises for services received as consideration for the share options during the vesting period. Lucas calculates the annual remuneration expense to be recognised in the income statement based on a static estimated percentage of leavers as follows:

> Number of options × Estimated percentage of remaining staff × Fair value of each share option × Numerator of the time fraction ÷ Total years (denominator of the time fraction) – Cumulative remuneration expense (the amount you've recognised since the share options began). (Where the time fraction is concerned, if the share options vest in four years and you're dealing with the first year, the time fraction is one year (the numerator) ÷ four years (the denominator) (¼).

Table 9-1   Calculation of Remuneration Expense

Year	Calculation	Remuneration Expense for the Year $	Cumulative Remuneration Expense $
1	48,000 options × 75% × $11 × 1 ÷ 3 years	132,000	132,000
2	(48,000 options × 75% × $11 × 2 ÷ 3 years) – $132,000	132,000	264,000
3	(48,000 options × 75% × $11 × 3 ÷ 3 years) – $264,000	132,000	396,000

This example is fairly simplistic because I assume that management's assessment that 25 per cent of staff would leave over the three-year vesting period is accurate. But unless you've amazing psychic powers, you aren't going to be able to see into the future. So I need to take this example one step further.

The same facts as in the previous example apply, but now consider that:

✔ In Year 1, 25 employees leave and Lucas revises its estimate of total leavers over the three-year vesting period from 25 per cent (100 employees) to 20 per cent (80 employees).

✔ In Year 2, another 23 employees leave. Lucas revises its estimate of total leavers over the three-year vesting period from 20 per cent to 15 per cent (60 employees).

✔ In Year 3, another 13 employees leave.

So the fun and games really start now because expectations aren't quite as clear cut. Table 9-2 shows what the calculation looks like:

Table 9-2	Calculation of Remuneration Expense		
Year	Calculation	Remuneration Expense for the Year $	Cumulative Remuneration Expense $
1	48,000 options × 80% × $11 × 1 ÷ 3 years	140,800	140,800
2	(48,000 options × 85% × $11 × 2 ÷ 3 years) − $140,800	158,400	299,200
3	(40,680 options × $11) − $299,200	148,280	447,480

You can see that a total of 61 employees (25 + 23 + 13) forfeited their rights to the share options during the three-year vesting period. As a result, when the share options vested, a total of 339 employees (400 – 61) received 120 share options, which resulted in 40,680 share options vesting in Year 3 at $11 per share.

Tackling the deferred taxation issues in a share-based payment

Some countries grant a tax allowance for share-based payment transactions. But the amount of the tax allowance is unlikely to be the same amount that's charged to the income statement under IFRS 2. This difference in amounts is because the tax allowance is often based on the option's *intrinsic value*: the difference between the fair value of the shares (the current price at which the shares are worth) and the exercise price (the price which is paid) for the shares. In many instances, you need to recognise a *deferred tax asset*, which represents the difference between the tax base (the value of the transaction that's subject to taxation) of the employee who's receiving the share-based payment's services received to-date and the carrying amount (the amount you state in the financial statements), which is normally zero.

In Chapter 6, I cover the issue of deferred tax assets, which occur when a company receives tax relief in advance for an accounting expense or income that isn't taxed until received. You can only recognise deferred tax assets if the company will have sufficient taxable profits in the future against which you can use the deferred tax asset. This concept applies to deferred tax assets that arise because of share-based payments.

Here are the steps to follow when handling a deferred tax asset.

Step 1: Recognise that a deferred tax asset exists

First, you need to know that you're dealing with deferred tax.

Gabriella Garments operates in a country where the tax authority grants an allowance equal to the intrinsic value of share options at the date they're exercised. Gabriella Garments grants share options to its employees with a fair value of $1.5 million at the date of the grant. The tax authority gives a tax allowance for the intrinsic value, which is $1.9 million. Gabriella pays tax at 26 per cent and the share options vest in two years' time.

So here you can see that the tax authority is giving an allowance for the intrinsic value of $1.9 million at 26 per cent. The carrying amount of employees services received to date is zero. Therefore, a deferred tax asset (representing the tax relief that the tax authority will grant Gabriella Garments in the future) arises.

Step 2: Calculate the deferred tax asset

You calculate the deferred tax asset as follows:

> Intrinsic value of the share option × Rate of tax the company pays × Time-fraction

In the Gabriella example, to calculate the deferred tax asset you take the intrinsic value of the share option ($1.9 million) and multiply this value by the rate of tax the company pays (26 per cent) and multiply by the time fraction (the share options vest in two years' time and you're dealing with the first year, so the time-fraction is 1 year ÷ 2 years). The deferred tax asset is $247,000.

Step 3: Work out the split of the deferred tax asset between the income statement and the statement of changes in equity

You split deferred tax assets between the income statement and equity as follows:

- ✔ If the estimated, or actual, tax deduction is less than, or equal to, the cumulative expense recognised, credit the deferred tax asset to the income statement.

> ✔ If the estimated, or actual, tax deduction exceeds the cumulative expense recognised, recognise the excess tax benefits directly in a separate component of equity.

To work out the split of the deferred tax asset between that of the income statement and that of the statement of changes in equity, here's what you do:

1. **Multiply the expense that has been recognised in the financial statements by the rate of tax paid by the company.** The result is the tax relief granted by the tax authority and is the portion of the deferred tax asset calculated in 'Step 2: Calculate the deferred tax asset' that goes to the income statement.

2. **Put the balance of the deferred tax asset calculated in 'Step 2: Calculate the deferred tax asset' into the statement of changes in equity.** You can prove this figure by taking the intrinsic value of the share option, deducting the expense you recognise in the income statement, multiplying the difference by the rate of tax the company pays and finally multiplying by the time-fraction.

In the Gabriella example, you need to split the deferred tax asset between the portion that goes as a credit to the income statement and the portion that you report in the statement of changes in equity (part of it goes to the statement of changes in equity because the credit entry of the $1.5 million expense is in the equity section of the statement of financial position). Gabriella recognises the $1.5 million expense in the income statement for the share option. Because the intrinsic value of the share options of $1.9 million exceeds the cumulative expense that has been charged of $1.5 million, Gabriella charges part of the deferred tax asset to equity – as per the second bullet point in the earlier list. (If, in the future, the expense exceeds the intrinsic value, Gabriella would take the amount recorded in equity to income.)

To work out the split of the $247,000 deferred tax asset between that of the income statement and that of the statement of changes in equity, Gabriella multiplies the expense that has been recognised in the financial statements by the rate of tax paid by the company:

$1.5 million $\times$ 26 per cent $\times$ 1 $\div$ 2 = $195,000

Of the $247,000 deferred tax asset calculated in 'Step 2: Calculate the deferred tax asset', Gabriella credits $195,000 to the income statement. Then Gabriella credits the balance of $52,000 ($247,000 – $195,000) to equity. You can prove the figure as follows:

($1.9 million – $1.5 million) $400,000 $\times$ 26% $\times$ 1 $\div$ 2 = $52,000 to equity

Understanding Retained Earnings

Retained earnings are profits that the company has built up over time that it has reinvested into the business. Retained earnings are the sum of:

- **Post-tax profit:** The profit after tax has been charged (usually the last monetary figure in the income statement referred to as *Profit for the year*).
- **Post-dividends profit:** What's left after a company pays dividends to its shareholders out of the post-tax profit.
- **Other retained profits:** Those that have been reinvested in the business since the company started on day one.

Retained earnings act in much the same way as your personal finances. You receive your monthly salary (or weekly wage), you pay out all your bills, you keep some dosh for yourself to spend and you (hopefully) put the rest into a savings account. Think of the money you keep in your savings account as your *retained earnings*; in other words, your *equity* (because your savings belong to you). Sometimes you spend more than you get and you borrow some money out of your savings to cover such costs. This principle is similar to the one that companies follow: in some years, a company's expenses may exceed its income, resulting in a loss, and the company's retained earnings are affected but it still needs to pay a *dividend* (a return to the shareholders on their investment).

You find retained earnings in the equity section of the statement of financial position, which is a snapshot of the financial position of a company at the close of business *at any one point in time* (for example at the year-end) – for example, 'Statement of Financial Position *as at* 31 December 2011'. You get the retained earnings figure from the statement of comprehensive income, which accumulates all income and expenses *over the year* (so 'Statement of Comprehensive Income *for the year ended* 31 December 2011'). After you close the books for the year-end, you clear out all the balances in revenue, income and expenses and put the residual total into the retained earnings account. The cycle begins again on the first day of the new financial year. (For more on the financial statements, head to Chapter 1.)

Making a loss and paying dividends

When shareholders put money into a company, they're making an investment in that company. Their priority is then to get a return on their investment (like when you put money into an interest-paying bank account, and the return you get is the interest). A shareholder's return is often paid by way of a dividend and a dividend is *always* paid out of post-tax profits.

Sometimes, even the best laid plans go horribly wrong and a company may hit on hard times (particularly in times of recession or economic difficulty). The end result may be that the company makes a post-tax loss for the year, but the shareholders still want a dividend.

The good news is that it's not the end of the world if the shareholders want a dividend when the company has sustained an overall loss for the year. If the company has been profit-making over the last few years and built up a good level of retained earnings, the company can still pay out a dividend because it has accumulated profit that it can use. Clearly, this accumulated profit reduces even further if the company pays a dividend, but that doesn't stop the company paying the dividend. A company can use retained earnings that it has built up over a number of years since the business started because these retained earnings are *distributable* to the shareholders.

However, you can't pay out a dividend *in excess* of the retained earnings figure. Such a dividend is unlawful because not enough retained profit exists to be paid out. You can't go overdrawn with the retained earnings as you can with a bank account!

If a business incurs a post-tax loss in a year, the company's expenses exceeded the income it received. This post-tax loss reduces accumulated retained earnings by the value of the loss incurred. Any dividends the company subsequently paid out also reduce retained earnings further by the value of the dividends.

Treetops Tree Cutting Services had a balance on retained earnings at 1 January 2011 amounting to $75,000. The financial statements for the year ended 31 December 2011 show a post-tax loss amounting to $30,000. The shareholders want a dividend of $10,000. In this example, Treetops can pay a dividend because the company has sufficient amounts of retained earnings, despite a loss being incurred. The closing retained earnings at 31 December 2011 look like this:

Opening balance at 1 January 2011	$75,000
Loss for the year	($30,000)
Dividend paid to shareholders	($10,000)
Closing retained earnings at 31 December 2011	**$35,000**

Be particularly careful if a company has been loss-making for a few years, or it sustains a serious loss in a year and this loss turns retained earnings into a negative figure (a debit balance on the statement of financial position). This situation means that the statement of financial position may be technically insolvent and dividend payments are essentially illegal. In the event of a liquidation or bankruptcy, shareholders may have to repay dividends.

Knowing when to put transactions directly to retained earnings

Generally speaking, you rarely put transactions directly to retained earnings. Retained earnings are a form of equity, and transactions such as the following go directly to 'other comprehensive income' in the income statement (not to the statement of changes in equity):

- ✔ Actuarial gains and losses on defined benefit pension plans (flick to Chapter 7 for details)

- ✔ Exchange differences arising on translating foreign operations

- ✔ Gains on property revaluations (properties covered by IAS 16, not investment properties covered by IAS 40)

- ✔ Income tax relating to components of other comprehensive income

- ✔ Share of other comprehensive income of associates (I cover associates in Chapter 12)

Occasionally, you put transactions directly to retained earnings, which means that you also include the transactions in the statement of changes in equity, which shows the changes that were made to the equity section of the statement of financial position (in other words, changes in the shareholders' funds). Here are some transactions that go to retained earnings:

- ✔ Change accounting policy (applied retrospectively as per IAS 8 – see Chapter 2 for accounting policy changes)

- ✔ Discover a prior-period error that requires correction under IAS 8 *Accounting Policies, Changes in Accounting Estimates and Errors* and thus restate the opening retained earnings figure (flick to Chapter 2 for more on accounting policies, estimates and errors)

- ✔ Switch to IFRS from domestic Generally Accepted Accounting Practice (GAAP) – here you're derecognising assets and liabilities that were permissible in domestic GAAP but aren't allowed in IFRS, or vice versa (Chapter 3 looks at the switchover from national accounting standards to IFRS)

- ✔ Revalue non-current assets (see the following section)

Revaluing Non-Current Assets

Non-current assets are those assets that a company uses in its day-to-day business operations to generate income for the company – for example, a manufacturing company has lots of machinery that it uses to manufacture goods for selling to customers to generate income for the business. The assets are non-current assets because the company expects to use them in the business for more than a year. Non-current assets are *tangible* (you can kick them) or *intangible* (they're invisible). (For more on non-current assets, head to Chapter 4.)

IAS 16 *Property, Plant and Equipment* covers non-current assets. Two possible measurement techniques exist: the *depreciated historic cost model*, where you initially recognise your non-current asset at cost and then write off this cost to the income statement by way of *depreciation* over the estimated useful life of the asset; and the *revaluation model*, where you state the non-current assets in the financial statements at fair value at each year- or period-end. This section looks at what happens when a company decides to use the revaluation model for some (or all) of its non-current assets.

If a company's non-current assets go up in value, then the overall value of the company increases. Because the company's value has increased, the share-holders' could (potentially) get more cash if they sold the company than they could *before* the revaluation took place. So the company reflects the increase in non-current assets in shareholders' funds (the equity section of the statement of financial position). This situation is a bit like when your house increases in value – the price goes up, so the *equity* you have in your house also increases. A company's assets go up in value, so the shareholders' funds (equity) increases.

Dealing with the revaluation reserve account

You take any fluctuations in the value of non-current assets that use the revaluation model to the *revaluation reserve* account in the equity section of the statement of financial position. You use the revaluation reserve account only for items of non-current assets that are subjected to the revaluation model under IAS 16. So when you carry an item of property, plant and equipment (PPE) at valuation and the value of the item of PPE goes up, the debit goes to the relevant item of PPE in the non-current assets section of the statement of financial position to increase the value of this non-current asset, and the credit goes to the revaluation reserve.

Here are the steps to take when dealing with a non-current asset under the revaluation model:

1. **Get hold of the up-to-date value of the non-current asset.** If a building is subject to the revaluation model, the valuation report contains the value.

2. **Compare the up-to-date valuation with the carrying amount of the non-current asset in the statement of financial position.** If the up-to-date

valuation is *higher* than the carrying amount, you have a revaluation *gain*; if the up-to-date valuation is *lower* than the carrying amount, you have a revaluation *loss*.

3. **For revaluation gains:**

   - **Debit the non-current asset in the statement of financial position with the difference between the carrying amount in the financial statements and the up-to-date valuation amount.**

   - **Put the credit entry to the revaluation reserve account.**

4. **For revaluation losses:**

   - **Credit the non-current asset in the statement of financial position with the difference between the carrying amount in the statement of financial position and the up-to-date value.**

   - **Put the debit to the revaluation reserve account, but only to the extent that the debit reduces any previous revaluation gains (credits) of the same property that's seen a fall in value to nil.**

   - **Put any remaining loss to the income statement.**

If you've an investment property, accounted for under IAS 40 (see Chapter 4), you take any fluctuations in the fair value of the property straight to the income statement – don't set up a revaluation reserve in equity for these fluctuations. Some local GAAPs require you to send gains and losses in the fair value of an investment property to a revaluation reserve in the equity section of the statement of financial position, but IFRS doesn't.

On 31 December 2010, Leyla Enterprises had a building that it carried in the financial statements using the revaluation model. On this date, the carrying amount (the amount stated in the statement of financial position) of the building was $100,000. On 31 December 2011, the valuation agency carried out a valuation of the building and confirmed that the building had increased in value to $110,000.

In order for Leyla Enterprises to incorporate the uplift of this building in the financial statements, it needs to:

Debit buildings (non-current assets) $10,000
Credit revaluation surplus (in equity) $10,000

Now, if in the subsequent year the building suffers a temporary fall in value (so, for example, if the valuer says in the following year that the building is worth $107,000), you don't send the fall in value (the loss) straight to the income statement. Instead, you credit the building in non-current assets to reduce its carrying amount to $107,000, and the corresponding debit entry can go to the revaluation surplus account, which then reduces the revaluation reserve account down to $7,000.

If the valuer said in the following year that the building was only worth $95,000 (not $107,000), meaning that the building has suffered a $15,000 revaluation loss, you credit the building in the statement of financial position with $15,000 ($110,000 minus $95,000) and debit the revaluation reserve account with $10,000 (to clear the revaluation reserve down to nil) and the remaining $5,000 ($15,000 less $10,000) would go to the income statement.

This concept is fairly straightforward when you've one item of PPE stated at revaluation, but what if you've more than one asset stated at valuation? I take a look at this issue in the following section 'Offsetting two assets in the same class'.

Offsetting two assets in the same class

When a company chooses to use the revaluation model, for consistency it must subject all the non-current assets in that class of non-current assets to the revaluation model. So if a company owns five buildings and the directors decide that they want to use the revaluation model for the company's buildings, the company subjects every building to the revaluation model.

Buildings going up and down in value is extremely common, and one building may go up in value while another goes down. The question, therefore, arises as to whether you can offset a loss on one building against the gain on another. The simple answer to this question is no!

You must look at each asset within an asset class in isolation. So, you follow the steps I provide in the earlier section 'Using the revaluation reserve account' for each individual asset.

Westhead Interiors has two buildings, both of which are subjected to the revaluation model. On 31 December 2010, Shop 1 was valued at $100,000 and Shop 2 was carried at $150,000. The revaluation reserve account in respect of both shops was as follows:

Shop 1	$35,000
Shop 2	$49,000

On 31 December 2011, the valuation agency said that Shop 1 had decreased in value and was only worth $60,000, whereas Shop 2 had increased in value and was now worth $155,000.

You need to look at the two shops in isolation. You know that Shop 1 has suffered a significant decline in value and needs to be reflected in the statement of financial position at $60,000. What you *don't* do is simply credit non-current assets (buildings) with $40,000 and charge the income statement with $40,000, because you need to deal with the revaluation reserve as well.

The entries in respect of Shop 1 are:

Credit non-current assets (buildings) $40,000
Debit revaluation surplus $35,000
Debit impairment loss (income statement) $ 5,000

In respect of Shop 2, the entries are:

Debit non-current assets (buildings) $ 5,000
Credit revaluation surplus $ 5,000

You can see that if you start offsetting losses against gains for different assets, the books are going to get into a bit of a mess!

If Shop 1 in the example goes up in value in the next year, you can recognise the gain in profit or loss, but only to the extent that it reverses the $5,000 loss charged. For example, if the value of Shop 1 went up by $30,000 to $90,000 in the 31 December 2012 valuation, you'd credit $5,000 to the income statement to reverse the effects of the prior year loss, and credit the remaining $25,000 to the revaluation surplus.

Moving the revaluation reserve into retained earnings

When you carry a non-current asset at valuation, sometimes you need to put some entries from the revaluation reserve account into the retained earnings account. (See the previous section 'Knowing when to put transactions directly into retained earnings' for other examples of transactions that go to retained earnings.)

The revaluation reserve account can't just stay on the statement of financial position sitting pretty! You write it back to retained earnings over the expected useful life of the asset. The idea behind this action is that when you write off the asset(s) to which the revaluation surplus relates to nil, the revaluation reserve in respect of those assets is also nil.

Here's what you do:

1. **Debit the item of non-current asset(s) that's increased in value with the difference between the cost price and the revalued amount and credit the revaluation reserve account with the same amount.**

Ethan Enterprises Co has a year-end of 31 December. On 1 January 2009, Ethan Enterprises Co buys an item of plant for $10,000 and the expected useful life of this item of plant is 10 years with nil *residual value* (an estimate of how much the asset will be worth at the end of its useful life). On 1 January 2011, the item is revalued to $18,000.

To get the revaluation into the books, here are the entries:

Debit property, plant and equipment cost	$8,000
Credit revaluation reserve	$8,000

2. **Reverse out any previous accumulated depreciation charges by debiting accumulated depreciation charges in the statement of financial position and crediting revaluation reserve with the same amount.**

Ethan Enterprises bought the item of plant for $10,000 on 1 January 2009 and estimated the useful life of this plant to be ten years with nil *residual value* (an estimate of how much the asset will be worth at the end of its useful life). Therefore, in the 31 December 2009 financial statements the depreciation charge was $1,000 ($10,000 ÷ 10 years) and in the 31 December 2010 financial statements there was another $1,000 depreciation charge, so Ethan has charged $2,000 worth of depreciation since acquiring the item of plant. You reverse out the accumulated depreciation on revaluation as follows:

Debit accumulated depreciation	$2,000
Credit revaluation reserve	$2,000

3. **Charge depreciation on the revalued amount over the expected useful life of the non-current asset by crediting depreciation charge in the statement of financial position and debiting depreciation expense in the income statement.**

The item of plant has a useful life left as at 31 December 2011 of eight years so the depreciation charge going forward becomes $2,250 ($18,000 ÷ 8). You do the normal annual charge as at 31 December 2011, which is:

Debit depreciation charge (income statement)	$2,250
Credit accumulated depreciation (non-current assets)	$2,250

4. **Move the *excess* of the depreciation charge that you'd have charged had the non-current asset not been revalued over the depreciation charge that you've charged following the revaluation exercise to retained earnings by debiting revaluation reserve with the excess and crediting retained earnings.**

    Had Ethan Enterprises not revalued the item of plant, Ethan would have charged another $1,000 depreciation in the 31 December 2011 financial statements. However, because of the revaluation, Ethan has charged $2,250 worth of depreciation (see Step 3). Ethan needs to transfer the difference between the depreciation charge *after* the revaluation ($2,250) and the depreciation that would have been charged if the revaluation had not taken place ($1,000) of $1,250 from the revaluation reserve account into the retained earnings account as follows:

Debit revaluation reserve account	$1,250
Credit retained earnings account	$1,250

As you can see, the revaluation reserve account doesn't just sit there. You have to do something with it every year. If Ethan Enterprises Co sold the item of plant before the end of its useful economic life, it would transfer any remaining balance left on revaluation reserve in respect of the sold item into retained earnings also.

Part III
Consolidating and Investing

The 5th Wave — By Rich Tennant

"If we cut our dividend, reduce inventory and time travel to the 13th century, we should be able to last another year."

In this part . . .

*L*ots of companies just stand alone; but sometimes a company buys a controlling stake in another company or simply invests funds in another organisation. This makes life a little trickier because the company needs to account for these sorts of investments in its financial statements.

In this part of the book, I examine the concept of *consolidated* financial statements (in other words where two, or more, sets of financial statements are combined) and the situations that arise when consolidated financial statements are required. I also look at some of the more complicated consolidation issues, including when a parent company sells off one (or more) of its subsidiary companies. I then move on to consider associates and joint ventures, and how you account for these.

Chapter 10

Getting Your Head Around the Basics of Consolidation

. . . .

. . . .

*E*very company has to prepare financial statements: to understand how the business has performed over the accounting period, to assess how much tax it has to pay on its profits and to inform shareholders who have a vested interest in the company. Preparing financial statements for an individual company is one thing, but preparing them for a *parent company* (one that owns another company or companies, or holds the majority of shares in another company or companies) is a little more taxing. Why? Because IFRS requires the parent company to prepare not only its own separate financial statements, but also consolidated financial statements. The *consolidated* statements combine the parent company's financial results with the results of the other company (or companies) that it owns or of which it's the major shareholder.

Now, consolidated financial statements can be complicated to deal with. So in this chapter I give you a good grounding in the basic concepts and objectives of these statements and help you understand the need for separate financial statements. I then take you through the methods involved in consolidated financial statements and round off by flagging for you some crucial need-to-know aspects of consolidations.

This chapter looks at the basic consolidation processes, and Chapter 11 looks at some fairly complex consolidation issues, but I don't go into every eventuality where consolidated financial statements are concerned because the area of consolidations is vast. If you're happy with the basics and want some more detailed information then *The Interpretation and Application of IFRS* by Bruce Mackenzie *et al.* (Wiley) is a good source of information, covering all the areas of consolidated financial statements.

Knowing the Objectives of Consolidated Financial Statements

The need for consolidated financial statements can arise due to IFRS provisions or companies legislation, or both (for more on UK companies law, see the sidebar 'UK law and consolidated financial statements').

The accounting standard that governs how you prepare the consolidated financial statements is IAS 27 *Consolidated and Separate Financial Statements*, and this standard is one that you need to understand well. When faced with preparing consolidated financial statements, many people try to cut corners or just dive in and start combining two statements of financial position and two statements of comprehensive income. What you need before you even contemplate consolidating is to understand the concept behind consolidated financial statements.

UK law and consolidated financial statements

Legislation may dictate when consolidated financial statements have to be prepared. In the UK, the Companies Act 2006 requires medium-sized groups to produce consolidated financial statements (boo!), whereas previously only large groups had to. So many accountants who previously needn't have produced a set of consolidated financial statements for their company or their client now have to do so.

In the UK, a group may qualify as small or medium-sized for a financial year. Groups qualify as small, and are therefore exempted from the requirement to prepare consolidated financial statements, or medium-sized, which means they have to prepare consolidated financial statements, if they satisfy any two of these conditions:

✔ Net turnover doesn't exceed £6.5 million for small groups or £25.9 million for medium-sized groups (*net* means that you don't include intra-group sales). Gross turnover doesn't exceed £7.8 million for small groups or £31.1 million for medium-sized groups (*gross* means that you include intra-group sales). A company may satisfy this criteria on the basis of gross *or* net figures. Check the gross size criteria first and then (only if required) the net size criteria.

✔ Net balance sheet total doesn't exceed £3.26 million for small groups or £12.9 million for medium-sized groups (*balance sheet total* is non-current (fixed) assets plus current assets). Gross balance sheet total doesn't exceed £3.9 million for small groups or £15.5 million for medium-sized groups (*gross* means that intra-group receivables (debtors) and payables (creditors) haven't been adjusted). A company may satisfy the qualifying criteria on the basis of gross *or* net figures, but should check the gross size criteria first and then (only if required) the net size criteria.

✔ The group's average number of employees doesn't exceed 50 employees for a small group or 250 employees for a medium-sized group.

If you've never come across consolidated financial statements before, I strongly advise you to carefully digest this section. In order to appreciate *how* consolidated financial statements are prepared, you need to understand *why* they're prepared.

Seeing how individual group companies report as one

Under IFRS, you have to prepare consolidated financial statements when a parent company controls another company or controls a number of other companies. First, you work out which companies (investees) are owned by the parent company, and then you determine whether the parent has control over the investee (I look at the area of control in the later section 'Working out who has control of a subsidiary, and when'). If the parent has control over the investee, the investee is known as a *subsidiary*.

Figure 10-1 shows a simple group structure. You can see that Company A owns 100 per cent of Company B and 100 per cent of Company C. Therefore, Company B and Company C are both subsidiaries of Company A because Company A controls both Company B and Company C because it owns 100 per cent of each company's net assets.

Figure 10-1:
A simple
group
structure.

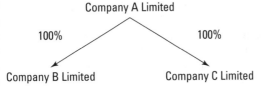

IAS 27 says that when a parent company has a subsidiary, or subsidiaries, it must consolidate the financial results of the subsidiary entities with the financial results of the parent entity. In other words, the parent entity must produce consolidated financial statements in addition to its own financial statements. The question to address at this point is why.

The overarching objective of IAS 27 (and the new IFRS 10 *Consolidated Financial Statements*, which I look at in Chapter 19) is that the consolidated financial statements must show the results of the group as if it were a *single* reporting entity – in other words, one big entity (organisation/company) without the parent–subsidiary relationship(s).

I place emphasis on the word *single*. This is because in many group situations members of the group trade with each other, by which I mean that they buy and sell goods or services from and to each other. It may also be that one company in the group makes a loan to another company in a group and charges interest. When it comes to doing the consolidated financial statements you have to eliminate all this *intra-group trading* (I look in more detail at this process in the later section 'Eliminating intra-group trading on consolidation').

In Figure 10-2, I take the example of Company A in Figure 10-1 and add in a bit of trading between the members of the group.

Figure 10-2:
Simple
group
showing
Co B selling
goods to
Co C.

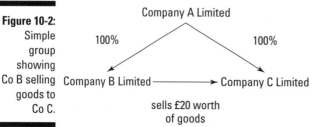

You can see that Company B has sold $20 worth of goods to Company C. Therefore, Company B's revenue figure includes $20 worth of sales to Company C and Company C's purchases figure includes $20 worth of purchases from Company B. This sale and corresponding purchase must be cancelled in the consolidated financial statements by reducing Company B's sales by $20 and reducing Company C's purchases by $20 because the consolidated financial statements must show the results of the group as if it were a *single* trading company.

Sales and purchases between group members are merely intra-group *transfers* for consolidated financial statement purposes. You can't recognise them as *revenue* (funds received from the selling of goods or rendering of services) until they're sold to customers outside of the group structure.

Looking at some exemptions

A parent with a subsidiary (or subsidiaries) doesn't always have to prepare consolidated financial statements. Some exemptions within IAS 27 (specifically at paragraph 10) say that a parent doesn't have to (but can) present consolidated financial statements provided that it meets the following conditions:

- The parent company itself is a wholly owned subsidiary company, or a partially owned subsidiary company of another parent, and its owners, including those who don't have the power to vote, have been told and don't object to the parent not presenting consolidated financial statements.

- The parent company's debt or equity instruments (for example, shares) aren't traded on a public market (like the London Stock Exchange).

- The parent company hasn't filed, or isn't in the process of filing, its financial statements with a securities commission or other regulatory organisation for the purposes of issuing any class of instruments (for example, shares) in a public market.

- The ultimate or any intermediary parent of the parent produces consolidated financial statements that are available to the general public and that comply with IFRS.

A company must meet the same criteria when it adopts the new IFRS 10. You can find the conditions in IFRS 10 at paragraph 4(A).

You need to understand that no exemptions are available in the following situations:

- When a parent *does* produce consolidated financial statements and a subsidiary operates in a different business to that of its parent

- When severe long-term restrictions are in place on the part of the subsidiary to transfer funds to the parent

- When a subsidiary that had been previously consolidated is now held for sale (the standard says that when a previously consolidated subsidiary is held for sale, you apply the provisions in IFRS 5 *Non-Current Assets Held for Sale and Discontinued Operations* – flick to Chapter 4 for the lowdown on IFRS 5 issues)

Working out who has control of a subsidiary, and when

A parent company only has a subsidiary when the parent *controls* that subsidiary. If the parent doesn't have control, it doesn't have a subsidiary. Then it accounts for its investment in a company as an associate under IAS 28 *Investments in Associates* (see Chapter 12) or as a simple investment as a financial asset under IAS 39 *Financial Instruments: Recognition and Measurement* (see Chapter 5).

So what's control all about then? *Control* is the power to govern the financial and operating policies of the subsidiary company so as to obtain benefits from its activities. If the parent possesses this power over a subsidiary, then IAS 27 and the new IFRS 10 apply (subject, of course, to the exemptions I discuss in the previous section 'Looking at some exemptions').

IFRS 10 says that a company has control of another company (the investee) if (and only if) it has *power* over the investee, which means that the investor has

✔ Rights that enable it to direct the subsidiary's activities

✔ Exposure, or rights, to variable returns from its involvement with the investee

✔ Power over the investee to such an extent that it affects the amount of return the investor receives from the investee

One of the main ways of checking whether or not the parent has control is by looking at the ownership interest the parent has in the investee. If the investor owns more than 50 per cent of the voting rights of the investee, it can have control. However, such a quantitative benchmark isn't the only indicator of control being obtained. Also consider who has the power to remove or appoint the directors holding a majority of the voting rights.

Alicia Enterprises owns 60 per cent of the net assets of Lisa Enterprises. This is a clear case of control being obtained because Alicia owns more than 50 per cent of the net assets of Lisa.

Alicia Enterprises owns 40 per cent of the net assets of Lisa Enterprises. Alicia has the power to appoint or remove the directors of Lisa holding a majority of the voting rights at all meetings of the Board on all, or substantially all, matters. In this instance, control is obtained because of Alicia's right to remove or appoint the directors holding a majority of the voting rights, despite the fact that Alicia Enterprises only owns 40 per cent of the net assets of Lisa Enterprises.

Creating Separate Financial Statements

When a parent–subsidiary relationship exists, consolidated statements are required. You may be thinking, 'Hooray! So we cut down the paperwork and just put together one big statement to cover all the companies.' Sorry to burst your bubble, but actually you produce the consolidated statement *and* individual financial statements for each company within the group (including the parent company). So each company has its own separate financial statements, and when these separate financial statements are finalised the subsidiary's financial statements are consolidated with the parent's financial statements to produce the consolidated statements.

Understanding why to bother doing separate financial statements

Separate financial statements are necessary for preparation of the consolidated financial statements. If the subsidiary company doesn't produce its own financial statements then how can the results of the subsidiary be consolidated with those of the parent? The simple answer is – they can't!

If a company doesn't produce its own financial statements, it also won't have a clue about how it has performed in the year (in other words, if the company has made a profit or a loss) or how financially sound the company is. The amount of money in the bank account at the end of the year isn't an indication as to how well a company has performed over the accounting period.

Seeing what's in separate financial statements but not consolidated ones

When a company (the investor) decides to invest in another company (the investee), it pays money to the investee in return for a share of the investee's net assets. The investor has to account for the transaction accordingly in its accounting records, so it

- ✔ Credits cash at bank (to reduce the money in the company's bank account or increase an overdrawn balance)
- ✔ Debits non-current asset investments in the statement of financial position

The investor's statement of financial position shows an increase in non-current assets (being the investment) and a reduction in the bank balance, or an increase in an overdrawn balance (to pay for the investment).

All that's fairly straightforward until the time comes to prepare the consolidated financial statements. Then, you show the results of the group as a *single* reporting entity. As a result, in the consolidated financial statements you eliminate the non-current asset investment and this then forms part of the goodwill calculation. *Goodwill* is the excess of the purchase price paid over the net assets you've acquired in the subsidiary – so you remove the cost of the investment and substitute this instead for goodwill in the consolidated financial statements. (Head to Chapter 11 for more on goodwill.)

Here's how the accounting works:

On 1 January 2012, Smyth Sunblinds purchased an 80 per cent share of Clare Canopies for $30,000. The entries in the books of Smyth Sunblinds are:

Credit cash at bank	$30,000
Debit investment (non-current asset)	$30,000

When the consolidated financial statements are being prepared, money used to invest in the subsidiary is removed from the non-current assets of the statement of financial position and included in the goodwill calculation. At the date Smyth Sunblind acquired Clare Canopies, the value of Clare Canopies' net assets was $20,000, consisting of $10,000 share capital and $10,000 retained earnings. You work out the goodwill arising as follows:

Cost of investment		$30,000
Net assets acquired:		
Share capital	$10,000	
Retained earnings	<u>$10,000</u>	
	$20,000	
	x 80%	<u>($16,000)</u>
Goodwill arising on acquisition		<u>**$14,000**</u>

In the consolidated financial statements, the $30,000 cost of investment disappears and instead is replaced by the goodwill of $14,000.

Group Accounting: The Fundamentals

Group accounting can seem daunting, because it's bigger than accounting for an individual company. But in this section I give you plenty of how-to guidance: how to eliminate intra-group transactions, handle unrealised profits in inventory, eliminate intra-group receivables, and manage dividends to parties with an interest in the company.

The financial statements of all subsidiaries to be used in preparing consolidated financial statements should, wherever practicable, be prepared to the same financial year-end as those of the parent and should also cover the same financial period. Where the reporting date of a subsidiary differs from that of the parent, prepare additional financial statements to the same date as those of the parent for use in preparing the consolidated financial statements. If it's not practicable to use additional financial statements, use the subsidiary's financial statements, providing that its year ended not more than three months before, or after, the relevant year-end of the parent.

Eliminating intra-group trading on consolidation

Intra-group trading refers to the situations when one member of a group buys or sells goods or services or makes a loan to another member of a group. Intra-group trading can take place between a parent and a subsidiary, or vice versa or between two (or more) subsidiaries. Intra-group trading is probably *the* most common issue you face as you prepare group financial statements.

In order to prepare the consolidated financial statements for the parent and subsidiary (or subsidiaries) that present the results of all the companies in the group as a single reporting company, eliminating the effects of intra-group trading is essential. The point is to enable the consolidated financial statements to show the results of the group purely from its activities with the outside world.

If you don't eliminate the effects of intra-group trading, the financial statements are significantly distorted (revenue and costs are overstated), which may lead the user to make the wrong conclusions about the company.

Intra-group sales and purchases are merely transfers of goods between one member of a group and another. They may be reflected as a sale and purchase in the individual subsidiary's accounting records, but the sale of the same goods can only be recognised as such when they're sold to third parties (in other words, customers *outside* the group structure).

Elimination of intra-group trading is easy when you've a parent with one subsidiary. The concept itself doesn't change when you've more than one subsidiary, but you do a little bit more digging around.

1. **Work out the value of intra-group sales between members of a group. Intra-group sales in one group company need to be intra-group purchases in the other group company's books.**

    For example, if one company sold another goods costing $100,000, the company the sold the goods has included the $100,000 in its sales figure, and the company that bought the goods has included $100,000 in its purchases figure.

2. **For the consolidated financial statements, reduce the value of revenue by the amount of intra-group sales and reduce the value of purchases by the same amount.**

   In the example in Step 1, you simply remove $100,000 from the intra-group sales figure and from the value of purchases.

Dealing with unrealised group profits at year-end

Unrealised profits usually occur when one member of a group (the seller) sells goods to another group member (the buyer) at cost to the seller plus the seller's profit margin, and the buyer still has some (or all) of these goods in its inventory at the year-end. The seller's sales price to the buyer includes an element of profit. If all (or part) of these goods remain in the buyer's inventory at the year-end, the inventory is valued at cost to the buyer when the buyer does its inventory count. This *cost* includes an element of the seller's profit. If you don't eliminate the seller's profit, then the inventory valuation in the consolidated financial statements is overstated (by the value of the seller's profit margin).

IAS 2 *Inventories* (see Chapter 4) says that you value inventory at the *lower* of cost or net realisable value (what an asset would be worth in an arm's-length transaction where both parties act independently and have no relationship to each other). You have to eliminate the seller's profit because it is *unrealised* – that is, it hasn't turned into cash. Unrealised profits in inventory become realised when that inventory is sold to parties outside of the group structure (in other words, the buyer's customers). By eliminating this unrealised profit in the consolidated financial statements, you bring the inventory valuation back down to cost to the group.

Here's how you eliminate unrealised profit in the consolidated statement of financial position:

1. **Work out the unrealised profit.**

   For example, say Norah owns 80 per cent of Stella. During the accounting period, Norah transferred goods to Stella for $6,000, which gave her a profit of $3,000. All these goods were included in Stella's inventory at the year-end. The unrealised profit is $3,000. (If half the goods were sold and half remained in inventory, the unrealised profit would be $1,500.)

2. **Debit group retained earnings by the unrealised profit.**

   You do this in the equity section of the consolidated statement of financial position.

3. **Credit inventory by the unrealised profit.**

Consider the impact the direction of the sale has on the overall consolidated results. IAS 27 (and IFRS 10) requires you to eliminate unrealised profits in full from the inventory value. But what about the other side of the double entry? The whole amount can be suffered by the parent company's shareholders by reducing the inventory value in the consolidated statement of financial position and the statement of comprehensive income (this action would, of course, reduce the profit for the year and hence the accumulated profit/retained earnings figure).

In this respect, the direction of the sale (parent to subsidiary or subsidiary to parent) is irrelevant. However, you can share the adjustment between the parent's shareholders and the non-controlling interests (those that own the remainder of the shares in the subsidiary). You reduce the inventory value in the consolidated statement of financial position and the consolidated statement of comprehensive income, and then give the non-controlling interest its share by making an adjustment in the books of the group company that made the sale to the other group company (in other words, a *seller adjustment*). This is when the direction of the sale becomes important.

Remembering amounts owed by and to group companies at year-end

The elimination of the effects of intra-group trading means that when all the work is done, the consolidated financial statements show the net effect of each group company's results purely from its activities with the outside world in one set of financial statements.

The elimination of intra-group sales and intra-group purchases is one thing, your bookkeeping knowledge tells you that if you make a sale on credit to someone, the other side of the entry is to trade receivables (those that owe you money). Conversely, if you purchase goods on credit from a supplier, the other side of the entry is to trade payables (those you owe money to). Exactly the same sort of principle applies to intra-group sales and purchases.

Intra-group sales and purchases (particularly towards, or at, the year-end) often give rise to intra-group receivables and payables, which you need to eliminate as part of the consolidation process. The elimination process also means that any intra-group loan balances need eliminating as well as any intra-group finance charges that have been made. The earlier section 'Eliminating intra-group trading on consolidation' shows you how.

Lynn owns 100 per cent of the net assets of Ian. Extracts from the financial statements of each individual company as at 31 December 2011 are as follows:

	Lynn	Ian
	$	$
Trade receivables	70,000	22,000
Trade payables	35,000	10,000

Ian owed Lynn an amount of $5,000 at the year-end. You're dealing with the consolidation adjustments required to the Lynn Group consolidated financial statements at the year-end. In the *individual* financial statements, the $5,000 is shown as a receivable in Lynn's financial statements and as a payable in Ian's financial statements. The following is how the extract from the Lynn Group consolidated statement of financial position for the year ending 31 December 2011 looks:

	$,000
Trade receivables (70 + 22 – 5)	87
Trade payables (35 + 10 – 5)	40

Admittedly, consolidated financial statements are somewhat fiddly and can get more complicated with larger, more complex companies. However, after you master the art of elimination of intra-group trading/balances, while keeping in mind the fundamental objective of consolidated financial statements, they become much more easier to deal with (and enjoyable – honest!).

Dealing with dividends to non-controlling interests

Non-controlling interests (NCIs) are those that own the balance of the shares that are *not* owned by the parent. You may have heard these interests referred to as *minority interests* in the past, but this term was dropped in 2008 in favour of non-controlling interests.

If you invest money, you want a return on that investment – a bit like you expect when you put savings into a savings account at the bank. Well, NCIs have also invested in the same company as the parent, and just because they don't control the company like the parent can, they still expect a return on their investment. *Dividends* are a form of return on an investment.

A company that's controlled by a parent but that has other investors (the NCIs) often pays dividends to *all* its shareholders. In the consolidated financial statements, the issue is which amounts to recognise in respect of this dividend that the subsidiary company is declaring at its year-end. Here's what to do:

1. **The subsidiary company records the total amount of dividend payable to both the parent company and the NCIs in its own individual financial statements by crediting dividends payable and debiting equity.**

2. **In the *individual* financial statements of the parent company, the parent records its share of the dividend as a receivable by debiting dividend receivable and crediting profit or loss.**

3. **During the consolidation process, the amount of the dividend payable to the parent (in Step 1) and the receivable recognised in the parent's individual financial statements (Step 2) is an inter-company balance, which you eliminate during the consolidation process.**

   The receivable in the parent is a payable in the subsidiary, so each cancels the other out.

4. **The consolidated statement of financial position shows the *parent company's* dividend only (if the parent has declared one at the year-end) as well as the non-controlling interest's (NCIs) share of the subsidiary's dividend.**

Howarth Holding Co purchased an 80 per cent controlling stake in Smyth Subsidiary Co Ltd on 1 January 2012. In this simple example, Howarth Holding Co (the parent) owns 80 per cent of the net assets in Smyth Subsidiary Co, and the NCIs own the remaining 20 per cent.

If Smyth Subsidiary Co proposes a dividend to its shareholders at the year-end (which is usually the case, because dividends are a return on an investor's investment), then clearly the parent (Howarth Holding Co) will receive its share, which represents 'reserves-in-transit'. Howarth Holding Co must record this dividend receivable by debiting dividend receivable and crediting profit or loss.

However, Smyth Subsidiary Co's individual financial statements record the dividend *payable* to both Howarth Holding Co *and* the NCIs (think of it as the gross dividend from Smyth's point of view). Howarth Holding Co shows its share of the dividend as a receivable in its individual financial statements. In the consolidated financial statements, the dividend receivable and payable by Smyth to Howard are inter-company balances and must be cancelled. Therefore, the consolidated statement of financial position only shows:

- ✔ The parent's (Howarth Holding Co) proposed dividends
- ✔ The non-controlling interest's share of Smyth Subsidiary Co proposed dividends

Important changes to IAS 27

In May 2011, the IASB issued new standards relating to consolidated financial statements. It hasn't replaced IAS 27 in its entirety, but it has made significant changes to it.

The consolidation guidance currently in IAS 27 has been replaced by IFRS 10. Therefore, IAS 27 only deals with separate financial statements and the IASB has renamed this IAS 27 *Separate Financial Statements*. The new IFRS 10 has been issued with the objective of introducing a single consolidation model for all companies that's based on control, regardless of the nature of the investee. The IASB believes that these changes will provide much clearer and more consistent guidance for more complex structures. IFRS 10 is effective for accounting periods commencing on or after 1 January 2013, but can be adopted earlier if you want.

Other new IFRS also relate to when a company has an interest in other companies:

✔ **IFRS 11** *Joint Arrangements*: See Chapter 13.

✔ **IFRS 12** *Disclosure of Interests in Other Entities*: The disclosures in the new IFRS 12 are highly comprehensive and largely beyond the scope of this book. As a quick summary, IFRS 12 requires disclosures relating to significant judgements and assumptions, interests in subsidiaries, interests in joint arrangements and associates and interests in unconsolidated structured companies. IFRS 12 goes into a lot of detail as to the types of disclosures needed and its objective is to require the reporting company to disclose information to such an extent that the user of the financial statements can understand the nature of, and risks associated with, its interests in other entities and the effect of those interests on its financial position, financial performance and cash flows. IFRS 12 is applicable for accounting periods commencing on or after 1 January 2013, but you can adopt it earlier if you prefer.

Chapter 11

Getting to Grips with More Complex Consolidation Issues

· ·

· ·

*C*onsolidated financial statements combine a parent company's financial results with the results of the other company (or companies) that it owns or of which it's the major shareholder. The idea is that the consolidated statements show the results of the group as a single reporting company.

Consolidated financial statements are quite complicated. If you're unfamiliar with consolidations or your knowledge is a bit rusty, I suggest you read Chapter 10, which explains the basics, before diving into this one.

The purpose of this chapter is to get to grips with some of the complexities of consolidation. I examine what happens when a parent company decides to sell a subsidiary, and take a look at some of the issues that arise during a sale of a company (such as contingent consideration). Sometimes a parent may sell off part of a subsidiary, or even buy more of the shares in a subsidiary, so I examine what happens in respect of changes in ownership. I examine the two ways you can calculate goodwill arising from a business combination, and I round off by demystifying two areas that at first glance seem tricky: deemed disposals and step acquisitions.

Consolidated financial statements can become a complete nightmare to deal with if you don't adopt a logical approach. Many people subscribe to a step-by-step approach. However, what works best for some may not necessarily work for others. Whatever method you adopt, if you find that you're struggling with the concepts of consolidated financial statements, take a breather and think about each transaction on its own and the effect the transaction has on the consolidated statement of financial position or the consolidated statement of comprehensive income. A logical and methodical approach always works best; trust me!

Disposing of a Subsidiary

Companies sell their ownership in other companies for various reasons:

- ✔ To raise finance
- ✔ Because the subsidiary company is surplus to requirements and no longer fits into the group's portfolio of companies
- ✔ Because the subsidiary company was previously making losses before the parent took it over and the parent has turned it around so wants to sell to make a return on its investment

Whatever the reason, when a company disposes of a subsidiary, it must account for the disposal.

Selling a subsidiary outright

Some companies may sell off a subsidiary company outright, as opposed to selling off parts of a subsidiary (see 'Selling off parts of a subsidiary', later in the chapter). The following sections break down the accounting process down into steps for you. I use an example of what happens in a fairly uncomplicated scenario to help you follow the steps in practice – you can see that the concept isn't that bad (honestly!).

The Holmes Group is a highly diverse group of companies. Four years ago, it acquired a controlling interest in the net assets of Aidan Enterprises. Because of the group's diversity, the management of the Holmes Group has decided that Aidan Enterprises no longer fits into the group's portfolio and has decided to sell the subsidiary off in its entirety. The Charlotte Group has agreed to purchase Aidan Enterprises from the Holmes Group for a sum of $100,000. Immediately before the date of disposal, the net assets of Aidan Enterprises were valued (and carried in the statement of financial position of the Holmes Group) at a value of $98,700. The sale of Aidan Enterprises completed on 23 December 2011, and you're preparing the accounting entries for the disposal to be included in the Holmes Group individual financial statements for the year ended 31 December 2011.

The subsidiary company that has been sold (Aidan Enterprises) had its net assets valued immediately prior to the sale at $98,700. You carry this investment in the individual financial statements of the Holmes Group at this value at this date.

Step 1: Remove the subsidiary from the books

To remove a subsidiary from the books, you will need to credit the investment in the subsidiary in the investor's statement of financial position and debit the disposal account in the income statement.

In the example, you need to remove the value of the investment from the individual financial statements of the Holmes Group and put the other side of the entry into a disposal of non-current assets account in the income statement as follows:

	Debit ($)	Credit ($)
Investment in Aidan Enterprises		98,700
Disposal account	98,700	

The journal narrative in the accounting records is: *Being disposal of the net assets of Aidan Enterprises.*

If you don't remove the investment in Aidan from the books of the Holmes Group, their non-current assets (investments) are overstated! Think of when a company sells a car – if it doesn't remove the car from the statement of financial position, its vehicles (and non-current assets) are overstated.

Step 2: Deal with the sales proceeds

The sales proceeds received went into the bank account, which is a debit. Therefore, the other side of the entry (the credit) goes to the sale of non-current assets account in the income statement.

You don't treat the disposal proceeds as revenue. IAS 18 *Revenue* says that revenue is income received from the normal course of business – disposing of a subsidiary company in this way isn't normal (in other words, it hasn't arisen in the ordinary course of business – but is a sort of one-off transaction), hence you treat the disposal as a gain rather than as revenue.

In the example, Charlotte Group has paid Holmes Group $100,000 for Aidan Enterprises, so the entries in the Holmes Group individual books are as follows:

	Debit ($)	Credit (£)
Cash at bank	100,000	
Disposal account		100,000

The journal narrative in the accounting records is: *Being cash received for the disposal of Aidan Enterprises.*

Step 3: Find the resulting figure in the sale of non-current assets account

This figure is the gain or loss you made on the disposal of the subsidiary. If this figure is a debit balance, you made a loss; if the figure is a credit balance, you made a profit.

In the example, the individual financial statements of the Holmes Group now show no investment in Aidan Enterprises, and the income statement shows a profit on disposal of the subsidiary as follows:

Net assets of the disposed subsidiary	$98,700
Sales proceeds received	($100,000)
Resulting profit on disposal	**$1,300**

If you're a bit rusty with your debits and credits and doing things like disposing of non-current assets, why not pick up a copy of *Bookkeeping For Dummies* by Paul Barrow and Lita Epstein (Wiley)? This book is handy to have by your side (in addition to this one, of course) in case you need to go back to basics once in a while, which, let's face it, everyone needs to do sometimes.

Selling off parts of a subsidiary

A company may only sell part of a subsidiary, but still retain an interest in it. For example, if a subsidiary company has a number of divisions, the parent may not need one (or maybe more) divisions because it does the same work or the work the division does just isn't needed in the parent's business. In this instance, the company may sell off part of a subsidiary to a company that can benefit from it. When this happens, the parent retains control of the subsidiary, or loses control of it (I discuss retaining and losing control in 'Accounting for Changes in Ownership', later in the chapter). *Control* is the power to govern the financial and operating policies of the subsidiary company.

When you sell part of your subsidiary, you need to check the remaining percentage that you own. A subsidiary (when you own more than 51 per cent of the voting rights) may become an associate (which I discuss in Chapter 12) because your share of the voting rights is less than 51 per cent but more than 20 per cent. But in some cases, you may still own a majority of the voting rights, hence continue to recognise your investment as a subsidiary.

Theresa's Trainers owns 90 per cent of Ballards Boots. Theresa's Trainers has been approached by Stella's Slippers to buy the manufacturing division of Ballards Boots. Theresa's Trainers has agreed to sell off part of its shareholding in Ballards Boots to Stella's Slippers. After Theresa's Trainers completes the sale to Ballards Boots, Theresa's Trainers owns 68 per cent of Ballards Boots. This situation is a clear case of a parent selling off part of a subsidiary company. Theresa's Trainers still has control of Ballards Boots because Theresa's Trainers still owns more than 51 per cent of the voting rights in Ballards Boots.

When a parent sells off part of a subsidiary but still retains control of that subsidiary, the sale transaction is a transaction between the owners. In other words, you account for the sale within the equity section of the statement of financial position. (I look at changes in ownership in the later section 'Accounting for Changes in Ownership'.) Here's what you do:

1. **Adjust the carrying amounts (those stated in the financial statements) of the controlling and non-controlling interests to reflect the changes in their relative ownership interests in the subsidiary company.**

   Controlling interests are those with control; *non-controlling interests* are the third parties that own the remainder of the subsidiary's shares.

2. **Recognise any difference between the amount by which the non-controlling interests are adjusted and the *fair value* (market value) of the sales proceeds directly in the equity section of the statement of financial position.**

   The subsidiary's assets (including goodwill) and liabilities don't change because the transaction is one between the shareholders; the subsidiary still has the same amount of shares and net assets in issue – this is just a transfer of shares between controlling interests and non-controlling interests. (Remember, an *asset* is something that belong to an organisation; a *liability* is something that a company owes to another person or another company.) This also means that you don't recognise any reduction in a parent company's ownership of a subsidiary as a gain or loss in the statement of comprehensive income.

Subjecting sale proceeds to contingencies

Contingent consideration is money that's due to the parent company but is withheld by the party that's purchased the subsidiary for certain reasons. Usually, consideration becomes contingent (in other words, withheld) depending on whether the company achieves certain outcomes. For example, the subsidiary company may have to hit a certain profit level in the following year (or maybe two, or more, subsequent years) before it will release the withheld money to the selling parent. Contingent consideration is usually a liability in the buyer's statement of financial position, but it could be an asset if a right in the sale contract requires a return of some of the consideration to the buyer.

The buyer may settle contingent consideration in the future by cash or by shares. You need to know how the contingent consideration is to be settled because the accounting treatments are different:

- ✔ **Cash:** If the contingent consideration is to be settled in cash, then the party acquiring the subsidiary recognises a *liability* in its accounts (because it owes the seller money that's going to be settled in the future), and the selling party recognises a *receivable*. The acquirer recognises any change in the fair value of the contingent consideration within profit or loss.

- ✔ **Shares:** If the contingent consideration is to be settled in shares, the acquirer recognises the contingent funds within equity. The acquirer recognises any change in the fair value of the contingent consideration on eventual issue within equity.

So if you've bought a company and the terms of the agreement say that you're entitled to withhold a certain amount of money until the company you've bought achieves certain milestones, and you agree that if the subsidiary achieves these milestones you'll cough up hard cash, then you recognise this contingency as a liability.

Bennett's Bathroom Company (Bennett) acquired a 100 per cent stake in Kim's Kitchen Company (Kim) on 1 January 2012 when the fair value of the net assets of Kim was $116,000. The terms of the share purchase agreement are that Bennett will pay $100,000 immediately on completion of the sale, and if Kim's pre-tax profit is over $150,000 for each of the next two years, the balance of $16,000 will become payable in cash.

In this scenario, the $16,000 is the contingent consideration and the entries in the books of Bennett at the completion date are as follows:

	Debit ($)	Credit ($)
Investment (non-current asset)	116,000	
Cash at bank		100,000
Provision for liabilities		16,000

If Kim's profits don't hit the benchmark contained in the share purchase agreement and it then transpires that the contingent consideration isn't payable, Bennett reverses the provision and subsequently records it in the statement of comprehensive income as a gain.

Accounting for Changes in Ownership

When a company sells off part of a subsidiary as opposed to selling the entire thing, two possible outcomes exist: the parent still has control of the subsidiary or the parent loses control of the subsidiary. This section takes a look at what you need to do when you sell off some of your subsidiary but still have control, as well as what happens when you lose control of the subsidiary. Sometimes it may be the case that you buy more of the shares in the subsidiary, so I take a look at how to account for additional ownership interest. (For a deeper look at the parent–subsidiary relationship and control, take a look at Chapter 10.)

Under IAS 27 (and IFRS 10), a parent has to consolidate the subsidiary company's results with its results from the date on which the parent first achieves control to the date on which control is lost.

Be particularly careful with the date on which control is obtained because the day on which you part company with the cash to pay for your share of a subsidiary may not be the same date on which you obtain control. IAS 27 and IFRS 10 deal with the effects of the combination on consolidation, but it's actually IFRS 3 *Business Combinations* that deals with the date of acquisition. The *date of acquisition* is the date on which control is first obtained. This date may be different from the date on which cash is coughed up by the parent to the seller of the subsidiary because sometimes it may take a couple of days for the funds to clear the seller's bank account!

Keeping control of a subsidiary

When a parent's ownership in a subsidiary company increases or decreases and it still has control, the parent accounts for the transaction as an equity transaction; in other words, as a transaction between the owners. What this means is that you won't see any effect of the transaction in the income statement, nor will the transaction affect the original calculation of goodwill (see the later section 'Accounting for goodwill') or the assets and liabilities in the subsidiary. The transaction affects the equity section of the statement of financial position (equity equals owners' interest, which is why it's a transaction between the owners).

A parent has a subsidiary when it controls the financial and operating policies of that subsidiary. This control is usually achieved with an ownership of 51 per cent or more of the voting rights in the subsidiary. So if a parent owns 80 per cent of the net assets in a subsidiary, clearly it has control. The remaining 20 per cent belongs to non-controlling interests that form part of the equity section of the consolidated statement of financial position. If the parent sells off some of this subsidiary to a third party, but still retains control, then ownership interest reduces but non-controlling interests increase.

Here are the steps to deal with a partial disposal of a subsidiary when the parent still retains control:

1. **Work out (in percentage terms) how much the non-controlling interests have increased.**

   If you've sold 20 per cent of your subsidiary, non-controlling interests have increased by 20 per cent.

2. **Credit the percentage you found in Step 1 of your sales proceeds to non-controlling interests in the equity section of the consolidated statement of financial position.**

   So if controlling interests have increased by 20 per cent, credit 20 per cent of sales proceeds to non-controlling interests.

3. **Credit the balance of the sales proceeds to the equity section of the consolidated statement of financial position.**

   So if your sales proceeds were $100 and non-controlling interest increased by 20 per cent (see step 2) then $20 will go to non-controlling interests ($100 x 20%), the rest $80 ($100 less $20) will go to equity.

Pixies Pictures holds a 90 per cent interest in Eric's Interiors. Eric's Interiors has net assets of $4,000. Pixies Pictures sells 10 per cent of its ownership interest in Eric for $500 to the non-controlling interests. Pixies Pictures still retains control of Eric's Interiors after the partial disposal to the non-controlling interests. The entries in the equity section of the statement of financial position for Pixies Pictures Inc are as follows:

	Debit ($)	Credit ($)
Cash at bank	500	
Non-controlling interests ($500 x 10%)		50
Equity		450

The journal narrative in the books is: *Being sale of 10 per cent of subsidiary company.*

Losing control of a subsidiary

In many situations, a parent may sell off (part of) a subsidiary to an extent that the parent's remaining holding is less than 51 per cent. The parent still retains an interest in the company being sold, but the interest isn't enough to give the parent control.

When a company loses control of a subsidiary, you need to do the following:

1. **Derecognise the assets (including any goodwill) and liabilities of the subsidiary at their carrying amount at the date on which control is lost.**

On 20 December 2011, Cahill Crutches (Cahill) owned 100 per cent of Wilkinson's Walking Sticks (Wilkinson). On 31 December 2011, Cahill sold 85 per cent of Wilkinson (therefore retaining a 15 per cent interest). The net assets of Wilkinson immediately prior to the disposal were $500.

Cahill needs to remove its old investment in Wilkinson. Immediately prior to the sale, the net assets of Wilkinson were valued at $500, which was the amount of the investment in Cahill's statement of financial position. To remove this investment, Cahill needs to credit the investment in the statement of financial position with $500 and debit the disposal account in the income statement with $500.

2. **Recognise the fair value of the sales proceeds received, if any, from the transaction.**

The sales proceeds received is the amount of money you've received from selling your share of the subsidiary company.

Cahill sold its share in Wilkinson for $750. So Cahill debits cash at bank with $750 and credits the disposal account in the income statement with $750.

3. **Recognises any investment retained in the former subsidiary company in the statement of financial position at the investment's fair value at the date on which control is lost.**

If you retain a shareholding between 20 per cent and 50 per cent, the former subsidiary becomes an associate, which you account for under IAS 28 *Investments in Associates* (flick to Chapter 12 for accounting for associates). Where a subsidiary becomes an associate, you debit 'Investments in associate' in the non-current assets of the statement of financial position. Where the remaining investment is less than 20 per cent, you account for the investment as a simple investment under IAS 39 *Financial Instruments: Recognition and Measurement* (more on IAS 39 and financial assets in Chapter 5). Where the investment is a simple investment, you show it in non-current assets in the statement of financial position.

Following the sale, Cahill accounted for its remaining 15 per cent holding in Wilkinson as an available-for-sale investment under IAS 39. At the date of disposal, the fair value of Cahill's 15 per cent available-for-sale investment was valued at $130.

Cahill includes the remaining 15 per cent available-for-sale investment as a non-current asset in the statement of financial position by debiting available-for-sale investments with $130. The credit entry goes to the disposal account, which represents Cahill's retained interest in Wilkinson (by effectively reducing the $500 *full* disposal debited to the disposal account in Step 1).

4. **Reclassify to profit or loss (or, if needed, transfer directly to retained earnings) the amounts identified in other comprehensive income.** *Retained* **earnings are profits that the company has built up over time that it has reinvested into the business.**

   You debit (clear to nil) any credit balances shown in other comprehensive and the other side of the entry (the credit) goes to the income statement or directly to retained earnings. Similarly, you credit (clear to nil) any debit balances in other comprehensive income and the other side of the entry (the debit) goes to the income statement, or directly to retained earnings.

   Wilkinson had previously revalued its property, and recognised a revaluation gain in the revaluation reserve account (more on the revaluation reserve account in Chapter 4). It therefore reported $20 in other comprehensive income. Cahill debits the revaluation reserve account with $20 and credits the disposal account in the income statement with $20.

5. **Recognise any resulting amount (the difference) as a gain or loss in profit or loss attributable to the parent company.**

   When you dispose of a subsidiary, you invariably dispose of it at a profit (which is a credit in the income statement) or at a loss (which is a debit in the income statement). The *profit or loss* is the difference between the money you received from the buyer and the value of the subsidiary in the books.

   The example with Cahill Crutches and Wilkinsons Walking Sticks shows that:

   - The value of the net assets of Wilkinson that Cahill has sold is $500 (Step 1). This is a *debit* to the disposal account (the credit side going to the investment in Wilkinson in the statement of financial position).

   - Cahill sold 85 per cent of the net assets in Wilkinson for $750 (Step 2). This is a *credit* to the disposal account (the debit side going to the bank account).

   - Cahill has retained a 15 per cent interest in Wilkinson, which has been valued at $130 (Step 3). This is a *credit* to the disposal account representing the value retained (the debit side going to investments in the statement of financial position).

   - Wilkinson had revalued a property resulting in a revaluation gain of $20, which Cahill put into profit or loss by moving from the revaluation reserve account into the disposal account (Step 4). The $20 revaluation gain is a *credit* to the disposal account (the debit going to the revaluation reserve account).

You work out the gain or loss on disposal by finding the difference between all the debits in the disposal account and all the credits in the disposal account like this:

Disposal Account	Debit	Credit
Net assets in Wilkinson disposed (Step 1)	500	
Sales proceeds received (Step 2)		750
Interest in Wilkinson retained (Step 3)		130
Gain on property revaluation (Step 4)	___	20
	500	900
Gain on disposal (Step 5)	400	___
	900	900

The gain of $400 that you take to the income statement is the difference between the gain on the interest disposed (the 85 per cent holding in Wilkinson) and the gain on the interest Cahill has retained in Wilkinson (the 15 per cent holding). If you really want to make sure that the gain (or loss as the case may be) Cahill recognises in the income statement is correct:

1. **Take the disposal proceeds of $750 and deduct from this amount the actual amount of the investment it has disposed of (85 per cent of $500 = $425) which equals $325, then add the transfer of the revaluation reserve account to the income statement of $20.**

   The result is $345.

2. **Look at what Cahill has retained, which is a 15 per cent interest valued at $130, and deduct from this 15 per cent of the revalued net assets of Wilkinson ($500, so the deduction is $75).**

   The result is $55.

3. **Add the results together.**

   So, $345 + $55 = $400. This gives you the gain that Cahill has recognised (as well as giving you comfort that the gain in the income statement is correct).

Buying more ownership interest

When ownership interest increases, it means that the parent company has bought more shares in the subsidiary. An increase in ownership interest has the effect of reducing non-controlling interests. For example, if the parent currently owns 60 per cent of a subsidiary, non-controlling interests own the remaining 40 per cent. If the parent then decides to purchase an additional 20 per cent of the subsidiary's shares (therefore bringing the parent's ownership interest to 80 per cent), the non-controlling interests own only 20 per cent.

If you increase your ownership in a subsidiary, you record the transaction within the equity section of the consolidated statement of financial position by crediting cash at bank and debiting non-controlling interests. You debit non-controlling interests because these reduce due to the additional shares you've bought in the company.

On 31 December 2011, Casper's Curtains owned 80 per cent of Ingots Interiors. At that date, the net assets of Ingots Interiors was $4,000 and the carrying amount of the non-controlling interests in Ingots Interiors was $800. On 31 December 2011, Casper's Curtains acquired a further 10 per cent of Ingots Interiors for $400, which increases its total interest to 90 per cent. Casper's Curtains records its ownership of Ingots Interiors as follows:

	Debit ($)	Credit ($)
Non-controlling interests ($800 × 10% ÷ 20%)	400	
Cash at bank		400

The journal narrative in the books is: *Being purchase of additional 10 per cent in Ingot Interiors.*

Accounting for Goodwill

In terms of a business combination, *goodwill* is the excess of the purchase consideration (the money, generally) paid and the net assets that a company has acquired in a subsidiary. In a nutshell, goodwill is a balancing figure!

Back in January 2008, the International Accounting Standards Board (IASB) made a few tweaks to IFRS 3 and IAS 27 to allow two ways of calculating goodwill: the gross method and the proportionate method. I explain each in this section, and I take a look at impairment as well.

Don't muddle your standards when it comes to goodwill. You account for goodwill arising from a business combination under the provisions in IFRS 3 *Business Combinations*. Yes, goodwill is a non-current asset and yes, goodwill is intangible, but you *don't* account for it as an intangible asset under IAS 38 *Intangible Assets*. Goodwill does include the obvious things like brand and reputation of a company, but in a business combination there's more to it such as the value to be paid in order to control the entity and the bringing together of synergies.

Working out goodwill . . . the new method

Under the new (*gross*) method, on the date of acquisition you compare the fair value of the entire subsidiary company (including the non-controlling interests) with the fair value of the net assets acquired. Using this method produces a goodwill figure that's attributable to both the parent's interest in the subsidiary *and* the non-controlling interest's share of the goodwill.

In order to be able to use the gross method of goodwill, you need to know the fair value of the non-controlling interests. If you're using this book as a student revising for financial reporting exams and this method will be in your examination, you find the fair value of the non-controlling interests in the body of the scenario or within the question requirement. If you're using this book in the capacity of a professional accountant, the fair value of the non-controlling interests should be available in the subsidiary's valuation report.

To calculate the goodwill using the new method, here's what you do:

1. **Work out how much you paid for your investment in the subsidiary company.**

   Susan's Steak Houses acquired an 80 per cent controlling stake in Neil Noodle Company on 31 December 2010 for a purchase consideration of $100,000. On that date, the fair value of the non-controlling interests were valued at $20,000 and the fair value of the net assets of Neil Noodle Company were $90,000. At the year-end 31 December 2011, the net assets of Neil Noodle Company were $120,000.

   The purchase price for the 80 per cent controlling stake is $100,000.

2. **Add the figure in Step 1 to the fair value of the non-controlling interests.**

   You can calculate the fair value by taking the value of the non-controlling interests as they were when you acquired your share in the subsidiary. In the example, you take the purchase price of $100,000 and add it on to the fair value of the non-controlling interests in Neil Noodle Company of $20,000.

3. **Deduct the fair value of the net assets acquired when you bought your share in the subsidiary.**

   In the example, you deduct the fair value of the net assets acquired when Susan's Steak Houses bought its controlling stake in Neil Noodle Company, which was $90,000. This results in goodwill of $30,000: $100,000 (Step 1) plus $20,000 (Step 2) *minus* $90,000.

4. **Update the fair value of the non-controlling interests at the next year-end by giving them their share of post-acquisition profits (their share of the profit for the current year-end).**

   You calculate the non-controlling interests at the year-end 31 December 2011 by updating the fair value of the non-controlling interests at the date of acquisition by giving them their share of the *post-acquisition profit* (in other words, their share of the profit for the year-ended 31 December 2011). These post-acquisition profits are the rise in the net assets of Neil Noodle Company since the date of acquisition, which you calculate as follows. On acquisition (31 December 2010) the net assets were $90,000; post-acquisition (31 December 2011) they were $120,000. The profit for the year-ended 31 December 2011 is therefore $30,000.

You then give the non-controlling interests their share of the post-acquisition profits. Fair value of non-controlling interests at acquisition is $20,000. Add on the share of post-acquisition profit $6,000 (20% × $30,000), and the result is $26,000.

Sticking to the old method of goodwill calculation

The gross method of calculating goodwill (see the previous section) is optional, and if you don't like it then you can always stick to the old, proportionate method.

If you're using this book as a student of financial reporting examinations, you must pay attention to the question requirements. Be careful not to calculate goodwill under the old method if the question requires you to calculate goodwill under the gross (new) method because you'll be penalised for doing so!

The traditional measurement of goodwill on the acquisition of a subsidiary is the excess of the fair value of the purchase proceeds over the fair value of the net assets you acquire. This method only determines the goodwill that's attributable to the parent company.

Using the same numbers in the example in the previous section (Susan's Steak Houses), assume now that you're required to calculate the goodwill arising on acquisition of Neil's Noodle Company under the proportionate method. The cost of investment is $100,000. Deduct from this the net assets acquired (80% × $90,000 = $72,000) and you get a goodwill figure of $28,000. The figure for non-controlling interests at the year-end 31 December 2011 is simply the non-controlling interests share of the year-end net assets, which is 20% × $120,000 = $24,000.

Comparing the goodwill calculation methods

Table 11-1 compares the effect of both the new and the old method according to the figures from the examples in the preceding two sections.

Table 11-1	Comparing the Old and New Methods of Goodwill Calculation		
	Goodwill ($)	Non-controlling Interests ($)	Difference ($)
Gross method	30,000	26,000	4,000
Proportionate method	28,000	24,000	4,000

It's no coincidence that the difference in the goodwill and non-controlling interests under both the new and the old method is $4,000. This difference is simply the goodwill that belongs to the non-controlling interests. To put it in numerical terms:

Fair value of the non-controlling interests of Neil's Noodle Company at the date of acquisition (per scenario)	$20,000
Non-controlling interests holding	x 20%
Goodwill attributable to the non-controlling interests	**$4,000**

For those of you who like to know the double-entry (debits and credits) to account for the non-controlling interests share of the goodwill, the entries are as follows:

	Debit ($)	Credit ($)
Goodwill (non-current asset in statement of financial position)	4,000	
Non-controlling interests (equity section of statement of financial position)		4,000

The journal narrative in the books is: *Being non-controlling interests share of goodwill in Neil's Noodle Company.*

Considering impairment of goodwill

Financial statements have to convey reliable information because otherwise users are misled. An important concept to keep in mind is that a company can't carry its assets in the statement of financial position at any more than their *recoverable amount* (the amount that an independent third party would realistically pay for the asset). (I look at how to calculate recoverable amount and at asset impairment in Chapter 5.)

IFRS 3 doesn't allow you to *amortise* goodwill, which means write goodwill off over its estimated useful life. But you can't just leave it and do nothing; instead you have to test your goodwill annually to see whether its impaired. When an asset is *impaired*, it means that its value has reduced through factors other than normal write-downs of the value (for example, trade receivables may be impaired when a customer tells you he can't pay). The standard that deals with asset impairment is IAS 36 *Impairment of Assets*.

When you have goodwill that has suffered impairment, you need to write the balance of the goodwill down to its recoverable amount. The bit that you're writing off goes to the income statement as an impairment loss. An impairment loss is more or less the same thing as additional depreciation and you treat it as such.

If the impairment loss is significant (in other words, material) to the financial statements, you need to show it as a separate line item on the income statement so that users can see the effect it has had on profit (or loss).

Holdbright Enterprises owns a 90 per cent holding in Starbright Enterprises. The business combination in 2011 resulted in Holdbright Enterprises recognising goodwill in the consolidated statement of financial position amounting to $50,000. Due to the recent recession, the directors of Holdbright have estimated that the value of the goodwill in Starbright is now only worth $30,000.

In this example, the goodwill in Starbright has suffered an impairment of $20,000 ($50,000 minus $30,000) and the financial statements need to show this impairment. To do this, you credit goodwill (to reduce the value of the goodwill in the consolidated statement of financial position) and debit impairment loss in the income statement.

Dealing with Deemed Disposals

The word *deemed* means 'to regard as' or 'consider'. For many (trainee) accountants starting out in the world of financial reporting, such terms may be somewhat ambiguous. 'To regard as' implies an element of uncertainty – in other words, the term isn't as absolute as 'it was' or 'it is'. A *deemed disposal* is a bit of a hybrid: a disposal has occurred, but not in the traditional 'money changes hands' fashion.

A *deemed disposal* arises when the interests of a parent in a subsidiary company are reduced for reasons other than a sale of the subsidiary. Deemed disposals can arise for many reasons, but they commonly occur when

> ✔ The group doesn't take up its full allocation when the parent makes a rights issue of shares. (See Chapter 16 about rights issues.)
>
> ✔ The group doesn't take up its share of a bonus issue made by the subsidiary. (You may have heard these shares referred to as a scrip dividend; flick to Chapter 16 for more details on bonus issues.)
>
> ✔ Debt holders exercise an option to convert their loans into shares (convertible debt).
>
> ✔ The subsidiary simply issues shares to third parties.

Accounting for a deemed disposal

The accounting for a deemed disposal can often be complex – particularly for much larger, more diverse companies. Clearly, when a parent's ownership is diluted because the subsidiary has issued more shares, the first thing you need to do is to work out whether the subsidiary is still a subsidiary, or whether you need to treat it as an associate in accordance with IAS 28 *Investments in Associates* (see Chapter 12) or a simple investment under IAS 39 *Financial Instruments: Recognition and Measurement* and IFRS 9 *Financial Instruments* (see Chapter 5).

When you're dealing with a deemed disposal, you need to

1. **Work out the percentage of what you previously owned.**

2. **Work out the percentage of what you now own.**

3. **Compare the percentage in Step 2 to determine whether you still have control or not.**

   You have control if you own more than 50 per cent of the shares. If you own less than 51 per cent of the shares, you don't have control.

Pauline's Pantry (Pauline) owns 600,000 of the 1,000,000 shares in Pat's Pies (Pat) giving Pauline a 60 per cent holding in Pat. Pat's net assets in the consolidated financial statements of Pauline are $100 million. When Pauline acquired Pat, goodwill arose amounting to $12 million, which has not suffered any impairment. Pat issues a further 500,000 shares to a third party investor for $90 million, resulting in Pauline's share falling from 60 per cent to 40 per cent (600,000 shares ÷ 1.5 million shares). Because Pauline's ownership falls from 60 per cent to 40 per cent, Pat is no longer a subsidiary of Pauline because Pauline's ownership is less than 51 per cent but more than 20 per cent. Pat therefore becomes an associate of Pauline. (See Chapter 12 for more on associates.)

You can see that Pat has merely issued shares to an unconnected party, which has diluted Pauline's ownership interest to such an extent that Pat loses its subsidiary status in Pauline's consolidated financial statements – this situation is a deemed disposal because Pauline hasn't actually sold any of its shares off.

You calculate the resulting gain or loss on the deemed disposal as follows:

1. **Work out the effective interest in your investment *after* the deemed disposal has occurred.**

   This figure gives you the value of your ownership in the investment following the deemed disposal and you need this in Step 3 to work out whether you've made a gain or loss after the deemed disposal.

   To find the effective interest after the deemed disposal, use this mathematical equation:

   Revised percentage holding × (Net assets of subsidiary + Cash raised from share issue) + (Goodwill on initial acquisition × Revised percentage holding ÷ by previous percentage holding)

2. **Work out the effective interest in your investment before the deemed disposal has occurred.**

   This figure gives you the value of your ownership in the investment before the deemed disposal and you need this in Step 3 to work out whether you've made a gain or loss after the deemed disposal.

   Here's the formula you need:

   Previous percentage holding × Net assets of subsidiary + Goodwill on initial acquisition.

3. **Determine whether you've made a gain or a loss by taking your effective interest in the investment *after* the deemed disposal (Step 1) and deduct it from the effective interest in your investment *before* the deemed disposal (Step 2).**

   The difference between the two is your gain or loss. You recognise a gain or a loss on a deemed disposal in the statement of comprehensive income.

Accounting for a deemed partial disposal

When a company issues more shares to outside investors, the parent doesn't always lose control. In such cases, you account for the deemed disposal as a transaction between the shareholders. In other words, in the consolidated statement of financial position:

1. **Debit cash at bank (to represent the money coming in from the additional share issue).**

2. **Credit non-controlling interests (to represent the additional non-controlling interests).**

3. **Send the balance to equity.**

Using the same facts as the example of Pauline and Pat in the previous section, Pauline owns 600,000 of the 1,000,000 shares issued in Pat, resulting in a 60 per cent interest. Pat then issues a further 90,909 shares to a third party for $17 million. In this example, Pauline's interest in Pat is diluted from 60 per cent to 55 per cent (600,000 ÷ 1,090,909). Pauline still controls Pat because the holding is more than 50 per cent and, therefore, Pat is still a subsidiary of Pauline.

Pauline accounts for this deemed disposal as a transaction between shareholders. Pauline doesn't recognise any gain or loss and doesn't adjust any goodwill previous recognised on the acquisition of Pat. All Pauline does in the consolidated financial statements is simply:

	Debit ($m)	*Credit($m)*
Cash at bank	17	
Non-controlling interests		12.65
Equity		4.35

You may be wondering about the non-controlling interests figure. Previously, the non-controlling interests were 40 per cent (because Pauline owned 60 per cent) and the net assets of Pat are $100 million, so 40 per cent multiplied by $100 million equals $40 million. Non-controlling interests are now 45 per cent (because Pauline only owns 55 per cent following Pat's share issue), so 45 per cent multiplied by $117 million ($100 million net assets plus $17 million proceeds from the shares) equals $52.65 million. Therefore, $52.65 million less $40 million is an increase of $12.65 million.

Handling Step Acquisitions

You account for business combinations from the *date of acquisition* – the date on which the acquirer obtains control of the acquiree. The acquirer has control when it has the power to govern the financial and operating policies of an entity or business so as to obtain benefits from the acquiree's business.

Lots of investments in subsidiaries start their life as small interests in the companies concerned. You account for smaller investments under IAS 39 *Financial Instruments: Recognition and Measurement* (which I look at in

Chapter 5). As the business grows, the investor may increase its investment. Alternatively, larger stakes could give rise to significant influence or joint control, which you account for under IAS 28 *Investments in Associates* (which I cover in Chapter 12) and IAS 31 *Interests in Joint Ventures* (which I look at in Chapter 13). If the acquirer gains control of an investment that was previously accounted for under one of these standards, it has carried out a business combination in stages – known as a *step acquisition*.

Defining a step acquisition

Put simply, a step acquisition means that a business combination has been undertaken in stages, rather than all in one go. You may have heard the phrase referred to as *bought on the step* or *stage acquisition*; they're also known as *piecemeal* acquisitions.

Investments may be carried at cost and this cost is replaced by a share of net assets and goodwill when the investing company has an ownership interest that gives it control (and therefore consolidation is used) or when the investing company has significant influence, which is when equity accounting is used (see Chapter 12). Head to the 'Accounting for Goodwill' section of this chapter if you want to see this concept applied numerically.

Accounting for a step acquisition

You account for a holding of less than 20 per cent of the net assets as a simple investment in accordance with IAS 39 *Financial Instruments: Recognition and Measurement* and IFRS 9 *Financial Instruments* (I look at financial assets under IAS 39 in Chapter 5). This means that a subsidiary can start its life as a simple investment, and then grow to be an associate and then eventually a subsidiary.

Revising the revisions

Back in January 2008, the IASB revised IFRS 3 *Business Combinations* and part of this revision process was to look at the way in which companies account for step acquisitions. Prior to IFRS 3 being revised, the old IFRS 3 required the acquirer to measure the assets and liabilities of an acquiree (the party being acquired) involved in a step acquisition at fair value at every step of the transaction and to calculate a portion of goodwill. The revised version of IFRS 3 has removed this requirement and all step acquisitions now apply the revised version of IFRS 3 because this version was effective for accounting periods commencing on or after 1 July 2009.

Several years ago, Harley Holidays (Harley) acquired a 15 per cent holding in Tony's Tours (Tony) for $10,000. In 2011, Harley acquired a further 60 per cent for $60,000 when the net assets of Tony were $85,000. The non-controlling interests are included in the financial statements at their share of Tony's net assets, and on the date of acquisition the fair value of the 15 per cent holding was calculated at $12,000. What is the goodwill on the acquisition of Tony?

You can see that Tony used to be a simple investment (Harley owned less than 20 per cent of the net assets). Harley has since acquired a further 60 per cent, which means that Harley now owns 75 per cent of Tony, resulting in Tony now becoming a subsidiary. You need to use the gross method of goodwill calculation (see the earlier section 'Working out goodwill . . . the new method') because the non-controlling interests are included in the financial statements at their share of Tony's net assets at the date of acquisition. The goodwill calculation is as follows:

	$
Cost of additional investment	60,000
Non-controlling interests share ($85,000 x 25%)	21,250
Fair value of the previous 15% holding	12,000
Fair value of net assets of Tony	(85,000)
Goodwill	**8,250**

Humphries Holdalls (Humphries) acquires 75 per cent of Steph's Suitcases (Steph) in two stages. Humphries acquired 40 per cent several years ago for $45,000 when the fair value of the net assets of Steph were $85,000. Since the date of acquiring its 40 per cent, Humphries has recognised its share of Steph's post-acquisition profits amounting to $5,500, resulting in a carrying amount of $50,500. During 2011, Humphries acquired a further 35 per cent in Steph for a further $60,000 and the net assets of Steph when the additional 35 per cent was acquired were $115,000. Humphries includes non-controlling interests in the consolidated statement of financial position at their fair value of $35,000, and on the date Humphries acquired the additional 35 per cent, the previous 40 per cent holding was valued at $55,000.

Okay, quite a bit is going on here because initially Steph was an associate of Humphries, because Humphries only owned 40 per cent of Steph. But following the additional purchase of shares, Steph has now become a subsidiary because Humphries now owns 75 per cent.

Deal with the issues in two steps, starting with the effect on profit or loss and then the goodwill.

First, on the date of acquiring the additional 35 per cent in Steph, Humphries needs to recognise a gain of $4,500 in profit or loss. This is the difference between the previously held 40 per cent stake of $50,500 and the fair value of the initial 40 per cent holding, which has been valued at $55,000.

Next, work out the goodwill in Steph (now a subsidiary) as follows:

	$
Cost of additional investment	60,000
Non-controlling interests at fair value	35,000
Fair value of the previous 40% holding	55,000
Fair value of Steph's net assets	(115,000)
Goodwill	**35,000**

In the two examples in this section, the first simple investment became a subsidiary and then an associate became a subsidiary. Earlier in the chapter (see 'Accounting for Changes in Ownership'), I examine what happens when a parent that already owns a controlling share in a subsidiary purchases more shares in the subsidiary (thus increasing its holding). The parent clearly retains control, but remember that when this additional purchase happens the parent accounts for any further acquisition of shares within equity and adjusts the carrying amount of the non-controlling interest to reflect its new (reduced) percentage holding. This may be zero if the parent has bought all the non-controlling interests' shares.

Chapter 12

Tackling Associates

In This Chapter

▶ Understanding what an associate is

▶ Examining the equity method

▶ Pondering presentation issues

▶ Discussing disclosures

*A*ssociates are a type of investment. An investor has what's known as *significant influence* over an associate, but it doesn't *control* the associate. This lack of control sets associates apart from subsidiaries (companies that are controlled by the reporting company) and joint ventures (a contractual arrangement whereby two or more parties undertake an economic activity that's subject to joint control).

In this chapter I take you through the different sorts of entities that can be an associate, as well as looking at what *isn't* an associate. I discuss the concept of significant influence, and look at how you account for an associate in the financial statements. Finally, I take you through how you present associates within a set of IFRS financial statements.

The standard that deals with associates is IAS 28 *Investments in Associates*. In 2011, the International Accounting Standards Board (IASB) issued new standards relating to consolidated financial statements and joint ventures. They've changed the name of IAS 28 to *Investments in Associates and Joint Ventures* and this re-issued standard is effective for accounting periods commencing on or after 1 January 2013, but if you want to adopt it earlier then you can do.

Defining an Associate in IFRS

Understanding exactly what constitutes an associate ensures that you correctly account for various investments under the right standards. It would be pretty embarrassing if you got this decision wrong and then had the unenviable job of explaining to your boss or your client that you need to change the financial statements!

In a nutshell, an *associate* is an investment in an entity (the investee) in which the investor (the party who's pumped money into the company) has significant influence over the investee.

An associate is *not* a subsidiary, nor, by definition, can an associate be a joint venture. Head to Chapters 10 and 11 for information on subsidiaries, and Chapter 13 for details of joint ventures.

Seeing which entities are associates

The bigger the company and the higher the number of investments, the more difficult they become to account for. For many companies, such as venture capitalists, investing in other companies is their principal activity (in other words, that's the whole point of their existence). You need to be careful with venture capitalists, though, as you see in the next section.

Many investors have associates, and these associates can take the form of incorporated entities (companies that have limited liability in the eyes of the law). Alternatively, an associate can also be an unincorporated entity such as a partnership.

Looking at exemptions from IAS 28 requirements

For some companies, investing in other companies is the reason they're in business. *Business angels* (also known as *venture capitalists*) provide capital for a new business, usually in exchange for some ownership in the company or *convertible debt* (a loan given to a company that contains an option to convert the capital element of the loan into shares at a later date rather than paying the loan back in hard cash; for more on convertible debt, head over to Chapter 7).

A venture capital organisation, which may have hundreds (or thousands) of investments on the go at any one point in time, doesn't have to comply with the requirements in IAS 28 – so it doesn't have to consider all its investments as associates. In addition, if you work for a company (or have clients) that operate mutual funds, unit trusts and similar entities including investment-linked insurance funds, these funds are also exempt from the requirements of IAS 28.

But what exactly comprises a venture capital organisation, or mutual funds, unit trusts and similar entities including investment-linked insurance funds? IAS 28 doesn't define them. This was a deliberate decision by the IASB given the difficulty of producing a definition, and the IASB hopes that it can rely on accountants and auditors not to abuse the scope of the exemption.

The IASB introduced the exemption because they considered that for venture capital organisations, mutual funds, unit trusts and similar entities, the application of the equity method (a method of accounting for investments in associates; see the later section 'Using Equity Accounting') would produce information that isn't relevant to their management and investors. Venture capital organisations, mutual funds, unit trusts and similar entities generally account for their investments using fair values (basically, how much something's currently worth), and therefore the IASB felt that the application of IAS 39/IFRS 9 would produce more relevant information. In addition, it was felt that the financial statements of such companies would be less useful if changes in the level of ownership in an investment resulted in frequent changes in the method of accounting for the investment.

The exemption applies to venture capital organisations and other similar sorts of financial institutions whose main activities consist primarily of managing an investment portfolio made up of investments that are clearly unrelated to the investor's principal business. This is why mutual funds, unit trusts and similar companies including investment-linked insurance funds account for investments in associates under IAS 39 *Financial Instruments: Recognition and Measurement* and IFRS 9 *Financial Instruments*. I take a look at IAS 39 in Chapters 5 and 7.

Understanding Significant Influence

The previous section gives you a grounding in associates, but you need to know what actually gives rise to an associate. *Associates* are investments in an entity (the investee) where the investor has *significant influence*, which means that an investor is involved, or has the right to be involved, in the financial and operating policy decisions of the investee. The investor can't control the investee because to do so would give rise to a parent–subsidiary relationship under IAS 27/IFRS 10 (see Chapters 10 and 11).

Knowing the indicators of significant influence

To achieve significant influence, the investor (the party making the investment) obtains between 20 per cent and 50 per cent of the net assets in the investee.

Cain Concrete Co owns 25 per cent of the voting rights in Byrne's Brick Co. Because Cain Concrete Co owns less than 51 per cent of the voting rights of Byrne's Brick Co but more than 20 per cent, Cain Concrete Co has significant influence over Byrne's Brick Co, and therefore accounts for the investment under IAS 28.

If an investor receives *more* than 50 per cent of the net assets of an investee, the investor has control, so the investee becomes a subsidiary of the investor and you need to consolidate the financial statements of the subsidiary with those of the parent. I take you through consolidation issues in Chapters 10 and 11. If the investor obtains *less* than 20 per cent of the investee and you decide it doesn't have significant influence then you don't account for the investment under IAS 28; instead you account for the investment under IAS 39 *Financial Instruments: Recognition and Measurement* (which I look at in Chapters 5 and 7).

But just because the investor owns less than 20 per cent of the investee doesn't automatically mean that it doesn't have significant influence. Significant influence can arise if the following are in evidence:

- ✔ Interchange of managerial personnel
- ✔ Material transactions between the investor and the investee
- ✔ Participation in the policy-making processes
- ✔ Provision of essential technical information
- ✔ Representation on the board of directors, or equivalent governing body

So if the holding is less than 20 per cent, you can presume that the investor doesn't have significant influence and the investment is to be accounted for under the provisions in IAS 39/IFRS 9, *unless* such significant influence is clear, for example in representation on the board.

Calling significant influence into question

You can call significant influence into question with or without a change in ownership levels. For example, the investor and investee may contractually agree that significant influence can be lost at a certain point in time. Or the loss of significant influence may occur when an associate becomes subject to the control of a government, court, administrator or regulator.

Significant influence may also be called into question in the following situations:

- ✔ The investor has failed to obtain representation on the investee's board of directors.

- ✔ The investee is opposing the investor's attempts to exercise significant influence.

- ✔ The investor is unable to obtain timely financial information or can't obtain more information than shareholders that don't have significant influence.

- ✔ A group of shareholders that hold the majority ownership of the investee operates without any regard to the views of the investor.

Losing significant influence

An investor can lose significant influence for a variety of reasons; for example, it may be the case that the investor agrees to hold 25 per cent of the voting rights for a certain period of time, after which 10 per cent passes to another third party, resulting in a loss of significant influence on the part of the investor.

When significant influence is lost, here's what you do:

1. **Measure any remaining investment at fair value.**

2. **Write off any difference between the *carrying amount* (the amount the investment is stated at in the financial statements) of the investment in the associate and the re-measured amount to profit or loss.**

3. **Account for the investment in accordance with IAS 39/IFRS 9.**

Diane Drain Company owns a 25 per cent holding in Stewart Street Cleaning Company. On 31 December 2011, the carrying value in Diane's financial statements was $20,000. The terms of the agreement are that, on 31 December 2011, Diane transfers 15 per cent of its holding in Stewart to an unconnected third party. The fair value of Diane's revised investment in Stewart as at 31 December 2011 was calculated to be $7,000.

In this scenario, Diane Drain Company writes down the investment in Stewart from $20,000 to $7,000, so Diane writes off $13,000 to profit or loss in the income statement. As significant influence has been lost, Diane accounts for the remaining investment under IAS 39/IFRS 9 as a simple investment. Diane no longer applies the provisions in IAS 28 and won't account for the investment in Stewart using the equity method of accounting (see the following section 'Using Equity Accounting').

Many accounting standards inter-relate with each other. When a company loses significant influence in an investment, this situation indicates impairment also and therefore triggers the provisions in IAS 36 *Impairment of Assets*. See Chapter 5 to find out about asset impairment.

Using Equity Accounting

The *equity method* works by adjusting the cost value of the investment (which is recognised as a non-current asset in the statement of financial position) for the investor's share of the associate's profit (or loss) and any dividends received from the associate.

You account for associates using the equity method, regardless of the fact that the investor may not have any investments in subsidiaries and as such won't prepare consolidated financial statements.

If an associate uses accounting policies that differ from those of the investor, the investor makes adjustments to enable the associate's accounting policies to conform with those of the investor. This conformity is a requirement of the equity method.

Knowing the exemptions

You *don't* account for an investment in an associate using the equity method in the following circumstances:

- ✔ The investment is classified as held for sale (in other words, the investor is planning to sell the investment) in accordance with IFRS 5 *Non-Current Assets Held for Sale and Discontinued Operations* (see Chapter 4).

- ✔ The reporting company is a *parent* (in other words, a company with one or more subsidiary companies) exempt from preparing consolidated financial statements under the exemptions in IAS 27 *Consolidated and Separate Financial Statements* (now called *Separate Financial Statements*) and IFRS 10 *Consolidated Financial Statements* (see Chapters 10 and 11).

- ✔ *All* the following apply:

  - The investor is a wholly owned subsidiary, or a partially owned subsidiary of another company, and its other owners, including those not entitled to vote, have been informed about, and don't object to, the investor not applying the equity method.

- The investor doesn't trade its debt or equity instruments in a public market (a domestic or foreign stock exchange or an over-the-counter market, including local and regional markets).

- The investor didn't file, nor is it in the process of filing, its financial statements with a securities commission or other regulatory organisation, for the purpose of issuing any class of instruments in a public market.

- The ultimate or any intermediate parent of the investor produces consolidated financial statements that are available for public use and that comply with IFRS.

Bringing the investment on to your statement of financial position

When the investor has agreed to invest in an associate, the investor is clearly going to hand over money. The first part of the bookkeeping is dead easy – credit cash at bank. The debit then goes to non-current assets (long-term assets) in the statement of financial position as an investment. Simple!

Under IAS 28, you initially recognise an investment in an associate at cost and then you increase, or decrease, this amount to recognise the investor's share of the profit, or loss, of the investee after the date of acquisition. Here are the steps to follow in the investor's books:

1. **Record the investment by crediting cash at bank and debiting investments in the non-current assets section of the statement of financial position.**

2. **Deal with the profit or loss the associate makes:**

   - **Profit: Debit the investment in the non-current assets section of the statement of financial position and then credit income from associate in the income statement.**

   - **Loss: Credit the investment in associate in the statement of financial position and debit income from associate in the income statement.**

   I look at loss-making associates in the section 'Dealing with loss-making associates'.

On 31 December 2010, Rio Co invests a sum of $10,000 in Molly Co in return for a 25 per cent holding in the voting rights in Molly. On 31 December 2011, the resulting profit of Molly was $7,000. As at 31 December 2010, Rio's accounting entries look as follows:

	Debit ($)	Credit ($)
Cash at bank		10,000
Investment in associate	10,000	

The journal narrative in the books is: *Being initial investment in Molly.*

So, cash at bank clearly decreases. Now Rio offsets this decrease in current assets (or increase in a current liability if the bank account were to be overdrawn) by an increase in non-current assets (the investment in Molly).

The financial results of the investee (Molly) have been finalised and they show a $7,000 profit, 25 per cent of which belongs to Rio. So the value of the investment has seen an increase, which is also reflected in Rio's income statement as 'share of profit from associate' as follows:

	Debit ($)	Credit ($)
Investment in associate	1,750	
Statement of comprehensive income		1,750

The journal narrative in the books is: *Being 25 per cent share of Molly Inc profit.*

Receiving dividends from an associate

Dividends are the return on an investment that the investor receives. An investor receives its share of the associate's profit or loss and may *in addition* receive a dividend from the associate.

At first glance you may think that you add dividends and profits received together, but you don't. Dividends *reduce* the value of your investment (by crediting the investment in the non-current assets section, the debit goes to cash at bank) because a dividend is a return on this investment. So you credit the profit that you receive from your associate to your income statement as 'share of profit from associate' with the debit going to the investment in the non-current assets section of the statement of financial position.

Irene Interiors (Irene) owns a 35 per cent holding in Leyla's Luxurious Lounges (Leyla), which cost Irene $80,000 on 31 December 2010. On 31 December 2011, the profit of Leyla was $70,000 and it had proposed a dividend (prior to the year-end) of $10,000. How should the dividend be accounted for in Irene's books?

The dividend is the return on Irene's investment. The investment of $80,000 is increased for Irene's share of the profit of $24,500 ($70,000 x 35 per cent). The investment is then reduced by the value of the dividend $3,500 ($10,000 x 35 per cent) because the dividend is a return on this investment, hence it decreases the investment's carrying value. Therefore, you can calculate the carrying amount of the investment as at 31 December 2011 as follows:

	$
Initial cost	80,000
Share of profit	24,500
Dividends	(3,500)
	$101,000

In the consolidated statement of financial position:

- ✔ Account for dividends payable/receivable fully in the individual company financial statements.

- ✔ Include the receivable (an amount owed to the investor) for dividends owed to the investor from the associate(s).

- ✔ *Don't* cancel inter-company balances for dividends because the associate isn't part of the group – the associate is only an associate, not a subsidiary.

In the consolidated statement of comprehensive income, *don't* include dividends from the associate. You include the parent's share of the associate's profit after tax (the profit before dividends) under equity accounting as 'income from associate'.

Dealing with loss-making associates

When an associate makes a loss, an investor must recognise its share of the losses until its share of losses equals, or exceeds, its interest in the associate, at which point the investor no longer recognises its share of further losses.

If your associate makes a loss, you debit the income statement – because it's a loss and will reduce the organisation's profit, and anything that reduces the profit in the income statement, or increases a loss, is a debit. The credit entry goes to the investment in associate in the statement of financial position.

If the associate continues to make losses, there may come a time when the value of all the losses reduces your investment to zero. At this point, you don't recognise any future losses, because otherwise you end up with a negative non-current asset, which isn't correct.

On 1 April 2011, Bharat Co invests $5 million in exchange for a 30 per cent share of the equity of Lauren Co. In addition, Bharat also makes a loan to Lauren of $9 million, which is unsecured, and Bharat has not committed itself to any further funding. The financial statements of Lauren Inc as at 31 March 2012 show a loss of $20 million. How should Bharat account for the $20 million loss that Lauren has made during the year?

Bharat's share of the $20 million loss is $6 million ($20 million x 30 per cent). If the loan to Lauren is considered to be part of the investment in Lauren, then the carrying amount of the associate is reduced by $6 million from $14 million ($5 million investment + $9 million loan) to $8 million (the ownership interest is reduced to nil and the loan is reduced to $8 million). However, if the loan isn't part of the investment in Lauren, Bharat accounts for the loss as follows:

- ✔ The interest in Lauren is reduced from $5 million to nil.

- ✔ A loss of $1 million ($5 million less $6 million) remains unrecognised because Bharat didn't provide any commitments to further funding.

- ✔ Because the associate is loss-making, this loss is an indicator of impairment and Bharat should test the loan for impairment in accordance with IAS 36 *Impairment of Assets* (see Chapter 5 for more on impairments).

Accounting for the goodwill in your associate

Goodwill is the excess of the price paid over and above what you've got for your investment. Goodwill can also arise when you invest in an associate. Just because an investment may not be a subsidiary, but an associate instead, doesn't preclude goodwill arising on the acquisition date. (Flip to Chapter 11 to find out more about goodwill and subsidiaries.)

Here's how you calculate goodwill:

1. **Work out the percentage you own in the associate.**

   This percentage has to be between 20 per cent and 50 per cent for your investment to qualify as an associate.

2. **Take the net assets of the associate and apply the percentage you worked out in Step 1 to those net assets.**

   This calculation gives you the value of the net assets you've bought.

3. **Compare the value of the net assets you've bought in Step 2 to the cost of the investment.**

   The difference is the goodwill on acquisition of your associate.

You never write off goodwill over its estimated useful life; you always test annually for impairment under the provisions in IFRS 3 *Business Combinations* (see Chapter 11).

When you're dealing with the investment in an associate, you *don't* show any goodwill separately, but instead you include it in the carrying amount of the investment. Therefore:

   Carrying value = Share of net assets at acquisition + Goodwill + Share of post-acquisition profit or loss

Recognising transactions with an associate

When you have a group of companies, members of the group commonly trade with each other – they sell goods or services to each other. This trading is called *intra-group trading*. When one member of the group sells goods to another member of the group, the selling company recognises a receivable in its statement of financial position and the buying company recognises a payable.

You cancel out intra-group trading between parents and subsidiaries on consolidation to enable the consolidated financial statements to show the results of the group as if it were a *single* reporting company (see Chapters 10 and 11). But you *don't* cancel inter-company balances on the statement of financial position and you *don't* adjust revenue and cost of sales for trading with the associate because associates are *not* subsidiaries.

In the consolidated statement of financial position, you *must* show balances with associates separately from other receivables and payables. The associate is *not* part of the group so you don't need to show amounts owed to the group by the associate as assets and amounts owed to the associate by the group as liabilities.

If the investor sells goods to the associate (*downstream*) and the associate still has these goods in its inventory at the year-end, the associate's carrying value of this inventory includes the profit element of the sale by the investor. This element of profit is *unrealised profit – unrealised* because the inventory hasn't been sold to unconnected third parties (in other words, external customers). The unrealised profit element is included within the associate's inventory as well as in the investor's revenue figure. The investor must eliminate unrealised profits to the extent of the investor's interest in the associate.

A similar situation arises if an associate makes a sale of goods to the investor (*upstream*). The investor has to eliminate this unrealised profit on consolidation to avoid double counting when equity accounting the associate.

To remove the unrealised profit, you deduct the profit from the associate's profit before tax and *retained earnings* (profits that the company has built up over time that it has reinvested into the business; see Chapter 9) in the equity section of the statement of financial position, regardless of whether the sale is from investor to associate or vice versa.

Cahill Cars owns a 40 per cent interest in Breary's Buses. Cahill Cars sold goods to Breary's Buses for $200 that originally cost $150. All the goods are still in the inventory of Breary's Buses at the year-end. To eliminate the unrealised profit in the consolidated financial statements, you deduct the $50 from the associate's pre-tax profits in the statement of comprehensive income. The other side of the entry goes to the retained earnings section of the statement of financial position. The share of the net assets and post-acquisition profit is $20 ($50 x 40 per cent) lower under equity accounting.

Knowing what to do when an associate is up for sale

A company may decide to sell its investment in an associate for a variety of reasons. When selling an investment, the company has to follow the principles contained in IFRS 5 *Non-Current Assets Held for Sale and Discontinued Operations*. (I look at IFRS 5 issues and the selling of non-current assets in Chapter 4.)

You only use the principles in IFRS 5 when you're going to recover the carrying amount of your investment through selling the investment in the associate, rather than continuing to use the investment in the associate.

At the date the associate is classified as held for sale, the investor must stop using the equity method of accounting. Instead, the investor measures the investment

> ✔ At the *lower* of the investment's carrying amount
> ✔ At fair value less costs to sell

If the circumstances change and the investor decides that it no longer wants to sell the investment, it re-commences accounting for the investment under the equity method from the date it decided that the investment is no longer to be held for sale. The investor must also go back to the previous accounting periods and restate the financial statements from the date it first decided to hold the investment in the associate for sale.

Presenting Associates in the Financial Statements

IFRS 12 *Disclosure of Interests in Other Entities* will deal with disclosures for accounting periods commencing on or after 1 January 2013. IFRS 12 wants information that allows the users of the financial statements (external stakeholders) to evaluate

- ✔ The nature, extent and financial effect of any interests in associates
- ✔ The nature and effects of any contractual relationship with other investors who have significant influence over the associate
- ✔ The nature of, and changes in, the risks associated with its associates

Disclosing the correct amount of information for an associate

You can see from the introduction to this section that IFRS 12 disclosure requirements aren't exactly crystal clear. Unfortunately, the world of IFRS isn't that prescriptive because the standards recognise that every company is different. Fear not – here's a list of what *some* of the disclosures may include:

- ✔ The name of the associate
- ✔ The nature of the relationship
- ✔ Proportion of ownership
- ✔ Any significant restrictions on the part of the associate to transfer funds to the investor
- ✔ Any commitments that the reporting company has relating to its associates
- ✔ Any unrecognised share of losses of an associate

These disclosure requirements are only some of the requirements of IFRS 12. You also need to consider additional disclosure requirements such as the fair value of investments in associates when published prices are available and the reasons that an investor may not have significant influence despite the fact that the investor holds 20 per cent or more of the voting rights of an investee.

A reputable disclosure checklist gives you the exact disclosure requirements for your company's (or your client's) individual circumstances.

Showing associates in the financial statements

Investments in associates that you account for using the equity method (see the earlier section 'Bringing the Investment on to your Statement of Financial Position') are classified as non-current assets in the statement of financial position. You record your share of the profit (or loss) of the investment in the statement of comprehensive income. You show the aggregate of the investor's share of profit or loss of associates under the equity method. (*Profit or loss* in the context of associates means the profit attributable to the owners of the associates – in other words, it's after tax.) IFRS doesn't stipulate where to show the investor's share of the profit or loss; I recommend putting it after operating profit as 'Share of results of associated companies'.

Paul Plant Pot Co (Paul) owns an 80 per cent stake in Lynn Lily Co (Lynn) and a 40 per cent holding in Brian Begonia Co (Brian). The statements of financial position of each company as at 31 December 2011 are as follows:

	Paul ($)	Lynn ($)	Brian ($)
Investment in Lynn	850	-	-
Investment in Brian	650	-	-
Non-current assets	1,650	850	1,400
Current assets	2,250	3,350	3,300
	5,400	4,200	4,700
Share capital	1,000	400	800
Retained earnings	4,050	3,450	3,650
Liabilities	350	350	250
	5,400	4,200	4,700

Here are some additional notes:

- ✔ Paul acquired its shares in Lynn eight years ago when the retained earnings of Lynn were $570.
- ✔ Paul acquired its shares in Brian on 1 January 2011 when the retained earnings of Brian were $450.
- ✔ No evidence exists of any impairment of any of the investments.

You need to deal with the consolidation of Lynn and Brian's financial statements into Paul's financial statements on a step-by-step basis, because a lot is going on. The following sections outline the seven steps that you need to work through.

Step 1: Work out the group structure

An 80 per cent ownership gives rise to a subsidiary and a 40 per cent ownership gives rise to an associate due to significant influence (see the earlier section 'Understanding Significant Influence'). Figure 12-1 shows the group structure.

Figure 12-1: Group structure for Paul, Lynn and Brian.

Step 2: Work out the net assets of both companies at the date of acquisition and the reporting date

Here's the calculation:

	Reporting Date	*At Acquisition*
Lynn Lily Co.		
Share capital	$400	$400
Retained earnings	$3,450	$570
	$3,850	**$970**
Brian Begonia Co.		
Share capital	$800	$800
Retained earnings	$3,650	$450
	$4,450	**$1,250**

Step 3: Work out the goodwill on acquisition

For the acquisition of Lynn and Brian, the calculation is:

	Lynn	*Brian*
Cost of investment	$850	$650
Net assets acquired:		
(80 per cent × $970 (see Step 2))	($776)	
(40 per cent × $1,250 (see Step 2))		($500)
Goodwill	$74	$150

Step 4: Work out the non-controlling interests

Here's the calculation:

Lynn Lily Co only (20 per cent × $3,850)	$770

Step 5: Work out the retained earnings figure

You put the retained earnings figure in the consolidated statement of financial position. Here's the calculation:

Paul Plant Pot Co	$4,050
Share of Lynn (80 per cent × (3,450 – 570) (see Step 2))	$2,304
Share of Brian (40 per cent × (3,650 – 450) (see Step 2))	$1,280
	$7,634

Step 6: Work out the value that appears as 'investment in associate' in the consolidated statement of financial position

Here's the calculation:

Share of net assets (40 per cent x (800 + 3,650))	$1,780
Goodwill (see Step 3)	$ 150
	$1,930

Step 7: Put the consolidated statement of financial position together

The consolidated statement of financial position now looks as follows:

	$
Goodwill (see Step 3)	74
Investment in associate (see Step 6)	1,930
Non-current assets (1,650 + 850)	2,500
Current assets (2,250 + 3,350)	<u>5,600</u>
	10,104
Issued share capital (Paul only)	1,000
Retained earnings (see Step 5)	<u>7,634</u>
	8,634
Non-controlling interest (see Step 4)	770
Liabilities (350 + 350)	<u>700</u>
	10,104

Chapter 13

Juggling Joint Ventures

A joint venture is an economic arrangement between two (or more) parties. Both parties need give unanimous consent to decisions concerning the financial and operating policies of the joint venture. Many companies have joint ventures with other companies or individuals. Companies need to account for these joint ventures, like anything else. In this chapter, I cover the IAS dedicated to the issues related to joint ventures: IAS 31 *Interests in Joint Ventures.*

Understanding a Joint Venture

Before you can dive in to accounting for joint ventures, you need a good grounding in what exactly a joint venture is according to IAS 31, why parties engage in joint ventures and who has the power to control the joint venture. This section lays the foundations for a good understanding of the joint venture.

Looking at how IAS 31 defines a joint venture

IAS 31 recognises that a joint venture is a contractual arrangement when two, or more, parties come together and form an economic activity in which both parties have joint control. A joint venture isn't actually restricted by a legal structure, but a contractual arrangement must be in place that gives joint control between the venturers.

IAS 31 doesn't use the term *entity*, which you find in a lot of the standards. Instead IAS 31 refers to *economic activity*, because joint ventures can take many different forms and structures so the standard doesn't limit itself to simply those joint arrangements formed in a legal structure such as a limited company.

Thinking about why parties may form a joint venture

A party may enter into a joint venture for various reasons:

- ✔ To benefit from the partners' complementary skills
- ✔ To benefit from economies of scale
- ✔ To share costs
- ✔ To improve profits
- ✔ To share the risks of a project

Whatever a party's reasons for entering into a joint venture arrangement, it can do so through an incorporated company (in other words, a limited company) or an unincorporated company (for example, a partnership). Many joint ventures are so simplistic that they just don't need the creation of a separate vehicle to operate through.

Sometimes companies may work together to promote each other's products or services. These collaborations are often termed *strategic alliances*, and for the purposes of accounting, you can consider these to be joint ventures.

Comparing the definition of a joint venture and control

In a joint venture, a contractual agreement must be in place that gives each party within the venture joint control. You must consider the effect that control may have.

IAS 31 defines *joint control* as the contractually agreed sharing of control over an economic activity. The important thing to bear in mind is that this definition means that no one party within the venture can have overall control over the financial and operating policies of the joint venture. As such, IAS 31 defines *control* as the power to govern the financial and operating policies of an economic entity so as to obtain benefits from it.

In a joint venture, the venturers have joint control for their *mutual* benefit. Each party conducts its part of the contractual arrangement with a view to its own benefit. All the venturers have the ability to plan an active role in setting the strategic operating and financial policies of the joint venture, which means that their interest doesn't necessarily only occur at the outset of the arrangement; all the venturers have an ongoing say in all strategic decisions.

Accounting for Joint Ventures

After you establish that a joint venture is in place, that the contract confirms an agreed sharing of control over the venture and that all parties are unanimous in their decisions relating to the operating and financial policies, you need to account for the joint venture within a venturer's financial statements.

You account for joint methods using either the equity method or the proportionate consolidation method.

Knowing the three types of joint venture

IAS 31 identifies three types of joint venture:

- ✔ Jointly controlled operations
- ✔ Jointly controlled assets
- ✔ Joint controlled entities

Jointly controlled operations

In a jointly controlled operation, each venturer

- ✔ Uses its own resources
- ✔ Carries out its own part of a joint operation separately from the activities of the other venturer(s)
- ✔ Owns and controls its own resources (that it uses in the joint operation)
- ✔ Incurs its own expenses
- ✔ Raises its own finance

The contractual arrangement required in IAS 31 outlines how the venturers share the goods or service outputs of the joint operation (together with any revenues from their sale, and any common expenses) in order that the venturer can recognise these in its own separate financial statements

- ✔ The assets it controls (an asset is something that belongs to an organisation; I take a detailed look at assets in Chapter 4)

- ✔ The liabilities it incurs (a liability is something that a company owes to another person or another company; see Chapter 6 for details)

- ✔ The expenses it incurs

- ✔ Its share of the income earned from the sale of goods or services from the joint venture

Ethan Engineering Co and Breary Bodywork Co both agree to develop and manufacture a new brand of high-speed aeroplane. Ethan Engineering Co agrees to develop and manufacture the engines and Breary Bodywork Co agrees to develop and manufacture the body of the aeroplane. Each venturer pays the costs and takes a share of the revenue from the sale of the aeroplanes as per the agreement. In its individual financial statements, each venturer shows the assets that it controls and the liabilities that it has incurred, together with the expenses that it incurs and its share of the income from the sale of the aeroplanes.

You can see that when it comes to the accounting for a jointly controlled operation, the standard treats the operations as if the venturer conducted them independently. This explanation is why a venturer accounts for the assets it controls and the liabilities and expenses that it incurs independently in its own books. The accounting entries in the books of the venturer's own financial statements flow through into the consolidated financial statements *if* the venturer prepares them. (Chapters 10 and 11 look at consolidation.) No further adjustments, or consolidation procedures, are required.

The venturer has to account for its share of the income earned from the jointly controlled operation and this share is determined in accordance with the contractual arrangement.

Jointly controlled assets

When an asset is jointly controlled, each venturer must recognise

- ✔ Its share of the jointly controlled asset(s)

- ✔ Any liabilities that it has incurred on behalf of the joint venture

- ✔ Its share of any joint liabilities incurred by the joint venture

- ✔ Its share of income and expenses incurred by the joint venture

- ✔ Any expenses it has incurred in respect of its interest in the joint venture in its own financial statements

Dawn and Andy jointly own a property. Each party takes a share of the rents and bears a share of the running costs of the property. The shared items are the property itself, revenue from rents received, maintenance costs of the property, depreciation of the property and a share of the liabilities incurred jointly with the other venturers. The separate costs that Dawn and Andy incur are loan interest to finance their share of the property.

When it comes to the accounting for a jointly controlled asset, the standard apportions to each venturer its share of revenues, expenses, assets and liabilities. The venturer must recognise its share in its own financial statements and its accounting records. This treatment is the same sort as that for a jointly controlled operation; therefore, the accounting entries flow through to the consolidated financial statements *if* they're prepared. No further adjustments, or consolidation procedures, are required.

Jointly controlled entities

A jointly controlled entity is an incorporated company or an unincorporated setup (like a partnership) that's jointly controlled by the venturers.

Liza and Jermain set up a housing development company, L&J Properties, and each transfers in assets and liabilities to combine their activities. The contractual arrangement is that both Liza and Jermain have joint control and decisions relating to the financial and operating policies of the company have to be unanimous. Theirs is a jointly controlled entity as defined in IAS 31.

In terms of the accounting treatment of a jointly controlled entity, this point is where things become slightly more complicated. Generally, each venturer measures its interest in a jointly controlled entity in the consolidated financial statements using the proportionate consolidation or the equity method. I go into more detail about these two methods of accounting in the next section.

When a jointly controlled entity is classified as 'held for sale' in accordance with IFRS 5 *Non-Current Assets Held for Sale and Discontinued Operations* (see Chapter 4), it need not apply the proportionate consolidation method or equity method to any jointly controlled entities held for sale. Instead, it applies the accounting and presentation requirements of IFRS 5, from the date the jointly controlled entity qualifies as held for sale.

Using the equity accounting method for joint ventures

Two methods of accounting for jointly controlled entities exist – the equity method and the proportionate consolidation method. This section focuses on the equity method; the following takes you through the proportionate consolidation method.

The standard that actually defines the equity method is IAS 28 *Investments in Associates* (see Chapter 12). Here's how the equity method works using a stepped-out approach:

1. **Record your investment in the jointly controlled entity initially at the investment's cost price.**

   You do this by crediting cash at bank with the amount you've paid for your investment and debiting investments in the statement of financial position.

   On 31 December 2010, Victor Venturers invests in 50 per cent of Joint Venture Co, which cost Victor Venturers $100. Victor Venturers credits cash at bank with $100 and debit investments in the statements of financial position with $100.

2. **When you receive your share of the profit (or loss) from the joint venture, adjust the value of the investment in the statement of financial position.**

   If the joint venture makes a *profit*, increase your investment in the statement of financial position by debiting a profit to the statement of financial position and crediting the income statement with the profit.

   If the joint venture makes a *loss*, reduce the value of the investment in the statement of financial position by crediting the investment with the value of the loss and debiting the income statement also with the value of the loss.

Using the Victor Venturers example in Step 1, now assume that the profit of Joint Venture Co was $60. Because Victor Venturers owns 50 per cent of Joint Venture Co, Victor Venturer's share of Joint Venture Co's profit is $30 ($60 x 50 per cent). Here, Victor Venturers debits investments in the statement of financial position with $30 (therefore increasing the value of the investment to $130) and credits 'Share of profit of joint venture' in the income statement with $30.

Using proportionate consolidation

Proportionate consolidation is currently the preferred, benchmark treatment under IFRS (but not for long – see the later section 'Keeping Up with New Developments in the Accounting Standard'). Under the proportionate consolidation method of accounting, the statement of financial position of the venturer includes its share of the net assets of the joint venture and the statement of comprehensive income includes its share of the income and expenses of the joint venture. This method is usually referred to as an _aggregated line-by-line basis_. The standard currently permits different reporting formats to present proportionate consolidation of financial statements. The following sections show you how to use proportionate consolidation.

Step 1: Work out the goodwill that arose when you acquired your share of the jointly controlled entity

Goodwill is the excess of what you paid for your investment over what you acquired. You need to take the amount it cost you when you first invested in the jointly controlled entity and compare this with the net assets you've actually acquired. (See Chapter 11 for more on working out goodwill.)

Alex Co acquired 40 per cent of James Co as a jointly controlled entity on 1 January 2011 for $700 when the net assets of James consisted of share capital of $900 and _retained earnings_ (profits reinvested in the business) of $700. The investment cost Alex $700 and for this $700 Alex has acquired 40 per cent of the net assets of James, so that's 40 per cent of James's share capital of $900 and 40 per cent of James's retained earnings of $700. The goodwill is:

Cost of investment	$700
Less what Alex has bought:	
Share capital (40% × $900)	($360)
Retained earnings (40% × $700)	($280)
Goodwill	**$60**

Step 2: Move the share capital

You now prepare to consolidate your share of the jointly controlled entity's financial statements with your financial statements. You put the share capital into the consolidated statement of financial position, which is the _investor's_ share capital only.

In the example, the share capital of Alex on 31 December 2011 was 1,000 $1 shares. The share capital of James on 31 December 2011 was 900 $1 shares. In the consolidated statement of financial position, the share capital is Alex's share capital only of $1,000. Do not include any of James's.

Step 3: Work out the retained earnings figure to include in the statement of financial position.

You take the investor's retained earnings and add on to the investor's retained earnings the investor's share of the post-acquisition retained earnings of the jointly controlled entity.

Don't include any retained earnings that belong to the jointly controlled entity before the date of acquisition (known as pre-acquisition retained earnings) in the consolidated retained earnings figure because they don't belong to the investor (hence pre-acquisition).

In the example, immediately before the date of acquisition, James's retained earnings were $700. On 31 December 2011, the balance on James's retained earnings stood at $3,700 and Alex's retained earnings stood at $4,100.

To calculate the consolidated retained earnings, take Alex's retained earnings first (because they, of course, belong to Alex), deduct the pre-acquisition retained earnings (because all of these earnings belong to James) and finally add on Alex's share of James's post-acquisition profit. This calculation gives you the consolidated retained earnings figure:

Balance on Alex's retained earnings		4,100
James retained earnings	3,700	
Less pre-acquisition retained earnings	(700)	
	3,000	
	× 40%	1,200
		5,300

Step 4: Consolidate the financial statements of the jointly-controlled entity with the investor's financial statements

Proportionate consolidation is similar to consolidating a subsidiary (see Chapters 10 and 11) *except* that when you're doing proportionate consolidation for a jointly controlled entity you only consolidate *your share* of the assets, liabilities, income and expenses of the jointly controlled entity with your financial statements. If you own 30 per cent of a jointly controlled entity, then using proportionate consolidation you take your assets and include your share (30 per cent) of the jointly controlled entity's assets also.

Dealing with the separate statements of financial position

Using the example, the separate statements of financial position for both Alex and James as at 31 December 2011 are shown below:

	Alex Co ($)	James Co ($)
Investment in James	700	
Assets	4,800	4,850
	5,500	**4,850**
Share capital ordinary $1 shares	1,000	900
Retained earnings	4,100	3,700
Liabilities	400	250
	5,500	**4,850**

Putting together the consolidated statement of financial position

In the consolidated statement of financial position, the investment in James disappears because you used it in the goodwill calculation (see Step 1, 'Cost of investment'). Here's how the consolidated statement of financial position for Alex and James looks:

	Alex Co (S)
Goodwill (Step 1)	60
Assets (4,800 + (40% × 4,850))	<u>6,740</u>
	6,800
Share capital (Alex only – Step 2)	1,000
Retained earnings (Step 3)	5,300
Liabilities (400 + (40% × 250))	<u>500</u>
	6,800

Sorting the consolidated income statement

When you come to deal with the consolidated income statement using proportionate consolidation, the good news is that this is easy (feel free to cheer or breathe a sigh of relief!). Follow these steps:

1. **Take the income statement of both the investor and the jointly controlled entity.**

2. **Take the revenue of the investor and add on the percentage of revenue of the jointly controlled entity that belongs to the investor.**

   The income statement of Alex shows revenue of $20,000 and the income statement of James shows revenue of $8,000. In the consolidated income statement, the revenue figure is Alex's revenue figure of $20,000 *plus* 40 per cent of James's revenue, which is $3,200 ($8,000 x 40 per cent).

3. **Combine the costs for both the investor and the jointly controlled entity using the same approach as in Step 2.**

   The individual financial statements of Alex and James show the following costs:

	Alex	James
	$	$
Cost of sales	10,000	1,000
Administrative expenses	7,000	4,000

   In the consolidated income statement, you take 100 per cent of Alex's costs and add on 40 per cent of all James's costs like this:

Cost of sales (10,000 + (40% x 1,000)	$1,400
Administrative expenses (7,000 + (40% x 4,000)	$8,600

You do this calculation for all items in the income statements until profit after tax.

Don't get too used to the proportionate consolidation method – the method is about to be consigned to the history books, as I discuss in 'Keeping Up with New Developments in the Accounting Standard', later in this chapter.

Considering presentation in the financial statements

As well as presenting the information relating to joint ventures in the statement of financial position, you need to include some additional disclosure requirements within the notes to the financial statements. The notes to the financial statements are a vital component of the financial statements and contain detailed issues that the user needs to know about.

When you're dealing with a company with joint ventures, make sure that the financial statements contain the following disclosure notes:

- Any contingent liabilities that the venturer has incurred in relation to their interest in the joint venture (see Chapter 7 for more on contingent liabilities)

- The venturer's share of the contingent liabilities of the joint venture for which it is liable

- Any capital commitments of the venturer in relation to its interest in the joint venture and its share in the capital commitments that have been incurred

- The proportion of ownership interest held in each of its jointly controlled entities

- The method that the venturer uses to recognise its interests in jointly controlled entities

The above list isn't exhaustive (it includes just some of the basic disclosures that are needed) and you're well advised to use an up-to-date disclosure checklist to make sure that you're making the right disclosures.

In IFRS, you present interests in joint ventures in the statement of financial position within the category 'investments accounted for using the equity method'. For jointly controlled entities accounted for using the proportionate consolidation method, investments in joint ventures are incorporated within the parent company's statement of financial position (in the consolidated financial statements).

Keeping Up with New Developments in the Accounting Standard

In May 2011, the International Accounting Standards Board (IASB) introduced three new accounting standards on the areas of consolidations, joint ventures and disclosures and then went on to amend two existing standards – IAS 27 *Consolidated and Separate Financial Statements* and IAS 28 *Investments in Associates*. I discuss the changes to IAS 27 and 28 in Chapters 10 and 12 respectively. Here, I focus on the changes that apply to joint ventures.

Knowing what's changed and why

In terms of joint ventures, there has been quite significant change. The IASB has issued a new standard called IFRS 11 *Joint Arrangements*. In this new standard, jointly controlled assets no longer exist and the standard only differentiates between joint operations and joint ventures. A *joint operation* is an arrangement whereby the parties that have joint control have rights to the assets and obligations for the liabilities. A *joint venture* is an arrangement whereby the parties that have joint control have rights to the net assets.

The changes have come about to converge US Generally Accepted Accounting Practice (GAAP) and IFRS. IFRS 12 *Disclosure of Interests in Other Entities* covers what you need to disclose in respect of joint ventures.

Looking at how the changes affect companies with joint ventures

As well as removing jointly controlled assets, the new IFRS 11 withdraws the use of the proportionate method (see the earlier section 'Using proportionate consolidation' to see how the proportionate method works); this change means that companies that adopt the proportionate method of consolidation are going to have to change to the equity method.

Because the switch from the proportionate method to the equity method is a change in accounting policy, IAS 8 *Accounting Policies, Changes in Accounting Estimates and Errors* will kick in (see Chapter 2 for more on accounting policy changes). Some companies may not be happy about the withdrawal of the proportionate method, but the IASB believes that IFRS 11 will improve financial reporting. In fairness, this new method is unlikely to reshape a company's statement of financial position because (in most situations) accounting for individual assets and liabilities gives the same outcome as proportionate consolidation anyway.

Knowing when the changes take effect

The new IFRS 11 will have to be adopted by companies that fall under its scope for their annual accounting periods commencing on or after 1 January 2013.

If you want to adopt IFRS 11 earlier than 1 January 2013, you're perfectly entitled to.

Part IV
Disclosing Information in the Financial Statements

The 5th Wave
By Rich Tennant

"Cooked books? Let me just say you could serve this profit and loss statement with a fruity Zinfandel and not be out of place."

In this part . . .

The numbers clearly play a vital role in a set of financial statements but the fact is that the numbers are only part of the bigger picture. Users of the financial statements must be able to make rational decisions based on the information contained within these statements. For this reason, you have to make many disclosure notes within a set of general purpose financial statements.

In this part, I look at some of the more common disclosure notes you're likely to come up against in the world of accountancy. I start by examining related parties and why these transactions need disclosure. I then take a look at a controversial accounting standard relating to segmental information. And finally, I explore one of the most crucial accounting standards for analysts and investors: earnings per share.

Chapter 14

Reporting Related Parties

*W*hen put together, the words *related* and *parties* create one of the most common causes of headaches for accountants and auditors. *Related parties* are people or companies related to a company. A related party relationship exists when one party has the ability to control, or exercise significant influence over, the other party in terms of making financial and operating decisions.

Related party transactions can have a significant impact on an organisation's financial statements from the viewpoint of potential investors and others, like the tax authorities. For this reason, the International Accounting Standards Board (IASB) issued IAS 24 *Related Party Disclosures*, which is wholly a disclosure standard. You apply this standard to do the following:

✔ Identify related party relationships as well as the transactions between those related parties.

✔ Identify any outstanding amounts between a company and its related parties.

✔ Ensure that adequate disclosures are made in the financial statements concerning transactions between related parties.

In this chapter, I drill down further on the definition of a related party and look at how both control and significant influence play a part. Because companies often have connections with the close family of directors or management, I look at how these guys influence the impact of related parties on the financial statements. I then move on to consider how post-employment benefit plans affect the disclosures concerning related party transactions. And finally, I round off by going through the relevant disclosures you need to make.

IAS 24 was issued in 1984, but don't let this fact detract you from the importance of related party transactions. This standard is as relevant today as it was back then and has been updated since it was first issued.

Understanding Related Parties

Over the years, the definition of a related party has become more and more complicated because financial reporting itself has become more complicated.

In a nutshell, a *related party* is a company, or another person, that's related to the company whose financial statements you're preparing. 'Well, that's easy enough!' I hear you say. The problem is that the definition of a related party is very, very wide.

Under IAS 24, the reporting company is related to another company if any of the following conditions apply:

- The party and the reporting company are members of the same group. So a parent, a subsidiary and other subsidiaries in the group are all related to each other. (I cover parents and subsidiaries in Chapter 10.)

- A reporting company is an associate or joint venture of the other company, or an associate or joint venture of a member of a group in which the other company is a member. (Take a look at Chapter 12 for more on associates and Chapter 13 for details of joint ventures.)

- Both parties are joint ventures of the same party.

- The reporting company is a joint venture of a third party and the other company is an associate of the third company.

- The reporting company is a post-employment benefit plan (pension plan) for the benefit of the employees of the reporting company, or another company related to the reporting company.

- The reporting company is controlled, or jointly controlled, by a person or a close member of that person's family who

  - Has control, or joint control, over the reporting company

  - Has significant influence or is a member of the key management personnel of the reporting company or of a parent of the reporting company

  - Is a member of the key management personnel of the company

As you can see, defining a related party isn't as easy as people may think! And it's not just companies that may be a related party of the reporting company; people can also be a related party.

The following sections help you understand further what or who is a related party, and why you disclose their relationship.

Knowing why you disclose related party transactions

Related party transactions are subjective and can be quite easily hidden from accountants or auditors if management don't want others to know about them, particularly if the accountant or the auditor isn't alert enough to be on the lookout for undisclosed related party transactions. In some cases, something sinister may be happening, which is the reason why some members of management may not want shareholders to become aware of certain related party transactions. In other cases, management may not want to disclose information concerning certain related parties because it considers the information to be extremely sensitive.

The reason you need to make sure that related party transactions are adequately disclosed is that some transactions may not have been carried out in an *arm's length transaction* (one in which both parties act independently and aren't connected in any way with each other).

A related party relationship may have an impact on the financial position and results of the company because:

- ✔ Related parties may enter into transactions that unrelated parties may not consider appropriate, or commercially feasible.

- ✔ Amounts charged for transactions between related parties may not be comparable to amounts charged for similar transactions between unrelated parties (the prices may be higher or lower than those charged in an arm's length transaction).

- ✔ Transactions may not have taken place had the parties not been related parties.

Cars R Us buys and sells new and second-hand motor vehicles for sale to businesses and to the general public, and has a year-end of 31 March 2012. Two directors are involved in the running of the business, and on 1 February 2012 one of the directors purchased a vehicle from the company at a price that was significantly lower than the vehicle's market value.

If Cars R Us don't disclose this transaction as a related party transaction, users won't be any the wiser that a material transaction has occurred between the director and the company, particularly one where the director has obtained goods from the company on favourable terms. IAS 24, therefore, requires disclosure of such a transaction.

Looking at the disclosures required

IAS 24 requires as a minimum the following disclosures:

- ✔ The amount of the transactions
- ✔ The amount of outstanding balances, plus

  - Their terms and conditions, including whether they're secured, and the nature of the consideration set for settlement
  - Details of any guarantee(s) given or received

- ✔ Valuation adjustments for doubtful debts relating to amounts included in the outstanding balances
- ✔ The costs recognised during the year relating to bad debts or doubtful debts from related parties

So, in order to make the disclosures, you follow these steps:

1. **Go through the accounting records in fine detail and identify all the related parties that are connected to the company.**

2. **Go through the transactions with the related parties to identify whether they're material (significant to the financial statements).**

3. **Work out whether any money was owed to or by the related party at the year-end and consider settlement terms and details of any guarantees given.**

4. **Work out whether any amounts were included in the financial statements to cover the cost of any debts due from related parties that may not be received.**

5. **If amounts due from related parties in the year have been written off, disclose them where they're material.**

Considering materiality

Disclosure of related party transactions is required only if they're material. IAS 24 doesn't contain benchmarks for materiality. However, IAS 1 *Presentation of Financial Statements* (which I cover in Chapter 1) says that an item is material if its omission or mis-statement can individually, or collectively, influence the economic decisions of users taken on the basis of the financial statements as a whole.

You also consider materiality in the context of both the size and nature of transactions.

Be alert to the *nature* criteria – if a director is involved, it doesn't matter about the size of the transaction because transactions with directors are *material in nature*.

Related parties and tax implications

In some countries, if a company is associated with another one, this association has tax implications. For example, in the UK, if a company is under common control, you have to consider this control when calculating the company's liability to tax on its profits. In the UK, a company pays tax at the small companies rate (20 per cent from 1 April 2012) if its taxable profits are between £0 and £300,000. When taxable profits go over £300,000, the company pays tax at the main rate of corporation tax (currently, at the time of writing, 26 per cent but reducing by 1 per cent each year until it is 23 per cent in 2014–15). Marginal relief is given to companies if their taxable profits are at an annual rate that is above the lower limit (£300,000) but equal to, or below, the upper limit of £1,500,000.

Companies that transact with other companies that are deemed related parties may well find that the companies with which they enter into related party transactions are also classed as an associated company for the purposes of tax. What this classification does is reduce the limits for marginal relief by the number of associated companies. They're reduced by dividing the limits by the number of companies that are associated.

Related party disclosures can often tell tax authorities an awful lot about the company's calculation of its tax liability. Therefore, if you're involved in the computation of a company's tax liability that has related party issues, be extremely careful to also consider whether such related parties also give rise to an associated company. If you get this judgement wrong, and you claim excessive amounts of marginal relief, the tax authority imposes interest charges and possible penalties.

Simon's Sizzles operates a successful chain of restaurants and takeaway outlets throughout the country. It has two directors, Simon and Kim. The issued ordinary share capital of Simon's Sizzles is 100 $1 ordinary shares. On 1 January 2012, Simon transferred his entire holding of 50 $1 shares to a holding company, Simon Group Holding Company. Now on the face of it, $50 may not sound material in the context of a successful company. However, the transaction itself is material in nature because it relates to the director's shares, hence Simon must disclose this transfer in the financial statements.

Looking at example transactions

Because IAS 24 recognises that related party transactions can be extremely subjective and sensitive in some areas, it offers some examples of transactions that it considers to be related party transactions. The examples (which are not exhaustive) are:

- ✔ Purchases or sales of goods (finished or unfinished)
- ✔ Purchases or sales of property and other assets
- ✔ Rendering or receiving of services
- ✔ Leases

> ✔ Transfers of research and development
>
> ✔ Transfers under licence agreements
>
> ✔ Transfers under finance arrangements (including loans and equity contributions in cash or in kind)
>
> ✔ Provisions or guarantees of collateral
>
> ✔ Settlement of liabilities on behalf of the company or by the company on behalf of another party

IAS 24 doesn't contain any exemptions based on the sensitive nature of the transaction. As a result, related party transactions also include transactions such as dividend payments and the issue of shares under rights issues to major shareholders.

Considering examples of when related party relationships exist

Many companies enter into related party transactions and it must be emphasised that companies doing so doesn't mean that they're fraudulent transactions! The main issue concerning related parties and their disclosure is that of control. I look at what constitutes control and what gives rise to significant influence in the next section, 'Defining control in the context of related parties'.

Take a look at Figure 14-1. Company A is controlled by Mark because he owns 60 per cent of the voting rights. Company B is significantly influenced by Mark because he only owns 30 per cent. What related party disclosures does Company A need to make in the financial statements?

Company B is a related party of Company A so any transactions between the two need disclosures. If Mark only had significant influence over both Company A and Company B, the two companies wouldn't be related parties.

Figure 14-1:
Group
structure
showing
control and
significant
influence
for related
party
purposes.

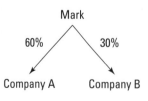

Now look at Figure 14-2. In terms of related parties, both Company A and Company B would be classed as related parties under IAS 24. However, if Mr and Mrs Byrne didn't have control over both companies, but only had (say) significant influence then Company A and Company B wouldn't be related parties.

Figure 14-2:
Group
structure
showing
husband-
and-
wife-run
company
for related
party
purposes.

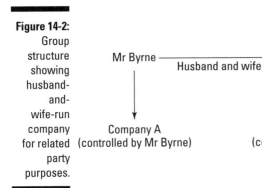

Mr Byrne ⟶ Mrs Byrne
  Husband and wife

Company A
(controlled by Mr Byrne)

Company B
(controlled by Mrs Byrne)

Defining control in the context of related parties

If the directors of a company have control over another company, they become related parties of each other. However, if the directors only have significant influence, the companies aren't related parties.

A company has *control* over another company if it has the power to govern the financial and operating policies of the other company so as to obtain benefits from the other company's activities.

One way of deciphering whether a company has control over another party is to look at the percentage of voting rights. If a company owns more than 50 per cent of the voting rights in the other party, it has control.

Alicia Art owns 60 per cent of the voting rights in Alex Art (thus Alex is a subsidiary of Alicia). The holding of 50 per cent or more of the voting rights in another company gives rise to a controlling stake in that company. Therefore, Alicia has control over Alex.

However, a company can also have control with a holding of less than 51 per cent of the voting rights if the company can govern the financial and operating policies of the other party.

Alicia acquires 45 per cent of Alex on 1 April 2011. The remaining shares are held by Ahmed (30 per cent) and Don (25 per cent). But the directors of Alicia have the ability to control and direct the day-to-day operating and financial policies of Alex. So Alicia has control over Alex.

Defining significant influence in the context of related parties

When a company doesn't have control, by virtue of its holding of voting rights or because it can't control the other company's day-to-day financial and operating policies, it may well have significant influence. IAS 24 says that one company is considered to have *significant influence* over another company if it has the power to participate in, rather than control, the operating and financial policy decisions of that other company.

The distinction between control and significant influence is important. Sometimes, two companies may become related parties when a person has control over both companies. However, the same two companies aren't related parties when that person only has significant influence, so you must assess control correctly.

Significant influence isn't the same as control. You can see whether significant influence exists by looking at the percentage holding in the party. If one party holds between 20 per cent and 50 per cent of the voting rights in another party, the party holding between 20 per cent and 50 per cent is deemed to have significant influence over that party.

Sanjay Sandwiches holds 30 per cent of the voting rights in Beth Baguettes. The board of Sanjay doesn't have the ability to control the operating and financial policies of Beth. In this instance, Sanjay has significant influence over Beth for two reasons:

- Sanjay owns 30 per cent of the voting rights in Beth and anything between 20 per cent and 50 per cent is considered to be significant influence.
- Sanjay doesn't have the ability to control the operating and financial policies of Beth, which means that Sanjay doesn't have control, but merely significant influence.

The existence of the ability to exercise significant influence over a company may be evidenced in one, or more, of the following ways:

- Dependence on another company for technical information
- Having material inter-company transactions between the two companies
- Interchange of managerial personnel between the two companies

 ✔ Participation in the policy-making process of the other company

 ✔ Representation on the board of directors of the other company

When you've significant influence over another company, you've what's known as an *associate* and you need to account for this associate under IAS 28 *Investments in Associates*. Flick to Chapter 12 for more on associates.

Looking at some grey areas – when related parties may not be related parties

IFRS places importance on the substance-over-form concept – this concept means that you report the commercial reality of a transaction, not its legal form. Well, if companies merely look to the legal form of a transaction or arrangement, this form alone may not correctly reflect what's *really* going on (the commercial reality). IAS 24 is one of those standards that particularly emphasises the concept of substance over form.

IAS 24 recognises that occasions may arise when (on the face of it) parties may seem to be involved in related party transactions, but, in fact, the standard deems them *not* to be related. The following parties aren't related parties:

 ✔ Two companies that have a director, or another key member of management personnel, in common or where a member of key management personnel of one company has significant influence over another company

 ✔ Two venturers who simply share joint control over a joint venture

 ✔ Certain agencies, companies or departments that play a role in the day-to-day business of the company, even when they participate in the decision-making process, such as providers of finance (banks and creditors), trade unions, public utilities and government departments and agencies

 ✔ A customer, supplier, franchisor, distributor or agent with whom a significant volume of business is transacted as a result of economic dependence

Establishing who falls under the scope of key management personnel

Key management personnel are those people within the company who have the authority to plan, direct and control the activities of the company. Directors (executive and non-executive) are key management personnel. IAS 24 requires transactions between the company and its key management personnel to be disclosed as related party transactions.

Non-executive directors don't have any day-to-day involvement in the running of a company. But transactions between the company and the non-executive directors do require disclosure as a related party.

Don't think that *every* single transaction between the company and key management needs disclosure. For example, if a company director buys a bar of chocolate from the company's canteen, this purchase is of absolutely no interest to anyone and it would be unreasonable to expect a company to make disclosure of such immaterial transactions. However, if an executive director purchases a building from the company at a price that's significantly lower than market value, this purchase requires disclosure because users of the financial statements are going to be interested in this transaction.

Key management personnel may enter into lots of smaller transactions with the company that, in isolation, may be immaterial to the financial statements. However, management should aggregate (total) those transactions and consider whether those items become material in totality and then consider the disclosures that may be needed.

Considering Close Family

You may have heard the phrase, 'You can choose your friends, but you can't choose your family.' It's true to say that you can choose your friends and on many occasions you can choose your related parties, but sometimes family and related parties are both one and the same. If they're the same, you must make sure that the financial statements reflect material transactions between the company and close family of an individual(s) who controls the company.

Knowing when close family become related parties

IAS 24 looks closely at close members of the family of an individual. It says that close members of the family of an individual are those who may be expected to influence, or be influenced by, that person in their dealing with the company. Essentially, IAS 24 considers the following to be close family:

- ✓ **An individual's domestic or civil partner:** Wives and husbands, unmarried couples and same sex partners.
- ✓ **Children and step-children:** The offspring from first, second, third (and so on) marriages.

✔ **Dependants of the individual, or the individual's domestic or civil partner:** Foster children, the elderly, infirm parents and, where they're dependent on the individual or the individual's partner, brothers, sisters, mothers-in-law or fathers-in-law, ex-partners receiving alimony and even more distant relatives such as cousins.

Realistically, you need to carefully consider any transactions that involve family, especially close family, for the purposes of related party issues.

Don't take the examples I cite of close family or relatives to be exhaustive. The scope of IAS 24 is wide. Anyone who's a member of the family (whether blood-related or not) is potentially a close family member for the purposes of IAS 24. They're close family members if they may be expected to influence, or be influenced by, the individual in their dealings with the company.

Seeing the influence that close family may have on a reporting entity

IAS 24 is intended to be a catch-all where family members and the company are concerned. Therefore, you need to consider any transactions or circumstances that involve family members to ensure correct and appropriate compliance with IAS 24.

IAS 24 considers close family to the extent it does because of the influences close family may have on the decision-making of the individual who has control of the company.

Paul Bury is the executive director of Bury Enterprises. He's married to Lisa Bury, who doesn't have an involvement in the day-to-day running of the company. Lisa Bury has decided that she's going to set up her own business as a nail technician and manicurist, offering services to the general public. She discusses the situation with Paul, who agrees to provide her with a small room in one of his commercial properties from which she can operate. Paul agrees not to charge Lisa any rent.

In this example, clearly Lisa has an influence over Paul, who's providing her with rent-free premises from which to operate her new business. The influence Lisa has wouldn't be the same if an unconnected third party were to approach Paul and ask him to provide rent-free premises – clearly, Paul wouldn't provide rent-free premises to someone he didn't know!

The influence that close family has over an individual can (and often does) have a major bearing on the financial statements because they've much more scope to receive goods or services from a company under more favourable conditions than would otherwise be the case for an unconnected third party. This is why IAS 24 identifies close family as a party that is always related party under the standard.

Disclosing the dependants of key management personnel

In situations when a company enters into transactions with dependants (as defined in IAS 24) of key management personnel, it must make sufficient disclosure within the financial statements of the transactions so that users have an understanding as to the transactions.

Where material transactions with the dependants of key management personnel are concerned, you don't aggregate these, especially where they're unusual or unique. The same applies to transactions between the company and key management themselves.

Like any other related party disclosure, disclosure includes

- ✔ The amount of the transaction(s)
- ✔ Outstanding balances as at the reporting date
- ✔ Any doubtful debt provisions made in relation to any outstanding balances
- ✔ Any doubtful debt expenses recognised in the income statement

Dealing with Post-Employment Benefit Plans

Post-employment benefit plans are pension plans provided to employees when they retire. (I look at post-employment benefit plans in a lot of detail in Chapter 7.) IAS 24 covers these in its definition of a related party because it says that a party is related to an entity if 'the party is a post-employment benefit plan for the benefit of employees of the entity, or of any entity that is a related party of the entity'. (IAS 24 doesn't actually indicate why a post-employment benefit plan is a related party of the entity. In my opinion, the reason is that the company sponsoring the post-employment benefit plan has at least significant influence over the plan.) So a company discloses pension plans within the notes to the financial statements.

But in many cases, directors and other key management personnel of a company pay into a pension plan that's nothing to do with the company or the group. For example, it may be that you've your own pension plan set up and your employer makes deductions from your wages and pays these deductions over, on your behalf, to your pension plan. But the company doesn't disclose the transaction as a related party transaction because the private plan is nothing to do with the company.

Jessica Robinson is an executive director of Robinsons Renovators, a large company with operations throughout the UK and Europe. Robinsons Renovators has several subsidiary companies and the company itself pays into a defined benefit pension plan for its employees and its executive and non-executive directors. Jessica Robinson is part of the company's pension scheme and sufficient related party disclosures are made in the company's financial statements concerning the company's payments into the defined benefit pension plan for its key management personnel. In addition to the company pension scheme, Jessica Robinson also has her own private pension plan to which she contributes $300 per month from her salary as a director. The company does not disclose the contribution as a related party transaction.

Only if the private pension plan became part of the company's pension plan would the plan then become a related party and thus require disclosure in accordance with IAS 24.

Disclosing Related Party Transactions

IAS 24 is a disclosure-only standard and requires extensive disclosures about related party transactions. The aim is to make sure that the user is fully aware of all material related party transactions. The following sections help you see what exactly to disclose.

Making full disclosure

Sometimes, directors read the draft financial statements and become aggrieved at some of the related party disclosures that have been made in the financial statements, particularly when these disclosures provide information about transactions not undertaken on an arm's-length basis. The directors may not want such transactions to be disclosed in the financial statements, and the requirements in IAS 24 to make such disclosures often adds to the reason that some entrepreneurs with small businesses choose not to operate as a company.

On occasion, a transaction falls under the scope of a related party transaction and has to be disclosed, but management demands that such a disclosure isn't made because they consider the information sensitive. But regardless of management's opinion, under IFRS you must disclose *all* related party transactions.

When transactions between related parties are undisclosed and the auditors become aware that related party transactions are material and haven't been disclosed, potential exists for the auditors' opinion to be *qualified* – in other words, they issue an unclean opinion on the financial statements. Usually, such an opinion (provided this issue is the only issue) states that a related party transaction(s) hasn't been disclosed, and except for this issue, the financial statements otherwise present fairly in all material respects. A qualified auditors' opinion is bad news: shareholders won't be too happy and will probably demand full and frank explanations! So management needs to be extremely careful to disclose all material related party transactions.

Disclosing information about transactions with key management

Many companies have transactions with key management that need to appear in the financial statements. Such transactions may include, for example, dividends to directors in their capacity as shareholders.

All transactions with directors are material and therefore should be disclosed. This is especially the case with dividends paid to the shareholders who are also the directors, because often dividends are material in amount as well. The disclosures you should make in respect of these transactions are

- ✔ The fact that dividends have been paid to the directors in their capacity as shareholder

- ✔ The amount of the dividend (you can express it as an amount of dividend per share)

- ✔ The amount of the dividend paid in the previous period

Here's an example disclosure. Cahill Enterprises is run by two directors – Jenny Cahill and Peter Cahill. The issued share capital is 100 $1 ordinary shares and each share contains full voting rights. The issued share capital is split 50/50 between Jenny and Peter. The year-end of Cahill Enterprises is 31 December 2011 and, on 31 October 2011, the management accounts for the third quarter ended 30 September 2011 were produced and they showed a considerable level of profit. Both directors have therefore made a Board resolution to pay themselves a dividend amounting to $10,000 each. This dividend is considered to be material to the financial statements, both in size and in nature. Cahill Enterprises makes this disclosure in the financial statements:

During the year, the company paid dividends on the ordinary shares amounting to $10 (2010: $15) per share to the directors in their capacity as shareholders.

Terminating staff or directors? What to disclose as related party transactions

Usually, the termination of staff doesn't warrant much (if any) disclosure as a related party transaction. However, where staff are key management, you need to make these disclosures in respect of their compensation.

✔ All employee benefits to which share-based payments (IFRS 2) applies (flick to Chapter 9 for more on share-based payments)

✔ All forms of consideration paid, payable or provided by the company, or on behalf of the company, in exchange for services rendered to the company

✔ Post-employment benefits such as pensions, other retirement benefits, post-employment life insurance and post-employment medical care (Chapter 7 details post-employment benefits)

✔ Other long-term employee benefits (for example, long-service leave, sabbatical leave, jubilee or other long-service benefits)

✔ Termination benefits (including compensation for loss of office, golden goodbyes and redundancy amounts)

Disclosing short-term employee benefits in the notes

The problem with employee benefits is that they can be vast depending on the type of company. Some companies offer many employee benefits; other companies (for example, small, owner-managed businesses) may not, simply because they can't afford them. But as general guidance, short-term employee benefits usually entail:

✔ Holiday pay

✔ Profit-sharing arrangements and bonuses

✔ Sick pay

✔ Wages and salaries

Short-term employee benefits can also include non-monetary benefits such as:

✔ Free or subsidised goods or services

✔ Housing

✔ Medical care

Any time you see the words *short-term* or *current*, generally such items fall due within 12 months after the reporting period. Insofar as short-term employee benefits are concerned, these usually fall due within 12 months after the reporting period in which the employees render the related services.

Figure 14-3 shows a typical disclosure note for Cordonisos Carpets, a large supplier of domestic and commercial carpets. The company's year-end is 31 December 2011, and during the year, it provided its key management personnel with salaries and share options as well as payments into a defined benefit pension plan. Three executive directors resigned their positions during the year and the company paid termination benefits in respect of these.

Cordonisos Carpets
Notes to the financial statements (extract) for the year ended 31 December 2011

Related party transactions
Key management personnel are defined as those persons having authority and responsibility for planning, directing and controlling the activities of Cordonisos Carpets, being the members of the Board of Directors.

Compensation of directors and other key management personnel

	2011	2011
	$,000	$,000
Short-term employee benefits	51	65
Post-employment benefits	14	13
Termination benefits	20	—
Share-based payments	30	42
	115	120

Figure 14-3: Example disclosure note.

Disclosing transactions between group companies

Many companies operate through group structures, especially larger companies, and in lots of instances each company within the group trades with the others. You may be familiar with the terminology *intra-group trading*. Well, this is what intra-group trading is all about – the buying and selling of goods between group companies.

If two members of a group trade with each other (one group member sells goods or services to another), you make disclosure of all the transactions that have taken place throughout the year by getting your hands on the sales and purchase ledger account of each group company and totting up the value of intra-group trading. In addition, you also need to disclose the amounts that are owed to and from each member of the group at the reporting date so that the user of the financial statements fully understands the impact all this intra-group trading has on the individual company's financial statements.

Whitaker Enterprises owns 80 per cent of the shares in two subsidiary companies – Heaton Enterprises and Westhead Enterprises. During the year to 31 December 2011, Whitaker Enterprises sold goods to Heaton Enterprises Ltd amounting to $200,000. Heaton Enterprises Ltd wrote off a debt owed by Westhead Enterprises Ltd amounting to $75,000. All amounts are considered material and no amounts are owed between any of the group companies at the year-end. Here's what Whitaker Enterprises discloses in the group financial statements:

> *During the year, Whitaker Enterprises sold goods amounting to $200,000 (2010: $150,000) to Heaton Enterprises. Whitaker Enterprises owns 80 per cent of the voting rights in Heaton Enterprises and all transactions were carried out on normal commercial terms. At the reporting date, an amount of $nil (2010: $nil) was owed to Whitaker Enterprises.*

> *Whitaker Enterprises owns 80 per cent of the voting rights in Westhead Enterprises. During the year, Heaton Enterprises, a company under common control, wrote off a debt owed by Westhead Enterprises amounting to $75,000 (2010: $nil). There were no amounts outstanding to or from Westhead Enterprises to any of the group members as at 31 December 2011 (2010: $nil).*

Chapter 15

Skilfully Segmenting Information

Some companies operate in a number of different classes of business, or have a variety of geographical locations. A typical example is that large supermarkets nowadays don't just sell food and groceries, they deal with all sorts of other things like mobile phones, TVs, domestic appliances and even loans and credit cards. For businesses such as supermarkets that operate in a number of different classes, financial information on each class of business, geographic location and regulatory or economic environments is useful for management and investors. This *segmental information* is mandatory for companies that trade their equity instruments (usually shares) in a public market (usually a stock exchange). The standard that deals with segmental information is IFRS 8 *Operating Segments*.

In this chapter, I help you to define and identify operating segments. I look at what happens in the event of errors or adjustments relating to previous accounting periods, and how you restate comparative segmental information. And I give you the low-down on how you disclose information about operating segments within the financial statements.

Understanding the Basics of Segmental Information

The main thrust of IFRS 8 requires a company to disclose information that enables the users of the financial statements to evaluate the nature and financial effects of the different types of business activities of a company, as well as the different economic environments in which it operates. And according to IFRS, the best approach is to spilt up the various parts of a business and provide information on each segment.

Defining an operating segment

Despite the huge amounts of controversy surrounding IFRS 8 (see the sidebar 'IFRS 8: The controversy' on this subject), this standard is still with us and is still mandatory for quoted (listed) companies. So those companies that fall under the scope of IFRS 8 need to identify their operating segments.

'But what is an operating segment?' I hear you ask. Well, basically an *operating segment* is a component of a company

- ✔ **That earns revenues and incurs expenses:** For example, through sales of goods or services.

- ✔ **That's regularly reviewed by the company's chief operating decision-maker:** The decision-maker is usually a chief executive, or a senior official of the company; for example, a board member. It can also be the manager of a segment; for example, a branch manager. (I talk more about the chief operating decision-maker in the section 'Understanding the management approach to reporting segmental information', a little later in the chapter.)

If the chief operating decision-maker just reviews, say, revenue for one particular area of the business, this action may not necessarily meet the definition of an operating segment because the decision-maker can't make decisions simply by looking at the revenue levels of a particular area of the business.

- ✔ **For which discrete financial information is available:** Generally, the criteria can be met with operating performance information only, such as gross profit by product line.

A segmental statement of financial position isn't necessary to arrive at the conclusion that discrete financial information is available.

Operating segments can become confusing. In Chapter 7, I examine defined benefit pension plans, which have pension assets and liabilities and contributions into the pension plan and payments out. Well, you may think that discrete financial information is available and therefore defined benefit pension plans meet the criteria for an operating segment – but defined benefit plans are *not* operating segments because they aren't components of the business.

Susan's Supermarkets sells a range of products and services:

- ✔ Clothing
- ✔ Domestic appliances
- ✔ Grocery
- ✔ Provision of loans and finance

Each of the above departments has its own revenue streams and incurs its own expenses and each departmental manager must report its results daily to the chief accountant.

In this example, the operating segments are each of the four different departments because each is essentially 'a company within a company'. You can identify the operations and the revenues and expenses separately from the main company, and each department reports results to the chief accountant as an identifiable component of the company.

Preparing to report about reportable segments

IFRS 8 requires that after a company has identified its operating segments, it then determines its reportable segments and its operating segments (or aggregations of operating segments) because you report segment information separately in the financial statements. *Reportable segments* are operating segments that meet *one* of the following specified criteria:

✔ The segment's reported revenue (from both external customers and inter-segment sales or transfers) is 10 per cent or more of the combined revenue (both internal and external) of all operating segments.

✔ The absolute measure of the segment's reported profit or loss is 10 per cent or more of the greater, in absolute amount of both

- The combined reported profit of all operating segments that did not report a loss

- The combined reported loss of all operating segments that reported a loss

✔ The segment's assets are 10 per cent or more of the combined assets of all operating segments.

IFRS 8 is the only IFRS that contains a materiality benchmark. It says that you must include at least 75 per cent of the company's revenue in reportable segments. Therefore, if the total revenue reported by operating segments constitutes less than 75 per cent of the company's revenue, you identify additional operating segments as reportable segments, even if they don't meet the quantitative threshold.

IFRS 8: The controversy

IFRS 8 was issued on 30 November 2006 and superseded IAS 14. Those companies that are mandated to apply IFRS 8 need to do so for accounting periods commencing on or after 1 January 2009, but earlier application was permitted.

When IAS 14 was being developed back in 1997, the previous standard-setter (which was the International Accounting Standards Consultancy) deliberately chose not to take a purely management approach to segmental reporting. The idea was to ensure that IAS 14 would give information that was more comparable between segments of a company and also between segments of different companies that operate in the same industry. IFRS 8 was deemed to be a totally unacceptable standard by many dissidents who believed that it was being used as a platform to increase the level of debate over the issue of convergence of IFRS with US GAAP. Certainly, the European Parliament commented at the height of the controversy that IFRS 8 would 'import into EU law an alien standard (US FAS 131) without having conducted any impact assessment'.

Understanding the management approach to reporting segmental information

Under IFRS 8, the chief operating decision-maker plays a key role (see the earlier section 'Defining an operating segment'). The chief operating decision-maker is a senior member of the management of a company and is responsible for making decisions about allocating resources to the segment and assessing the segment's performance. The chief operating decision-maker may be one person, for example the chief executive, or it may be a group of individuals.

The chief operating decision-maker's role in IFRS 8 is a deliberate attempt to use a management approach to segmental information. The approach gives consistency between what's reported in the financial statements and what's reported internally to management and is more consistent with information that's reported elsewhere (for example, in a management commentary) within the financial statements. The idea is that the user of the financial statements can effectively review the operations of a company 'through the eyes of management'. And the information reported to management internally about a segment is what management use for evaluating segment performance and allocating resources to it.

Identifying and Aggregating Reportable Segments

In order to present segmental information, you need to know how to go about identifying and aggregating reportable segments. I take you through all you need to know in this section, so you can handle IFRS 8 with confidence.

Dealing with the easy ones first: Single operating segments

Single operating segments are components of an entity about which separate financial information is available. This separate financial information is regularly reviewed by the chief operating decision-maker in deciding how to allocate resources to it and assess its performance.

For example, a holiday firm may operate an airline business to fly customers to and from their destination, a travel agency business where customers can book their holidays and a car hire business where customers can hire cars when they arrive at their destination. The operating segments in this example are the airline business, the travel agency business and the car hire business.

Tackling more complex reportable segments: Aggregating multiple segments

IFRS 8 suggests ten as a practical limit to the number of reportable segments that a company discloses separately because otherwise segmental information may become too detailed. But you can aggregate two or more operating segments into a single operating segment provided that in doing so you meet certain specified criteria:

- ✔ Aggregation is consistent with the core principle of IFRS 8.
- ✔ The segments have similar economic characteristics.
- ✔ The segments are similar in respect of:
  - The nature of products and services
  - The nature of the production process
  - Types or class of customer for the products and services
  - Distribution method
  - Where applicable, the nature of the regulatory environment (for example, banking or insurance)

Aggregation is permitted, but isn't required.

Looking at the whole step-by-step approach

Unfortunately, the process for determining reportable segments in real life isn't always straightforward (big sigh). However, in recognition of this fact, the International Accounting Standards Board (IASB) has included a useful flowchart in its *Guidance on Implementing IFRS 8 Operating Segments*, which you can download from www.ifrs.org.

The steps are as follows:

1. **Identify your operating segments.**

2. **Determine whether any operating segments meet *all* the aggregation criteria.** (For the criteria, see the section 'Tackling more complex reportable segments: aggregating multiple segments'.) If they do, aggregate them if you want.

3. **Review the identified operating segments and aggregated groups of operating segments and check whether they meet the quantitative threshold.** You treat those that meet the criteria as reportable segments.

4. **For the remaining segments, check whether any of the identified operating segments, or aggregated groups of operating segments, meet a *majority* of the aggregation criteria.** If they do, aggregate them and treat them as reportable segments, if desired, but make sure that the newly aggregated segment meets the quantitative thresholds.

5. **Test whether the external revenues of reportable segments so far identified represent 75 per cent or more of the company's external revenue.** If they do, aggregate the remaining segments into a segment named 'All other segments', which isn't a reportable segment in the context of IFRS 8. If they don't meet the 75 per cent threshold, identify additional reportable segments until the total of reportable segments reaches the 75 per cent threshold.

Disclosing long-term financial performance

The earlier section 'Tackling more complex reportable segments: aggregating multiple segments' explains aggregating (combining) operating segments. This aggregation usually happens when operating segments show the same long-term financial performance because they've similar economic characteristics. For such operating segments that show the same long-term financial performance, you expect to see information like long-term gross margins to be similar as well as other factors such as similar trends in the growth of products and management's long-term expectations for the product lines.

You can usually combine operating segments that show similar long-term financial performance provided that they meet the aggregation criteria I examine in the earlier section on that subject.

Be particularly careful with operating segments that show similar long-term financial performance and make sure that all the aggregation criteria are met. For example, you can't combine operating segments that have different sorts of underlying currency risks because this variation is indicative of different economic characteristics, hence aggregation isn't appropriate. Where you've operating segments that have different sorts of currency risks, follow a step approach:

1. **Identify your operating segments.**

2. **Scrutinise the operating segments to see whether some, or all, of them show similar long-term performance.**

3. **Identify those segments that operate in different currencies.** If you've a majority of segments operating in the same currency, you can't combine those with different currencies.

4. **Combine those segments that have similar economic characteristics.**

Phil's Pharmaceutical Company is a global supplier of medicinal products. It has identified six internally reported operating segments: Australia, France, Germany, Italy, the UK and the USA. It enjoys significant market domination in Australia and Germany and these two segments are extremely profitable. The remaining segments are quite volatile in terms of profitability and in recent months margins have eroded quite significantly.

Australia, the UK and the USA all operate outside of the euro zone, but Phil's Pharmaceutical Company can't combine them because they all have different economic characteristics. These exclusions then leave France, Germany and Italy for potential aggregation. Germany can't be included because this segment is far superior in terms of profitability than France and Italy. Therefore, Phil's Pharmaceuticals can only combine its operations in France and Italy for external segmental reporting purposes.

Looking at some practical examples of segmental reporting

When a company is mandated to apply IFRS 8, it must make entity-wide disclosures. It must disclose information about the following if the information isn't already provided as part of the reportable segment information:

- Products and services
- Geographical areas (if you take a look at some real-life financial reports, you often find that a company includes maps and other diagrams to show where operating segments are located)
- Major customers

The following sections offer an example in each area.

Segmental reporting by products (and services)

Don's Domestic Dealers sells domestic appliances and is a nationwide company. Its year-end is 31 December 2011 and the company has reported revenue for the year of $867,690 (2010: $879,790). It has identified six operating segments disclosed as in Table 15-1.

Table 15-1	Don's Domestic Dealers Reportable Segments	
Product	**2011 Revenue ($)**	**2010 Revenue ($)**
Fridge freezers	217,930	235,200
Cookers	235,820	232,830
Televisions	158,780	160,680
Audio	102,580	102,400
Washing machines	99,340	98,160
Repairs and servicing	53,240	50,520
Total sales	**$867,690**	**$879,790**

Segmental reporting by geographical area

Pauline's Plastic Company has just completed its first year of trade and has its head office based in a country we'll call Farland but has branches in the USA, Europe, China and Japan. The company has identified each of its branches as an operating segment of the company. The company's revenue for the year-ended 31 December 2011 amounted to $87,870 and the book values of its non-current assets were $62,385. Table 15-2 shows how the segmental disclosure may look for Pauline's Plastic Company:

Table 15-2	Pauline's Plastic Company Reportable Segments	
Geographical Location	*2011 Revenue ($)*	*2011 Non-current Assets ($)*
Farland	46,100	27,800
United States	10,102	–
Poland	9,283	17,820
China	7,145	9,185
Japan	15,240	7,580
Total	**87,870**	**62,385**

Segmental reporting by major clients

IFRS 8 requires disclosure as to the extent of the company's reliance on major customers. In this respect, the company must state:

- ✔ The fact that revenues from a single external customer account for more than 10 per cent of the company's total revenues (you don't have to disclose the identity of the customers)
- ✔ The total amount of revenues from each such customers
- ✔ The identity of the reportable segment(s) reporting the revenues

Pat's Perfume Co sells perfume and other ladies accessories to a range of leading high street stores. Pat's Perfume has identified perfumes and ladies accessories as operating segments. Revenue for the year-ended 31 December 2011 amounts to $1,725,000. During the year, the company sold $197,250 worth of perfume to its major customer, Teen Trends. Pat's Perfume Co makes the following disclosure in its financial statements:

> *Revenues from one customer of the perfume segment represents approximately $197,000 of the company's total revenues.*

Restating Comparative Segments

When a mistake is made in the financial statements that occurred in the previous period(s), you have to go back and change the financial statements to correct the error (see Chapter 2 for more on this). When a company applies IFRS 8, it must also go back and restate comparative segments. IAS 8 *Accounting Policies, Changes in Accounting Estimates and Errors* is the standard that covers this type of restatement.

Discovering errors and correcting comparative segmental information

When a material error is discovered that affects prior periods reported, you must retrospectively correct the error and the opening retained earnings figure to take account of the error. To achieve consistency and to ensure that the information contained within the segmental disclosures is consistent with the financial statements, you should also change the comparative segmental information.

When you've the correct information, you go back into the previous year's financial statements and physically amend the segment information. So, if an operating segment's costs were understated in the previous year, you amend the segmental information in the previous year to what it should be in order that the financial statements are comparable.

During the preparation of the financial statements of Frank's Furniture Company (a global supplier of domestic and commercial furniture), the accountant discovered that the sales system hadn't included the last two months' worth of sales in the previous financial year. The account considered the error to be material and therefore he applied retrospective correction. He also changed the comparative segmental information so that it was consistent with the restated financial statements for the comparative period.

Disclosing information about restated comparative segmental information

In addition to errors, you may also find other examples of where restatement is required.

If a segment is considered immaterial (insignificant) then it isn't reportable as an operating segment in the financial statements. However, think about an area of a business that sees significantly rapid growth in the year. In the previous year, the segment may have been insignificant (and therefore not reportable) but in the next financial year it may well become material and therefore reportable as an operating segment. When this happens, you have to go back into the previous year and report the same segment, even though it was immaterial in the previous year. Why? To achieve comparability in the financial statements.

Sometimes, the reverse occurs and a material reportable segment becomes immaterial. If management considers the segment to be of continuing significance, you must continue to report it as a separate reportable segment. But if management no longer view the segment to be of continuing significance, you needn't separately disclose it and you restate the prior year's segmental information to comply with the current year's presentation.

Disclosing Information About Segments in the Financial Statements

If a company has to apply IFRS 8, it also has to make extensive disclosures in the financial statements. For large, multi-national companies, disclosures about operating segments run to several pages. So if you have to deal with operating segment disclosures, the chances are that you need a disclosure checklist to hand in order to get the disclosures spot on.

The information a company discloses under IFRS 8 enables the users of the financial statements (the shareholders or external stakeholders) to evaluate

- ✔ The nature and financial effect of its business activities
- ✔ The economic environment in which it operates

The information needs to include:

- ✔ **General information**, such as products and services, geographical areas, regulatory environments or a combination of factors as well as whether aggregation of segments has taken place.

  A company should disclose the types of products and services from which each reportable segment derives its revenues; for example, a retailer of women's coats may have segments such as 'store label – coats' and 'designer label – coats'.

- ✔ **Information on segmentation,** including details of reported segment profit or loss, segment assets, segment liabilities and the basis of measurement.

- ✔ **Reconciliations** of total reportable segments revenues, total profit or loss, total assets, total liabilities and any other amounts.

The following sections focus on the segmentation information and the reconciliation.

Detailing the measurement basis used for segmental information

IFRS 8 requires a company to disclose an explanation that enables the users of the financial statements to understand the basis on which segmental information is measured. As a minimum, the explanation must cover the following:

✔ How segmental profit/loss, assets and (where reported) liabilities are measured.

✔ The basis of accounting for transactions between reportable segments (usually at market value, but sometimes, though rarely, at cost).

✔ The nature of any differences between the measurement of reportable segments' profits/losses and the pre-tax profit or loss that's reported in the company's income statement.

✔ The nature of any differences between segmental assets and (where reported to the chief operating decision-maker) segmental liabilities, and differences between these and the assets and liabilities in the company's statement of financial position.

✔ The nature of any changes from prior periods in the measurement methods used, as well as an explanation as to the effect of these changes.

✔ Any asymmetrical allocations to reportable segments. IFRS 8 gives an example of a company that may allocate depreciation expense to a segment but not allocate the related depreciable non-current asset to the segment.

Understanding the reconciliations used in segmental information

IFRS 8 requires reconciliations so that analysts and others can understand and interpret the segmental information properly in the context of the financial statements as a whole.

IFRS 8 requires companies to give reconciliations for each of the following:

✔ Total reportable segments' revenue to the company's revenue

✔ Total reportable segments' measure of profit or loss (before taxation and discontinued operations)

✔ Total reportable segments' assets to the company's assets

✔ Total reportable segments' liabilities to the company's liabilities (if applicable)

✔ All other material items, which must be separately identified and described

Figure 15-1 shows an example of segmental reconciliation information.

Westhead Group segmental reconciliations.

Revenue reconciliation	$
Total revenues for reportable segments	94,000
Sundry revenue	2,500
Inter-segment revenue eliminated	(9,000)
Company revenue	87,500

Profit or loss

Total profit or loss reportable segments	9,800
Inter-segment profit eliminated	(600)
Other expenses	(1,000)
Consolidation adjustment to pension expense	(500)
Company profit before income tax expense	7,700

Assets

Total assets for reportable segments	190,000
Other assets	5,000
Inter-segment receivable eliminated	(2,000)
Company's assets	193,000

Liabilities

Total liabilities for reportable segments	105,000
Unallocated defined benefit pension plan liability	60,000
Company's liabilities	165,000

All other material items

Also included in the reconciliation to the Westhead Group's consolidated totals for depreciation and amortisation for the years 2010 and 2011 are depreciation and amortisation of Heaton Enterprises Limited activities of $1,222 million and $2,140 million respectively

Figure 15-1:
Example segmental reconciliations.

IFRS 8 requires total reportable segments amounts for every other material item of information to the corresponding amount in the company's financial statements. Material reconciling items may occur because of different accounting policies, or for items such as depreciation and amortisation (methods of writing off the cost of assets over estimated useful life).

Chapter 16

Easing into Earnings per Share

*E*arnings per share, the amount of a company's profit that belongs to a single share, is probably one of the most important ratios that's widely used by financial analysts, investors and other users of the financial statements to get an idea as to the profitability of a company, as well as to value a company's shares. Earnings per share is such an important accounting ratio that an entire accounting standard exists on the very subject – IAS 33 *Earnings per Share*.

The reality is that in the world of IFRS, the earnings per share ratio is only really applicable to those companies that trade their shares on a stock market (for example, the London Stock Exchange) because such markets place a huge amount of emphasis on the earnings per share ratio.

Calculating Basic Earnings per Share

The way to calculate basic earnings per share isn't difficult in itself. What's important is that you pick up the right figures from the financial statements as well as understand what the earnings per share number is telling you.

Doing the basic calculation

The basic earnings per share (EPS) calculation is actually easy; all you do is divide earnings by shares. Simples! When you've got the number that gives you basic EPS, you usually present it as pence/cents per share to one decimal place. Here are the steps you follow:

1. **Find the profit for the year that belongs to the company (in other words profit after tax, dividends and any non-controlling interests share).**

2. **Find the amount of issued ordinary share capital from the equity section of the statement of financial position.**

3. **Divide the profit figure in Step 1 into the ordinary shares figure in Step 2. The result is the amount of earnings per share.**

Molly has 100,000 ordinary $1 shares in issue (I say *ordinary* shares, which means those shares that are subordinate to all other classes of shares, in order to distinguish them from *preference shares*, which have a debt component as well as an equity component attached to them). Molly's earnings for the purposes of IAS 33 earnings per share calculation are $75,000. The basic EPS calculation is earnings ($75,000) divided by shares (100,000), which equals 0.75 cents per share.

Establishing what basic earnings per share means

Companies that fall within the scope of IAS 33 must calculate basic (and diluted; see the later section 'Calculating Diluted Earnings per Share') EPS for the profit or loss of a company that are attributable to the shareholders of the company. A shareholder is extremely interested in basic EPS because it represents how much retained profit the company has generated for distribution to the shareholders. Now, you won't necessarily find that every penny, or cent, of retained profit for the year is dished out to the shareholders in the form of a dividend; invariably, only some of the post-tax profit for the year is given to the shareholders as a dividend and the rest is kept in accumulated retained earnings.

You can now see that basic EPS is literally a rough estimate of the amount of profit that you can allocate to one share in the company. In the example in the previous section, the profit was equivalent to 75 cents per issued ordinary share.

When you're dealing with the basic EPS calculation, you must make sure that you only use the ordinary shares.

Knowing which profit figure to use for the calculation

You calculate the EPS figure by taking a company's earnings and dividing these earnings into the number of ordinary shares issued. But when I say *earnings*, what exactly do I mean?

When a company produces a set of general purpose financial statements, one of the primary financial statements is the statement of comprehensive income (you may know it as the profit and loss account), which contains the company's income statement for the year.

At the bottom of an income statement, you essentially have two profit (or loss) figures: profit *before* tax and profit *after* tax.

When you're calculating the EPS figure, you need to use the profit *after* tax figure. You're wasting your time using the profit before tax figure because the tax authorities want their share of the profits, so to incorrectly use this figure would disproportionately inflate the EPS figure and have the shareholders (incorrectly) jumping for joy! It would also be somewhat embarrassing for the poor soul who had used the incorrect figure when she realised her mistake and had to 'fess up!

This point is important when the company just happens to be the parent of a group of companies that doesn't wholly own some, or all, of its subsidiaries (sometimes a parent may only own, say, 80 per cent of the voting rights in a subsidiary; the *non-controlling interests* have the other 20 per cent). When these situations arise, you must use the profit for the period that is *only* attributable to the parent entity's ordinary shareholders.

Also bear in mind that for the purposes of the IAS 33 calculation, 'earnings' means *after*-tax profit, *less* non-controlling interests less *preference dividends* (fixed dividends that, unlike ordinary dividends, you don't have to declare). Be sure that you use the correct figures because not to do so leaves you red faced with embarrassment.

Calculating basic earnings per share: A practical illustration

The calculation of basic EPS is fairly straightforward; the complexities arise when you've information overload – especially when you throw preference shares and non-controlling interests into the mix. Here's an example to show you how to calculate the basic earnings per share, using the three steps I introduce in the earlier section 'Doing the basic calculation':

Heaton Enterprises owns 75 per cent of the voting rights in Westhead Enterprises. Westhead Enterprises' post-tax profit for the year after it paid preference dividends to the holders of the preference shares and after the non-controlling interests took their share of the profit was $2 million. The consolidated income statement of Heaton Enterprises shows the following as at 31 December 2011:

	$,000
Profit before taxation	15,000
Taxation	3,900
Profit after taxation	11,100
Attributable to:	
Equity holders of the parent	$10,600
Non-controlling interest*	$ 500
	$11,100

* Heaton Enterprises owns 75 per cent of Westhead Enterprises, therefore non-controlling interests own the remaining 25 per cent. Westhead Enterprises post-tax profit was $2 million, so $2 million multiplied by 25 per cent is $500,000.

Heaton Enterprises has 12 million ordinary $1 shares issued and 3 million $1 preference shares.

Now, the steps:

1. **Find the profit that belongs to the parent.** This figure is shown under *Profit attributable to equity holders of the parent*. So the profit that belongs to the parent (earnings) is $10,600,000.

2. **Find the amount of issued ordinary share capital.** You must take only the *ordinary* shares – you ignore the preference shares for the purposes of the basic earnings per share calculation. So Heaton Enterprises has 12 million ordinary shares.

3. **Divide the earnings into the ordinary shares figure.** The calculation is therefore earnings ($10,600,000) divided by shares ($12,000,000), which equals 88.3 cents per share.

The earnings figure is the *numerator* (the top number in the fraction) and the relevant number of ordinary shares is the *denominator* (the bottom number in the fraction).

Understanding Weighted Average Number of Shares

When a company wants to raise finance, it has a number of options: go to the bank and ask for a loan, approach other finance houses such as venture capitalists or issue more shares. And if the company approaches the bank for a significant sum, the bank may request that the shareholders pump some of their money into the company, so the bank essentially meets the company halfway.

The calculation of basic EPS becomes a little more complicated when a company issues more shares in the year because you have to calculate a *weighted average number of shares* that have been issued in the period (this calculation takes into account changes in the number of shares that are in issue over the reporting period). A company usually issues more shares in the year by way of additional shares, a bonus issue or a rights issue. I discuss these types of issues in later sections in this chapter. In this section, I explain calculating EPS with weighted average number of shares.

When a company trades its shares on a stock market, the chances are the number of shares it has outstanding during the year changes frequently. For the purposes of the IAS 33 EPS calculation, unfortunately you can't just take the number of ordinary shares that are issued at the year-end and divide this number into earnings, as I explain in the earlier section 'Calculating Basic Earnings per Share'. If it were this simple, the EPS calculation would be meaningless. Instead, you calculate a weighted average number of shares and use this figure in the EPS calculation.

Barry's Builders has a year end of 31 December. On 1 January 2011, Barry's Builders had 10,000 shares in issue. On 30 June 2011, it issued a further 7,000 shares at market value. You're undertaking the EPS calculation for Barry's Builders for the year ended 31 December 2011 and need to calculate the weighted average number of shares in issue during the year to 31 December 2011.

Here's how you calculate a weighted average number of shares:

1. **Start from the first day of the reporting period and make a note of the actual number of shares in issue.**

   Barry's Builders had 10,000 shares in issue.

2. **Go forward until the date of the next issue of shares and work out how many months of the year (or period) the number of shares in Step 1 were in issue until the next lot of shares were issued.**

   Barry's Builders had 10,000 shares in issue from 1 January 2011 to 30 June 2011, which is 6 months out of a 12-month period, so the fraction is $\frac{6}{12}$.

3. **Take the number of shares in issue (from Step 1) and multiply these shares into the fraction you calculate in Step 2.**

   Barry's Builders had 10,000 shares in issue for 6 months out of 12 so the calculation is 10,000 shares multiplied by $\frac{6}{12}$, which equals 5,000 shares.

4. **For the new issue of shares, add the number of the newly issued shares onto the number of shares already in issue and then work out the number of months the total number of shares were in issue.**

Barry's Builders had 10,000 shares until 30 June 2011. It then issued another 7,000 shares, which means by the year-end 31 December 2011 it had 17,000 shares in issue (10,000 shares plus the additional 7,000 shares). Barry's Builders had 17,000 shares in issue from 1 July 2011 to 31 December 2011, which is 6 months out of 12, which gives you 8,500 shares (17,000 multiplied by $^6/_{12}$).

5. **Add the result of Step 3 and Step 4 together.**

This calculation gives you the number of shares (the *weighted average number of shares*) in the year to use in the earnings per share calculation.

Barry's Builders had a weighted average number of shares of 5,000 from 1 January 2011 to 30 June 2011, and a weighted average number of shares of 8,500 from 1 July 2011 to 31 December 2011. The weighted average number of shares for the period is therefore 13,500 (5,000 shares plus 8,500 shares).

Making Rights Issues

So far in the chapter, I consider fairly standard ways in which a company's capital structure can change. These changes are generally confined to the larger companies but many smaller companies may undertake their own 'internal' calculations relating to earnings per share, even though the EPS calculations aren't mandatory to smaller companies that don't yet use IFRS anyway.

In this section of the chapter, I take you through another way in which the capital structure of a company can change, which is that of a rights issue.

A *rights issue* is a way of raising finance by selling additional shares to existing shareholders in proportion to their current shareholding. Rights issues have become more common during the recent tricky economic times. As an incentive to the existing shareholders, the price at which the shares are offered in a rights issue is usually set at a discount to the current share price (the market value). However, companies can offer a rights issue to existing shareholders at market value if the company so chooses. If the shareholders choose not to purchase the additional shares, their shareholding becomes diluted.

Why make a rights issue? Put simply, rights issues are to raise finance. Banks and finance houses often require a company to make attempts to raise finance from other sources, and a rights issue is a way of raising this finance.

Before getting your head around how a rights issue works, you need to understand some of the associated terminology:

> ✔ **Actual cumulative (cum) rights price:** The price of the share with rights attached immediately *before* the rights issue.
>
> ✔ **Theoretical ex-rights price:** The expected share price immediately *after* the rights issue.

You need to be on alert where rights issues are concerned. If a company that has a lot of other borrowing makes a rights issue, this can be a bad sign; unless the company can show signs of improvement, changing its capital structure achieves little (if anything).

Getting to grips with the theoretical ex-rights fair value calculations

When a company issues ordinary shares during an accounting period at a discount to the market price (the discount is usually applied to entice existing shareholders to take up the offer of the rights issue), the weighting calculation must reflect that the discount is essentially a bonus issue (I talk about bonus issues more in the next section, 'Boning Up on Bonus Issues').

Only the discount element of the shares is a bonus element because, effectively, in a rights issue made at a discount, an element of a share (the discounted element) is made to the shareholder at no cost.

The notional capitalisation issue reflects the bonus element that is inherent in the rights issue and is measured by dividing *fair value* (the market value of the share) per share immediately before the exercise of rights by theoretical ex-rights fair value per share.

The fair value per share immediately before the exercise of rights is the *actual* closing value at which the shares are quoted on the last date inclusive of the right to subscribe for the new shares (the *cum rights* price). The ex-rights price is the *theoretical* price at which the shares would trade after the exercise of the rights in an ideal world (in other words, a world without any external influences).

You use the sum to adjust the number of shares in issue *before* the rights issue in order to make an adjustment for the bonus element inherent within the rights issue.

Apply the adjustment for the bonus element inherent within the rights issue for both the current period prior to the rights issue and the previous accounting period.

Taking a look at a practical example

The theory behind a rights issue appears to be fairly complex, but in reality after you master the reasons for the adjustments you have to make, the calculations become fairly easy.

When company makes a rights issue, it offers the issue to existing shareholders in proportion to their current shareholding. For example, a company may make a rights issue of one share for every four shares held by a shareholder. So if the shareholder takes up the rights issue, she previously had four shares and following the rights issue she now has five.

When a company makes a rights issue, it offers its existing shareholders the right to acquire new shares in proportion to their current holding at a price that's less than the share's market value. The company does so primarily to entice shareholders to make the purchase. Because it issues shares at a discounted price, this 'discount' represents a bonus element (the bit that's essentially free because of the discount). For this reason, you need to adjust the number of shares outstanding immediately prior to the rights issue for the bonus element inherent within the rights issue.

The financial statements of Jessica Joinery Co show the following distributable net profit attributable to shareholders:

31 December 2010	$2,100,000
31 December 2011	$3,500,000

On 1 January 2011, Jessica Joinery Co had 800,000 $1 ordinary shares in issue. On 1 April 2011, it offered its existing shareholders a rights issue in the proportion of one share for every five shares already held at a price of $6 per share. On that date, the actual fair value of Jessica Joinery Co shares was $10 per share.

The following steps help you calculate an adjustment factor that takes into account the fact that some of the shares made in the rights issue contain a bonus element (the part of the share that's given for free). You can then use this adjustment factor to calculate the earnings per share figure.

Step 1: Calculate the theoretical ex-rights value per share

The *theoretical ex-rights value per share* is the price at which the additional shares would be valued in an ideal world after they've been taken up. To calculate this:

1. **Take the number of shares originally in issue and multiply this figure by the market price of the share.** The market price of the share is the share price *before* applying any discount.

2. **Multiply the number of shares to be issued in the rights issue by the price at which you're issuing the shares.** Use the share price *after* applying any discount.

3. **Add the results of Step 1 and Step 2 together and then divide the result into the number of shares that will be in issue *after* the rights issue.** The result is the theoretical ex-rights fair value per share.

The following is the sum for the example:

$$(800,000 \text{ x } \$10) + (160,000^* \text{ x } \$6) \div 960,000 = \$9.33$$

* The rights issue is 1 share for every 5, therefore 800,000 shares already in issue multiplied by 1 share divided by 5 shares = 160,000.

Step 2: Calculate the adjustment factor

Because the shares are actually worth $10, but Jessica Joinery Co is offering them to the shareholders at a price of $6, you can see that an element of the share in the rights issue is being 'given' to the existing shareholders for nil consideration. You have to calculate the adjustment factor to determine this bonus element. You use this calculation:

Fair value per share immediately before the exercise of rights ÷ Theoretical ex-rights fair value per share.

Fair value per share immediately prior to exercise of rights ($10) divided by theoretical ex-rights fair value per share ($9.33) equals $1.07.

Step 3: Calculate the earnings per share

Now you've all the required information to hand, you can calculate the earnings per share. Doing so is a little trickier than simply dividing earnings into the number of shares. Here's what you do:

Earnings figure (profit *after* tax, preference dividends and non-controlling interests) ÷ (Shares in issue *before* the rights issue x Number of months in issue ÷ Number of months in the accounting period x Adjustment factor) (see Step 2) + (Shares in issue *after* the rights issue x Number of months the new number of shares have been in issue ÷ Number of months in the accounting period)

Here's how to calculate Jessica Joinery Co earnings per share for 2011 *after* the rights issue:

$$\$3.5m \div (800,000 \text{ x } 3/12 \text{ x } 1.07) + (960,000 \text{ x } 9/12) = \$3.75$$

For the previous year's earnings per share calculation (2010), you just take the earnings figure and divide it into the number of shares previously in issue (800,000) multiplied by the adjustment factor (1.07):

$$\$2.1m \div (800,000 \times 1.07) = \$2.45$$

For the bonus element of the shares involved in the rights issue, you must assume that they've always been in issue and therefore adjust the comparative, which is why you must apply the adjustment factor of $1.07 to the 2010 comparative year to arrive at a $2.45 EPS figure.

Boning Up on Bonus Issues

Bonus issues are a common way of changing a capital structure. The thing that distinguishes bonus issues from rights issues is that bonus issues are given free! Bonus issues of shares are also known as *scrip issues* or *capitalisation issues*. A *bonus issue* takes place when the company issues further shares to the shareholders in proportion to their existing shareholdings (in the same way as a rights issue). For example, a company may offer a bonus issue of one share for every five shares held.

Any change in capital structure doesn't affect the income statement – the change is merely to the company's capital structure. Also, where a company issues new shares by way of a bonus issue, the only effect is to increase the number of shares that are outstanding after the issue; the issue has no effect on earnings because no flow of funds results.

Understanding why companies give bonus issues

Now, why would a company want to give away shares for absolutely nothing? Well, the thing with bonus issues is that they're more common than people think! A bonus issue has a distinct advantage: the shareholders receive additional shares at no extra cost to them. Companies usually make bonus issues as an alternative to paying dividends to existing shareholders. The main advantage here is that, from the company's perspective, it helps preserve cash. Bonus issues are usually advantageous to companies that are under-capitalised because in situations when under-capitalisation occurs, the rates of dividends paid to existing shareholders are much higher. A bonus issue of shares, therefore, lowers the rate of dividend paid and thus preserves cash.

One of the other main advantages of making a bonus issue is that such issues have minimal costs attached to them. The company simply gives bonus issues to existing shareholders in proportion to their present holding.

So, in a nutshell, the shareholder receives additional shares at no extra cost to them, and the company may preserve cash by not paying a dividend! Everyone's a winner!

Calculating earnings per share after a bonus issue

When the number of shares issued changes during an accounting period, you must use the weighted average table to work out the weighted average number of shares that have been outstanding during the period (I explain in more detail in the earlier section 'Understanding Weighted Average Number of Shares'). But simply taking the number of shares outstanding at the end of an accounting period *doesn't* give the correct EPS figure.

When a bonus issue has taken place, you must assume that the shares have always been issued and therefore go back and change the comparative EPS amount, regardless of the fact that the bonus issue may have occurred part-way through the current accounting period. These assumptions are also consistent with the treatment for the bonus element of a rights issue that you see in the example of Jessica Joinery Co in the previous section 'Making Rights Issues'.

To get a revised earnings per share figure that takes into account the bonus issue, first you work out the earnings per share figure (the earlier section 'Calculating Basic Earnings per Share' explains how). Then you take into account the dilution of earnings per share figure. *Dilution* means a reduction. Because more shares have issued, you have to apportion the earnings figure to a higher number of shares. Here's how:

1. **Divide the number of shares issued pre-bonus issue into the number of shares issued *after* the bonus issue.**

2. **Multiply the result by the earnings per share figure.**

Sarmonia Enterprises has 100,000 $1 ordinary shares in issue on 1 January 2011. On 30 September 2011, it made a bonus issue of one ordinary share for every five shares held at that date. Post-tax profit (earnings) attributable to the equity holders of Sarmonia Enterprises was $85,000.

The bonus issue doesn't have any effect on the earnings figure, but it causes a dilution to the EPS figure because more shares have been issued, so pre-bonus, the EPS figure would have been:

$85,000 ÷ 100,000 = 0.85 cents per share

However, you need to take into consideration the bonus issue, which causes a dilution in EPS as follows:

0.85c x (100,000 shares (pre-bonus issue) ÷ 120,000 shares post issue*)
= 0.71 cents per share

* Shares in issue pre-bonus issue	100,000
Bonus issue (100,000 x 1 share ÷ 5 shares)	20,000
New number of shares	**120,000**

As you can see, if you ignore the dilutive impact of the bonus issue, your earnings per share figure is higher than it should be. This is because the bonus issue means more shares are in issue, so you have to divide the company's earnings into a higher number of shares than before.

Making retrospective adjustments

When you're dealing with a bonus issue (or the bonus element of a rights issue), you must assume that the bonus shares (or the bonus elements of a rights issue) have always been issued.

Because you have to assume that the bonus shares have *always* been in issue, you have to go back and restate the prior year comparative EPS because otherwise the financial statements present a fictitious EPS figure that's higher than it should be.

The IASB *Conceptual Framework* requires financial statements to contain various characteristics, one of which is the concept of comparability. If you don't go back and restate the comparative EPS figure, the current year's financial statements won't be comparable to the previous year's and users of the financial statements are misled – a situation to avoid at all costs!

Calculating Diluted Earnings per Share

When a company must apply IAS 33, the standard requires it to calculate and disclose both the basic and the diluted EPS figure in the financial statements. *Diluted EPS* is the figure *after* taking into account any shares that have not yet been issued but may be taken up in the future. Basic EPS is easy to calculate, but IAS 33 takes the concept one step further and also requires that you give shareholders additional information relating to potential dilution of their shareholding. (I cover the issues concerning disclosure of EPS in the later section 'Discovering the detailed disclosure requirements of IAS 33'.)

Understanding diluted earnings per share

Sometimes a company may have *potential ordinary shares* in issue, which means that although the shares haven't been issued, they may potentially become issuable at a later date. This situation is particularly the case with convertible debt.

The term *convertible debt* relates to a loan that the company has taken out, for whatever reason, and the terms of this loan contain an option for the loan provider to convert the capital element of the loan into shares at a later date.

Diluted EPS doesn't just arise because of convertible debt; it can also arise because the company has granted share options to subscribe for new shares. Another way in which diluted EPS can arise is when a company buys another company and settles the consideration in shares upon the satisfaction of certain conditions imposed in the sale agreement, which may occur at a later date.

The main thrust of IAS 33 and diluted EPS is to alert shareholders to the future impact on the EPS figure that exists now.

Knowing which profit figure to use for the calculation

When you come to calculate diluted EPS, you take the profit or loss that's attributable to the parent entity's ordinary shareholders, but you must adjust this figure for the *after*-tax effect of the following:

- ✔ Dividends or other items that relate to dilutive potential ordinary shares that you used in arriving at profit attributable to ordinary shareholders, such as dividends on dilutive ordinary preference shares

- ✔ Interest recognised in the period on dilutive potential ordinary shares, such as interest on dilutive convertible debt

- ✔ Any other changes in income or expense that would result from the conversion of the dilutive potential ordinary shares

'Why include all this?' I hear you ask. Well, when you convert potential ordinary shares into ordinary shares during the period, the company no longer incurs the interest and other expenses associated with those potential ordinary shares. Hence, the effect of the conversion is to increase profit (or reduce losses) attributable to ordinary shareholders as well as the number of shares in issue. The adjustments to earnings include not only the direct savings in servicing debt (interest) and the related tax effects, but also any other consequential changes in other income or expenses that arise as a result of the conversion.

Taking a look at a practical example

A common situation that may trigger diluted EPS is when a company takes out a loan where the capital element of that loan may be converted into shares at a later date. This isn't the *only* situation in which diluted EPS arises, but is a fairly common occurrence.

When you're dealing with diluted EPS, you need to look at the costs that the company is incurring now that are directly associated with the convertible loan. You then look at the costs that the company would save if the loan was converted into shares. For example, in this situation the first cost that would be saved is interest on the loan. This saving would then go to increase profit; and a common incentive for companies to make higher profits is to give the directors a bonus based on the amount of profit a company makes. You must consider any cost savings that would be made if the loan was converted into shares, together with any increases in profit-related bonuses, when calculating the earnings figure for the purposes of diluted EPS.

Zedcolour Trading Co has a $50,000 4 per cent debenture (a document that creates a debt) in place, each debenture having a nominal value of $1. The terms of the debentures are that the holders can convert them into shares at a rate of 1:1 at any time until 2019. The directors of Zedcolour Trading Co receive a bonus, which is based on 1 per cent of profit before taxation, and at 31 December 2011, the results showed a pre-tax profit of $90,000 and a post-tax profit of $63,000. For simplicity, I assume that the company pays tax at 30 per cent on its pre-tax profits.

For the purposes of calculating diluted EPS, you must adjust the earnings figures for the reduction in the interest charge that would occur if the debentures were converted (because such interests charges wouldn't be incurred). In addition, the bonus payment would also increase because profit would increase with no interest charges incurred. Therefore:

	$
Profit after taxation	63,000
Plus reduction in interest cost:	
($50,000 x 4%)	2,000
Less tax relief that would have been granted on the interest cost	
($2,000 x 30%)	(600)
Less increase in management bonus:	
($2,000 x 1%)	(20)
Add tax benefit:	
($20 x 30%)	<u>6</u>
Earnings for the purpose of diluted EPS	**<u>64,386</u>**

Note: This example is to illustrate the calculations using simple diluted EPS. It doesn't take into account the requirements of IAS 32 regarding the classification of convertible debentures as liabilities and equity.

Presenting Earnings per Share in the Financial Statements

The whole point of the calculation of EPS in IAS 33 is to make shareholders aware of the EPS figure, both basic and diluted. Yes, IAS 33 is a complicated standard to apply, and yes, the detailed calculations in real life are going to be fairly complex. But such complex issues don't eliminate the requirement of an organisation to disclose the EPS figures correctly. I take a look at the detailed disclosure requirements in IAS 33 in this section.

Knowing where to present earnings per share

A company that has to apply the requirements of IAS 33 must present both basic and diluted EPS figures on the face of the statement of comprehensive income, or if the company presents the components of profit or loss in a separate income statement, the company must disclose basic and diluted EPS on the face of the income statement. I provide a practical example of how a company can make these disclosures at the end of this section.

Disclosing earnings per share for discontinued areas of the business

Sometimes, a company may discontinue one of its operations for various reasons – usually, because the division becomes unprofitable. For example, a company with a manufacturing division and a retail division may close its manufacturing division because of rising costs and a need to restructure the business.

IAS 33 requires disclosure on the face of the statement of comprehensive income, or the separate income statement where this income is presented, of the basic and diluted EPS figures for discontinued operations. A company can also make such disclosure of the basic and diluted EPS within the notes.

Discovering the detailed disclosure requirements of IAS 33

If you're not savvy with the detailed disclosure requirements, get hold of a disclosure checklist.

Some of the more common disclosures for EPS are

- ✔ Basic and diluted EPS for profit or loss for the period attributable to the ordinary shareholders of the parent company
- ✔ Basic and diluted EPS for the discontinued operation(s) on the face of the statement of comprehensive income or separate income statement or in the notes
- ✔ Any events that change the EPS share calculations

When a company has changed an accounting policy that it applied retrospectively, or corrected a prior-period error (per IAS 8 – see Chapter 2), the company then adjusts basic and diluted EPS for the effects of these.

A company must also present basic and diluted EPS, even if the amounts disclosed are negative (in other words, a loss per share).

Taking a look at a practical disclosure illustration

An example disclosure for when a company doesn't have any discontinued operations (as defined in IFRS 5; see Chapter 4) and where the company's basic EPS figure, diluted EPS figure and total EPS figures (basic plus diluted EPS) are the same for operations that will continue in business looks like this:

Basic EPS for profit from continuing operations and for profit for the year	$
Diluted EPS for profit from continuing operations and for profit for the year	$
Basic and diluted EPS on profit from continuing operations and for profit for the year	$

On the other hand, if a company has a discontinued operation (see the earlier section 'Disclosing earnings per share for discontinued areas of the business'), and it discloses the EPS figures for profit or loss on the face of the statement of comprehensive income, disclosure may be as follows:

	2012	*2011*
Earnings per share:		
Profit from continuing operations	$	$
Profit from discontinued operations	$	$
Profit for the period	$	$
Diluted earnings per share:		
Profit from continuing operations	$	$
Profit from discontinued operations	$	$
Profit for the period	$	$

Part V
The Part of Tens

"I assume you'll appreciate the entreprenurial spirit behind our accounting methods."

In this part . . .

This part contains three very useful chapters that essentially pull together key information from all the chapters in the rest of the book. I start by taking a look at the mistakes of others and give you ten pitfalls that you must avoid at all costs if you don't want to run into trouble with your boss, your client, the tax authorities or professional regulators. Because disclosure notes are such a fundamental aspect of financial statements, I also consider ten of the most common disclosure requirements that you have to make in a set of financial statements prepared under IFRS. I finish off by looking at ten future developments in the world of IFRS that I think you should keep your eye on because change is constant in the world of accountancy and you can't afford to stand still.

Chapter 17

Ten Pitfalls to Avoid

*T*he accountancy profession is heavily regulated and accountants have to comply with strict rules when preparing financial statements. If your accountancy firm is a member of a professional body – for example, the Association of Chartered Certified Accountants (ACCA) or the Institute of Chartered Accountants in England and Wales (ICAEW) – then your firm is going to be subjected to quality control visits. These visits are usually referred to as *monitoring visits* or *quality assurance visits*.

A common misconception is that regulators concentrate on those clients that are subject to statutory external audit. Regulators are hugely interested in client files that aren't subject to the external audit requirement in order to ensure that companies apply accounting standards, regulations and legislation correctly.

Unfortunately, for some practitioners these visits go rather badly, and what relevant action the professional body takes against the firm depends on just how badly it views the firm's work. Action can vary from a simple slap on the wrist to more serious action, such as significant fines and even expulsion from membership.

This chapter looks at ten of the most common errors that regulators pick up in a set of financial statements, so you can be sure that you don't fall into the trap. For those of you who work in companies rather than accounting practices, use this section of the book to check your own financial statement disclosures to make sure that you don't run into difficulties with your auditors.

You can avoid many of the mistakes in this chapter by using reputable accounts production software. Also invest in a reputable, up-to-date disclosure checklist that helps you ensure that you're doing things right and reduces the risk of producing sub-standard work.

Reporting Incorrect Transactions with Related Parties

You must report all significant (commonly known as *material*) related party transactions in the financial statements (go to Chapter 14 if you need to refresh your memory about these). Related party disclosures are one of the top ten disclosure errors that regulators pick up on. Accountants can miss or incorrectly disclose things like directors' transactions and the organisation's controlling parties.

Make sure that you disclose all key management compensation:

- ✔ All employee benefits to which share-based payment applies (I talk about share-based payment arrangements in Chapter 9)

- ✔ All forms of consideration paid, payable or provided by the company, or on behalf of the company, in exchange for services rendered to the company

- ✔ Short-term employee benefits such as wages, salaries and any employer costs (such as employer's national insurance), paid annual leave, paid sick leave, profit-sharing and bonuses (provided that these benefits are payable within 12 months of the end of the accounting period) and non-monetary benefits such as health care, housing, car and free or subsidised goods or services

- ✔ Post-employment benefits such as pension, other retirement benefits, post-employment life insurance and post-employment medical care

- ✔ Long-term employee benefits (for example, long-service leave, sabbatical leave, jubilee or other long-service benefits)

- ✔ Termination benefits payable to employees

Treating Accounting Policy Changes Incorrectly

You apply changes in accounting policy retrospectively (so you go back to the earliest period reported in the financial statements and apply the changes as if the new policy had always been in existence). You apply changes in estimation techniques prospectively (in other words, you don't go back; instead, you apply the change in the current and succeeding accounting periods). (You can find more on changing policies in Chapter 2.) Unfortunately, sometimes those dealing with these changes get into a bit of a muddle.

When dealing with changes in policies and/or estimation techniques, take a moment to think about what you're actually doing. You're changing accounting policy if you're going to change any of the following criteria:

- ✔ Measurement bases
- ✔ Presentation criteria
- ✔ Recognition criteria

If you're not changing any of the above, you've a change in estimation technique; so don't go back, carry on moving forward.

Don't forget to make the correct disclosures if you're changing policies and/or estimation techniques. For changes in policies, here are the main (but not all; there are too many to list) disclosures to make in the notes to the financial statements:

- ✔ Amount of the adjustments
- ✔ Circumstances that led to the change
- ✔ Effects of the changes in accounting policy on both the current and prior periods presented
- ✔ Reasons that the new policy gives more relevant and reliable information
- ✔ The nature of the change in accounting policy

For changes in accounting estimate, don't forget to disclose:

- ✔ The nature of the change in accounting estimate
- ✔ If you find it impracticable to determine the amount of the effect of the change in accounting estimate, disclose this fact

Disclosing Inappropriate Accounting Policies

I certainly have a lot to say about accounting policies! The reason is that they're the bedrock of preparing financial statements and tell the user an awful lot about the way the financial statements are put together. However, one of the most common pitfalls (which is why I include it in my top ten) is disclosing every possible accounting policy known to man!

Financial statements prepared under IFRS must disclose those accounting policies that have a material impact on the financial statements, such as the company's policy on how it recognises revenue in the financial statements. In other words, a company must disclose the *critical* accounting policies. So having endless lists of accounting policies in the notes to the financial statements is pointless when the vast majority of them are inappropriate to the client or your organisation (not to mention the paper you waste, adding to your carbon footprint).

Consider an organisation that only buys non-current assets (fixed assets) outright; in other words, it doesn't use any sort of finance (such as hire purchase) as a means of financing its investment in non-current assets. In this example, why bother having an accounting policy for dealing with assets under hire purchase?

For the critical accounting policies, don't forget to include the measurement basis (or bases) used in preparing the financial statements.

Neglecting to Ensure That the Numbers Balance

Believe it or not, many sets of financial statements contain the most unforgiveable mistake in the world of accountancy: the statement of financial position (also known as the balance sheet) not actually balancing!

For many who use reliable accounts production software, this problem is extremely rare. However, for accountants who rely on spreadsheet packages and/or word-processing packages to produce their accounts, the problem can be particularly prevalent – especially if the preparer's double-entry knowledge (debits and credits) leaves a lot to be desired.

In some countries (for example, the UK), incorporated entities (companies rather than sole traders) have to file financial statements with a government agency (Companies House in the UK). These government agencies can (and do) reject financial statements where the statement of financial position doesn't actually balance, which can prove to be embarrassing.

If you're going to produce financial statements in a non-accounts production software package, make sure that you get the trial balance to agree first. Then, and only then, prepare the primary financial statements from a trial balance that's in balance. If the trial balance doesn't balance, your statement of financial position won't balance either.

Forgetting to Disclose Items Separately in the Statement of Comprehensive Income

Sometimes businesses encounter *unusual* events: they don't take place on a daily (or regular) basis. When these events occur, they give rise to one-off transactions that may happen again at some point in time or may not. When a company incurs a significant amount of expenditure in a period (or receives a significant amount of income) from events that don't normally take place in the ordinary course of business, it shows this expenditure or income *separately* on the income statement so that the user of the financial statements can clearly see that one-off events have given rise to a decrease (or an increase, as the case may be) in profit or loss for that particular year.

Consider a company that operates in the chemical industry. One night one of the main warehouses explodes due to a chemical leak and the cost to repair the warehouse is a significant sum. Clearly, chemical explosions aren't an everyday part of the company's usual trade, and therefore the company doesn't usually incur such costs on a regular basis. However, in the year that the company incurs the expense to repair the warehouse its repairs and renewals expenditure will be clearly significant. The company should show the costs of repairing the warehouse separately on the income statement so that the user can see exactly why profits have reduced significantly from the previous year (or losses increased, as the case may be).

IAS 1 *Presentation of Financial Statements* requires you to present each material class of similar items separately in the financial statements. You can aggregate items that aren't similar only if they're *individually* immaterial; in other words, they wouldn't cause the user of the financial statements to change his perception of the company or come to the wrong conclusions about the company.

Failing to Split Non-Current Liabilities

A *current liability* is one that falls due for payment within 12 months of the accounting period end (I discuss these liabilities in Chapter 6). Well, some liabilities may span more than one accounting period; for example, a bank loan. Your company may take out a bank loan and repay it over five years. You must ensure that you correctly classify this bank loan, otherwise regulators will be quick to slap your wrists.

If you've a liability that's due for payment more than one year after your period end, or is being paid in instalments over, say, three years (like a loan), then you must show such liabilities in the statement of financial position split between the portion due within 12 months (current) and the portion due after more than 12 months (non-current). This requirement is particularly important with bank loans, hire purchase agreements, mortgages and some deferred government grants. In addition, you always show these liabilities *net* of any finance costs (interest) involved.

If you get the split wrong, the statement of financial position shows a disproportionate amount of current or non-current liabilities. Showing such liabilities has a significant impact on your net current assets/liabilities (current assets minus current liabilities) because you overstate or understate your net current assets or net current liabilities and overstate or understate your long-term liabilities. If you overstate your net current assets, users think that you've got less liabilities becoming due within 12 months after the reporting date, which isn't actually the case.

Always cross-reference the amounts you show in the statement of financial position in respect of current and non-current liabilities to your working papers file to make sure that you've classified them correctly. If you're not sure, get someone else to review them for you.

Getting into a Muddle with Deferred Tax Assets

Deferred tax is essentially a means of accounting for the tax consequences on all current year transactions whether the tax consequences are current or deferred (I explain further in Chapter 6). Deferred tax is probably one of the biggest headaches that accountants suffer from. Many have forgotten the concept of deferred tax completely and others simply ignore it (at their peril, I may add). Accountants often think, 'Well, it's not paid to the tax authorities, so why bother?', but tax deferral definitely isn't as black and white as that.

One of the biggest mistakes in IFRS is to inappropriately recognise a deferred tax asset. Deferred tax assets are less common than deferred tax liabilities. They're rarer because you more commonly have temporary differences for things like non-current assets whose values in the financial statements may be higher in the financial statements than they are for tax purposes (due to things like accelerated capital allowances from the tax authority). Chapter 6 goes into much more detail on this issue.

IAS 12 *Income Taxes* contains an extremely strict rule in relation to deferred tax assets. You can only recognise a deferred tax asset if it's probable (in other words, more likely than not) that the company will make sufficient profit in the future to enable it to utilise the deferred tax asset.

The most common type of transaction that would give rise to a company recognising a deferred tax asset is unused tax losses that go towards reducing future years' tax liabilities to the tax authorities when the company makes subsequent profits.

Don't recognise deferred tax assets just for the sake of it. You must be convinced that the asset is recoverable (in other words, that it will be used up). In some situations, the mere existence of unused tax losses may indicate that the company will never be able to generate suitable taxable profit to utilise the deferred tax asset; for example, if the company is in financial difficulty.

Forgetting the Statement of Cash Flows

When you first switch over to IFRS, you may have to do things that you didn't previously, or vice versa. In some countries (for example the UK), the statement of cash flows (or cash flow statement in the UK) is optional for companies that meet certain criteria and are deemed small in the eyes of companies legislation (see 'Incorrectly Claiming Audit Exemption', later in this chapter, for these criteria). For other companies that aren't deemed 'small', the statement of cash flows becomes a mandatory primary statement.

If your company reports under IFRS, the bad news is that the statement of cash flows is a mandatory financial statement regardless of whether the company is small or not (big sigh!).

Switching across to IFRS can be a painful exercise for some companies – particularly those companies that haven't really done a lot of research and preparation for the switchover (this lack of preparation happens quite frequently, believe it or not!). Picture the scene: you're happily plodding along, preparing your accounts under IFRS, and then along comes the letter telling you that your professional body wants to come and inspect your files to make sure that you're doing everything you should be. The regulator inspects your files and informs you that you aren't doing things right at all. You're not preparing the statement of cash flows for your clients who report under IFRS. 'But I didn't have to when I reported under the old standards,' you innocently reply. That's not really going to get you off the hook!

Under the IFRS regime, the statement of cash flows is a mandatory financial statement and is given the same amount of prominence as that of the statement of comprehensive income (income statement) and the statement of financial position. Pleading ignorance to regulators (or clients, for that matter) isn't a get-out-of-jail-free card! Flip to Chapter 2 for more information about the statement of cash flows.

Many accounts production software programs are able to handle the preparation of the statement of cash flows, though doing so can be a bit fiddly when you use IFRS for the first time. The good news is that after you've produced a statement of cash flows once, you usually find it all much easier for succeeding accounting periods. You may also find it useful to see the movements in cash between the current and the previous year.

Incorrectly Claiming Audit Exemption

Many countries have thresholds that, when breached, mean that the company is automatically required to have its financial statements scrutinised by way of an audit by a firm of external auditors. The thresholds aren't absolute and requirements in the company's legal constitution (such as the articles of association) may stipulate that the company is to have an external audit, regardless of the levels of revenue or value of its gross assets.

In addition, where the company has been given a loan, the bank or financier may also demand that the company has an external audit in order to give reassurance that the company is able to meet its obligations under the loan.

Incorrectly claiming audit exemption is one of the worst things you can do. Not only do you receive a lambasting from the regulators, but you also look pretty silly in front of your client or your boss when you have to explain that you thought you could get away with not having an audit.

The problem regulators have with some accountants is that they misinterpret the criteria to determine whether (or not) a company is eligible for audit exemption. For example, in the UK a company can be classed as small when it meets two out of the following three criteria for two successive years:

- ✔ Turnover is less than £6.5 million.

- ✔ The statement of financial position gross assets (non-current assets plus current assets) don't exceed £3.26 million.

- ✔ The company has less than 50 employees.

Remember the old Meatloaf song 'Two out of Three Ain't Bad'? Apply this song to the small companies test: two out of three is the small companies test to see whether a company is *small* and therefore eligible to claim audit exemption. If a company is *not* small, it can't claim audit exemption.

The audit exemption test in the UK is a bit different. If you breach *either* the turnover threshold of £6.5 million *or* the balance sheet total threshold of £3.26 million, you must have an audit (so you can be classed as a small company in the eyes of the law, but you still need an audit because you fail on *either* the turnover test *or* the balance sheet total test). Don't apply the small companies test when figuring out whether (or not) you need an audit because the two tests are different (though there is talk in the UK of aligning the two tests to make the audit exemption test the same as the small companies test).

Other countries have different rules for determining an organisation's size, so please make sure that you check with your auditors or the legislation in your country. Note also that groups of companies also have different size limits, but here I just stick to individual companies.

Mistaking When to Amortise Goodwill

Goodwill is one of those accounting concepts that often throws accountants into a state of confusion.

Although goodwill is an *intangible asset* (in other words, you can't kick it), you don't deal with goodwill with under IAS 38 *Intangible Assets*. Instead, you account for goodwill under IFRS 3 *Business Combinations* (head to Chapters 10 and 11 for more on goodwill).

Many countries still use their own domestic accounting standards that may allow companies to write off goodwill over its estimated useful life (*amortise*) – usually, if its expected useful life is less than a prescribed threshold. For example, in the UK, Financial Reporting Standard 10 allows a company to amortise goodwill over its expected useful life if its life is deemed to be less than 20 years. But a huge difference exists between what domestic accounting standards may allow and what IFRS 3 allows. Mix-ups are responsible for many accountants getting into trouble with regulators and their clients, who may be one step ahead of them!

Don't amortise goodwill under IFRS 3 – you must test goodwill annually for impairment and then recognise an impairment loss if necessary. You need to do this test every year. Chapter 5 takes you through the accounting for goodwill.

IFRS for SMEs is notably different when it comes to goodwill amortisation. See Appendix B for details.

Chapter 18

Ten Disclosure Requirements Under IFRS

● ●

In This Chapter

▶ Knowing some of the key disclosure requirements

▶ Disclosing information about prior-period adjustments

▶ Taking stock: getting inventories and work-in-progress disclosures correct

▶ Sharing information about employee-related issues

● ●

I bang on a lot about disclosures in this book and how important they are, but the reality is that they *are* important because they convey crucial information about the numbers in the financial statements together with any significant events that have occurred in the year that the user of the financial statements should be made aware of. Crucial concepts underpinning the preparation of financial statements are how companies elaborate on the numbers in the financial statements, how easy the user finds it to understand those numbers and the effect those numbers have on the organisation. You apply these concepts primarily through the disclosures you make in the notes to the financial statements (and in other parts of the financial statements, such as in the Report of the Directors).

In this chapter, I take you through ten areas of the financial statements and give you a list of the main disclosures required. This chapter isn't meant to be a disclosure checklist, so keep a checklist by your side to make sure that you get the disclosures right.

The book *The Interpretation and Application of International Financial Reporting Standards* by Bruce MacKenzie and friends (Wiley), which I discuss in Appendix A, contains a disclosure checklist, and those of you who apply IFRS for SMEs (see Appendix B) can get hold of a disclosure checklist at www.ifrs.org.

Non-Current Tangible Assets

I discuss *non-current tangible assets* (assets used in a business that have a physical form – in other words, you can kick them) in Chapter 4. The main disclosures you must make in respect of property, plant and equipment (PPE) are as follows:

- The methods used for determining the gross carrying amount
- Depreciation methods used
- Useful lives of PPE or depreciation rates used
- Gross carrying amount and accumulated depreciation amounts at the beginning and end of the period
- PPE purchased during the period
- PPE classified as held-for-sale and other disposals of non-current assets
- Increases or decreases during the period resulting from revaluations and from impairment losses and reversals
- Depreciation charges for the period

Non-Current Intangible Assets (Goodwill)

I discuss non-current intangible assets (those assets that don't have a physical form) in Chapter 4. Here are the main disclosures that you need to make sure exist in the financial statements for goodwill:

- The gross amount and any accumulated amortisation and impairment losses at the beginning of the accounting period
- Any additional goodwill recognised in the period
- Goodwill that you plan to sell and classify as held-for-sale
- Impairment losses that you recognised during the accounting period in respect of goodwill following the annual or periodic impairment test
- Any other changes in the carrying amounts during the reporting period
- The gross carrying amount and accumulated impairment losses at the end of the reporting period

Prior-Period Adjustments

Prior-period adjustments are omissions from, and mis-statements in, the organisation's financial statements for one or more periods arising from a failure to use, or misuse of, reliable information. They can arise because of changes in accounting policies or errors (more on these in Chapter 2).

You may need to make many disclosures in the notes to the financial statements in respect of errors or changes in accounting policies and estimates. For prior-period errors, you must disclose:

- ✔ The nature of the prior-period error

- ✔ For each prior period presented, to the extent practicable, the amount of the correction for each line of the financial statements affected

- ✔ The amount of the correction at the beginning of the earliest prior period presented in the financial statements

- ✔ Where retrospective restatement of the financial statements isn't possible, an explanation and description of how you corrected the error

Where your organisation or client chooses to change an accounting policy (or policies) that has an effect on the current or any prior period, you need to make the following disclosures in the notes to the financial statements:

- ✔ The nature of the change in accounting policy

- ✔ The reason that applying the new accounting policy provides more reliable and more relevant information

- ✔ The amount of the adjustment for each line of the financial statements affected for the current and each prior period presented in the financial statements, to the extent practicable

- ✔ The amount of the adjustment relating to periods earlier than those presented in the financial statements, to the extent practicable

- ✔ The effect the change in accounting policy has had for each component of equity you've adjusted in respect of the change in accounting policy

- ✔ Where retrospective changes aren't practicable for a particular period – or for periods before those presented in the financial statements – the circumstances that led to the existence of that impracticability and a description of how and from when the organisation applied the change in accounting policy

Where an organisation or your client changes an accounting estimation technique during the accounting period, make sure that you disclose the following:

- ✔ The amount and nature of the change in an accounting estimate
- ✔ If relevant, that you find it impracticable to determine the amount of the effect that such a change in accounting estimate will have on future periods

Assets That You've Held for Sale

Assets that you've held for sale can encompass a couple of things: a business operation (for example, a subsidiary company) or property such as a building. For simplicity, I stick to normal day-to-day assets held for sale rather than go into the complexities of the disclosures you make for discontinued operations.

In respect of non-current assets classified as held for sale, or groups of non-current assets that are held for sale, you must disclose:

- ✔ A description of the non-current assets (or group of non-current assets)
- ✔ A description of the facts and circumstances of the sale, or leading to the expected sale, and the expected manner and timing of the sale
- ✔ Gains or losses recognised in the financial statements, and if not shown separately in the statement of comprehensive income, the line item in the statement of comprehensive income that includes that gain or loss

If you've a non-current asset (or group of assets) that meets the criteria as held for sale *after* the reporting date, you must make the same disclosures as those in the previous list in the notes to the financial statements.

For more on held-for-sale assets, visit Chapter 4.

Inventories and Work-in-Progress

In respect of inventories accounted for under IAS 2 (which I cover in Chapter 4), make sure that you disclose the following in the notes to the financial statements:

- ✔ The accounting policies adopted in measuring inventories
- ✔ The cost formula used (standard cost, the retail method, first-in first-out or average cost)

✔ The total carrying amount of inventories

✔ The carrying amount of inventories in classifications that are appropriate to the entity (classifications can include things like 'raw materials' and 'finished goods')

✔ The carrying amount of inventories that are stated at fair value less costs to sell

✔ The amount of inventories that have been immediately recognised as an expense in the income statement during the accounting period

✔ The amount of any write-downs of inventories recognised as an expense during the accounting period

✔ The amount of any reversals of any write-downs that have been recognised as a reduction in the amount of inventories

✔ The circumstances or events that led to the reversal of write-downs of inventories

✔ The carrying amount of inventories that have been pledged as security

Be careful that the inventories and work-in-progress you include are covered by IAS 2 *Inventories* and IAS 11 *Construction Contracts*. IAS 2 provides a detailed list of items that are beyond its scope.

Construction Contracts

Construction contracts can be a right pain to get right. If you're not sure what to disclose, by all means follow the guidance I give you in this section but also make sure that you look at what's in IAS 11 *Construction Contracts* or at least get hold of a reputable disclosure checklist.

For construction contracts that fall under the scope of IAS 11 (which I cover in Chapter 8), make sure that you disclose:

✔ The amount of contract revenue you've recognised as revenue in the accounting period

✔ The methods you've used to calculate contract revenue that you've recognised in the period

✔ The methods you've used to determine the stage of completion of contracts in progress at the end of your reporting period

In addition, consider those contracts that are still in progress at the end of the reporting period. Disclose

✔ The total amount of costs incurred and recognised profits minus recognised losses to date

✔ The amount of advances that have been received

✔ The total amount of retentions

After you've made these disclosures, you need to make sure that you've presented information in relation to construction contracts correctly in the statement of financial position (balance sheet), so make sure that you show

✔ Gross amounts due from the customer for contract work as an asset

✔ Gross amount due to customers for contract work as a liability

A company must also make disclosure of any contingent liabilities and contingent assets (in accordance with the provisions in IAS 37 *Provisions, Contingent Liabilities and Contingent Assets*) that may arise from items such as warranty costs, claims, penalties or potential losses. I cover IAS 37 issues in more detail in Chapter 7.

Employee Benefits

The problem with employee benefits (as defined in IAS 19 *Employee Benefits*) is that they're so vast. Employee benefits doesn't cover things like share-based payments, however, because these are accounted for under IFRS 2 *Share-based Payment* (I discuss share-based payment issues in Chapter 9). Given the significant disclosures that are required, I can't go into every single disclosure in this chapter, so I show you the main disclosures required in respect of a company that operates a defined benefit pension scheme, which I examine in Chapter 7.

In terms of defined benefit pension schemes, you must make sure that you disclose in the notes to the financial statements:

✔ The company's accounting policy for recognising *actuarial gains* (changes in the actuaries' assumptions) and losses

✔ A general description of the type of pension plan

✔ Components of the total expense in the statement of comprehensive income

✔ Principal assumptions used by the actuary

✔ A reconciliation of opening and closing balances of the present value of the pension obligation showing separately the effects during the period of

- Current service cost (the increase in the present value of the pension scheme's liabilities that are expected to arise from employee service in the current accounting period)

- Interest cost (the imputed cost caused by the unwinding of discount values because liabilities are closer to becoming settled)

- Contributions paid into the pension pot

- Actuarial gains and losses

- Benefits paid to members of the pension plan

- Past service cost (the increase in the present value of scheme liabilities and relating to employee service in prior periods as a result of new retirement benefits or improvements to existing retirement benefits)

- Curtailments (an event that significantly reduces the expected years of future service of present employees or eradicates for a substantial number of employees the entitlement of post-retirement benefits – curtailments can occur because of termination of contracts for services)

- Settlements (these relieve the employer, or the plan, of the responsibility for pension benefit obligations, or eliminate the risks to the employer or the plan)

The disclosures in the list are only a small part of the main disclosures required by IAS 19. Consult a professional or refer to a reputable disclosure checklist for the other major disclosure requirements so you get it right. If you need to brush up on your understanding of the terminology, refer to Chapter 7.

Share-based Payment Transactions

I examine share-based payment transactions in Chapter 9. Extensive disclosures exist in this area, so I can't cover every disclosure requirement, but the main ones that you need to be aware of are as follows:

- ✔ A description of each type of share-based payment arrangement that existed at any time during the period, including the general terms and conditions of the arrangement

- ✔ The number and _weighted average exercise price_ (average based on the number of shares granted at each value) of share options for each of the following groups of options:

  - Outstanding at the beginning of the period

  - Granted during the period

  - Forfeited during the period

- Taken up during the period

- Expired during the period

- Outstanding at the end of the period

- Exercisable at the end of the period

✔ For those share options that have been exercised during the period, the weighted average share price at the date of exercise

✔ For share options that are outstanding at the end of the period, the range of exercise prices and *weighted average remaining contractual lives* (an estimate of the amount of time it will take to fully expense the remaining amount of outstanding share options – number of months from the current period end date for each option grant multiplied by the unrecognised expense for that future period; divide the sum of the value for *all* grants by the total recognised expense)

Provisions and Contingencies

A *provision* is an actual liability that is subject to a degree of uncertain timing or amount. A *contingent* liability, on the other hand, is a potential liability that arises from something in the past whose outcome is based on uncertain future events. It can also be a liability that you don't recognise because the liability's not probable, or you can't reliably estimate the value of the liability. A contingent asset's existence will only be confirmed by uncertain future events that aren't within the control of the organisation. (Take a look at Chapter 7 for more detail on provisions and contingencies.)

You need to make major disclosures in respect of provisions and contingencies to enable the user to evaluate the effect of these on the financial performance and position of the organisation – particularly in subsequent periods when outcomes may become certain.

In respect of each class of provision, you must disclose the following:

✔ The amount of the provision at the beginning and the end of the period

✔ Additional provisions made in the period, including increases to existing provisions

✔ Amounts used during the period

✔ Unused amounts reversed in the period

Here are some additional disclosures you make in respect of provisions:

- ✔ A brief description of the nature of the obligation and the expected timing of any resulting settlements of the obligation

- ✔ Indications of any uncertainties about the timing or amount of the cash flows that you'll use to settle the obligations

- ✔ Any major assumptions made relating to future events

- ✔ The amount of any expected reimbursement and also the amount of any asset that you recognised for that reimbursement

Sometimes a company can't meet the criteria to recognise a provision and therefore it makes disclosure as a contingent asset/liability. In the notes to the financial statements you disclose:

- ✔ A brief description of the nature of the contingent liability

- ✔ An estimate of its financial effect (where practicable)

- ✔ An indication of the uncertainties relating to the amount or timing of any cash outflows (where practicable)

- ✔ The possibility of any reimbursement (where practicable)

In respect of contingent assets, you make additional disclosures:

- ✔ A brief description of the nature of the contingent asset at the end of the reporting period

- ✔ Where practicable, an estimate of the contingent asset's financial effect

Of course, a company may be reluctant to disclose its contingent liabilities/assets because by doing so it may seriously prejudice its position when involved in, say, a dispute. Where disclosure is likely to seriously prejudice the position of the company, it need only disclose the general nature of the dispute, together with the fact that additional disclosure may seriously prejudice the case.

Business Combinations

If you have to make disclosures relating to business combinations and business combinations is an area in which you lack experience, seek advice from your auditors or a professional, or use a reputable disclosure checklist. (I talk about issues relating to business combinations in Chapters 10 and 11.)

I'm sure that you can appreciate that the list of disclosure requirements for business combinations is long! Here, I cover the main disclosures in respect of current period acquisitions of subsidiary companies:

- The name and description of the *acquiree* (the party subject to the acquisition)
- The date of acquisition
- The percentage of voting rights acquired by the acquirer
- The primary reason for the business combination
- The acquisition-date fair value of the purchase proceeds transferred (also referred to as the *consideration transferred*, but it really means the amount of dosh the organisation's paid out) and the acquisition-date fair value of each major class of consideration (such as cash and other intangible or tangible assets used to buy the acquiree) or liabilities incurred (for example, contingent consideration)
- A general description in relation to *contingent consideration arrangements* (where you may stipulate that certain conditions have to be met before you release the balance of any more money, such as where the acquiree must make a certain level of profit in the next financial year)
- The amounts recognised as at the date of acquisition in respect of each major class of asset acquired and liability assumed
- The total amount of goodwill in the business combination that you expect to be deductible for the purposes of tax
- If your organisation is involved in a business combination that's been undertaken by way of a *bargain purchase* (where the proceeds to purchase are less than the fair value of the assets acquired), disclose

  - The amount of any gain recognised in accordance with IFRS 3 paragraph 34 and the line item in the statement of comprehensive income in which you recognise the gain

  - A description of the circumstances giving rise to the bargain purchase

- For each business combination where the parent owns less than 100 per cent in the acquiree, the amount of *non-controlling interests* (the other party that holds the balance of the shares) in the acquiree recognised at the date of acquisition and the measurement basis for that amount

Business combinations also cover the issue of goodwill (IFRS 3) – more on goodwill in Chapters 10, 11 and 17.

Chapter 19

Ten Future Developments in IFRS

In This Chapter
▶ Knowing how the standards are changing
▶ Seeing how amendments will affect accounting practice

*N*othing stands still in the world of financial reporting, and certainly not at the ivory tower known as the offices of the International Accounting Standards Board (IASB). In this chapter, I look at ten projects that the IASB is currently sifting through that may affect how the International Financial Reporting Standards (IFRS) and International Standards on Auditing (IAS) work in the future.

For all standards development issues, including new IFRS, that the IASB are planning and any withdrawals, regularly check the IASB's website www.ifrs. org (click 'Standards development' on the main navigation tab).

Keeping up to date with standards development can count towards your professional body's continuing professional development (CPD) requirements if CPD is relevant to your career. Bonus, eh?

Overhauling the Financial Instruments Standards

The banking industry has recently been slammed for the way in which it accounted for certain financial instruments, in particular complex ones, that people inappropriately manipulated. Critics have cited that the banks' failing was due in part to the creators of the financial instruments not understanding well enough how they should actually work.

In response to this criticism, the IASB is bringing in a new standard – IFRS 9 *Financial Instruments* – to replace IAS 39 *Financial Instruments: Recognition and Measurement* (which I go through in Chapters 5 and 7). Among other things, the new standard puts a lot more emphasis on fair value accounting for things like financial assets (which I look at in Chapter 5). The plan is that the new IFRS 9 takes effect on 1 January 2015.

Changing Fair Value Measurements

You hear the term *fair value* a lot in financial reporting; it means the value at which something is worth. IFRS 13 *Fair Value Measurement* kicks into play on 1 January 2013 and specifies exactly what fair value means, as well as setting out a framework to enable you to measure fair values. You'll also find the disclosure requirements in the new IFRS 13.

Re-jigging Consolidated Financial Statements

The IASB is stripping out all the consolidation guidance that's currently in IAS 27 *Consolidated and Separate Financial Statements* (which I cover in Chapter 10) and putting it into another standard called IFRS 10 *Consolidated Financial Statements*. IFRS 10 places more emphasis on control of a subsidiary than IAS 27. IAS 27 has been renamed *Separate Financial Statements* and the new IFRS 10 and amended IAS 27 are to take off for accounting periods commencing on or after 1 January 2013, but you can adopt them earlier if you want.

Revising How You Present Financial Statements

IAS 1 *Presentation of Financial Statements* (see Chapter 1) requires a statement of comprehensive income that comprises the normal income statement (profit and loss account) and a bit at the end called *Other Comprehensive Income*. For accounting periods commencing on or after 1 July 2012, you need to group items into those items that may potentially be reclassified to the income statement and those that can't be reclassified.

Leasing: The Future

Leasing is one of those issues in the world of accountancy that's been controversial since day one and the IASB is keen to stop things like *off-balance sheet finance* taking place, which is when instead of taking out a bank loan to buy an asset, a company leases an asset and charges payments to the income statement (head to Chapter 6 for more details).

The IASB is abolishing the concept of operating leases (whereby you simply charge all lease payments charged to the income statement as and when they arise). The plan is to introduce a new standard under which you treat all leases, regardless of whether risks and rewards have passed to the lessee or not, as a finance lease. This means that you'll bring all leases onto a company's statement of financial position and recognise a liability, which represents the payments due to the leasing company.

Transforming Revenue Recognition

The IASB is planning to clarify the principles involved in recognising revenue from contracts with customers (usually construction contracts, which I look at in Chapter 8). The planned changes involve bringing in a single model to calculate revenue under such contracts. If you're involved in such contracts, your job is likely to get easier because the change will reduce the number of requirements you've currently got to refer to in order to establish how much revenue to recognise for customer contracts.

Overhauling Joint Ventures

Companies that have joint ventures can currently use the proportionate method of consolidation to account for their joint ventures as well as the equity method. I look at joint ventures and the proportionate and equity methods in Chapter 13.

The IASB has issued a new standard, IFRS 11 *Joint Arrangements*, which bans the use of the proportionate method of accounting for joint ventures. IFRS 11 comes into play for your accounting periods commencing on or after 1 January 2013, so if you use the proportionate method of accounting for your joint ventures, you won't be able to continue doing so from this date.

Revising IAS 19

In 2011, the IASB amended IAS 19 *Employee Benefits*. The new IAS 19 is due to come into play for accounting periods that start on or after 1 January 2013; if you want to adopt it earlier, feel free. The changes mean:

- *Actuarial gains and losses*, which arise when actuaries' assumptions and actual events differ, will be called *remeasurements*.

- You recognise remeasurements in the Other Comprehensive Income section of the statement of comprehensive income – so the 10 per cent corridor (see Chapter 7) no longer applies.

✔ You recognise past service costs in the period when the plan is changed, and you include within past service costs gains and losses that arise from *curtailment* (an event that significantly reduces the expected years of future service of present employees or eliminates the future accrual of pension benefits).

Chapter 7 tells you more about IAS 19.

Understanding Changes in Insurance Contracts

For those of you who deal with insurance contracts, the first thing you need to know is that the current IFRS on insurance (IFRS 4 *Insurance Contracts*) is only an interim standard (which is why I don't cover it in this book). The IASB is going to issue a proper standard in 2012 to eliminate some of the inconsistencies contained in the interim IFRS 4.

If you work in an insurance environment, under the new regime you'll apply a measurement approach that

✔ Works out a current estimate of the future cash flows

✔ Uses a discount rate that adjusts the future cash flows for the time value of money (in other words, discounts them to present-day values)

✔ Uses an explicit *risk adjustment* (the compensation the insurance company requires to take on the risk of an insurance policy that has a degree of uncertainty attached to it in terms of the timing and amount of the cash flows)

✔ Uses a *residual margin* (the profit made by the insurance company on the policy, fixed at the start of the policy and released to the income statement over the period of the policy to stop the insurance company from reporting a profit right at the start of the policy)

Including a Bit of Flexibility in IAS 12

The IASB undertakes its Annual Improvements Project to improve the standards so that financial statements prepared under IFRS become more relevant and reliable. The IASB issued its last exposure draft relating to the project on 22 June 2011, and within it was an amendment to IAS 12 *Income Taxes* (I explain this standard in Chapter 6). (If you'd like to look at the exposure draft, you can download it from www.ifrs.org.)

The change relates to organisations that hold investment properties (which I cover in Chapter 4). IAS 12 requires an organisation to measure *deferred tax* (the future tax consequences of transactions that have taken place in the current period) on an asset, depending on whether the organisation expects to recover the *carrying amount* (the amount stated in the financial statements) of that asset through continued use in the business, or by way of selling the asset. The IASB recognises that many companies that have investment property struggle to decide whether the value of the investment property will be recovered through continuing use or by way of selling the investment property. So the IASB has decided to include a *rebuttable presumption* (an assumption that can be reversed) that the carrying value of an investment property will normally be recovered by way of selling the investment property.

This rebuttable presumption kicks in for accounting periods commencing on or after 1 January 2012 and is only likely to affect a small number of companies because not many companies have investment properties on the statement of financial position.

Part VI
Appendixes

"Hi, I'm Bob Darrel. I'm here to perform the audit of your books. Don't mind the vultures. They follow me everywhere."

In this part . . .

In this final part, I give you some snippits of useful information in the form of appendixes.

Because the world of IFRS is so vast, you've quite a lot to take in. After you get the basics under your belt, you may want to delve further into IFRS and build on the knowledge this book gives you. In Appendix A, you find a lot of additional sources of information that help you develop your knowledge.

Appendix B gives you handy guidance on the mini version of full IFRS (called IFRS for SMEs), which is designed for smaller companies that don't trade their shares on a stock market. You find out what IFRS for SMEs is, which companies it applies to and some of the notable differences between IFRS for SMEs and full IFRS.

And finally, in Appendix C I provide a quick-reference glossary of some of the key terms I use in the book – so you can get easily to grips with IFRS and accounting lingo.

Appendix A

Sources of Guidance

• •

*T*his appendix helps you find further information from various sources. I include reference material from the official standard-setters, articles from professional bodies, other publications referring to IFRS and International Standards on Auditing (IAS) as well as guidance on where you can ask questions and receive answers (many for free – bonus!).

On the Web

Here are some helpful websites that contain information that helps you comply with IFRS and IAS and keeps you up to speed with the latest developments in the world of financial reporting.

Accountancystudents.co.uk

The website www.accountancystudents.co.uk largely caters for people who are studying accountancy but also contains information that's relevant to qualified accountants. This site is an independent website for students of all the major professional bodies such as ICAEW/ACCA/AAT and such like. You can find lots of technical articles on IFRS and IAS and articles on the best way to approach and pass professional examinations.

In addition, the website contains links to other interesting websites where you can get the latest news on IFRS, such as Accountancy Age and AccountancyProfession.com. Also, if you're struggling with a particular aspect of IFRS or IAS that I haven't covered in this book, simply register for free and post a question in the discussion forums where someone's bound to know the answer and point you in the right direction.

AccountingWEB.com

AccountingWEB.com is the sister website of AccountingWEB.co.uk and is based in the USA at www.accountingweb.com. this site is in much the same format as AccountingWEB.co.uk (see next section) and a wide range of tax and financial reporting resources is available. The website devotes a whole section to IFRS, offering free technical summaries of the major content of IFRS and IAS. Registration is free of charge.

AccountingWEB.co.uk

AccountingWEB.co.uk is probably the leading accountancy website in the UK and contains a huge mass of information relevant to students, professional accountants and those who simply take an interest in the accountancy profession.

The website, www.accountingweb.co.uk, is a one-stop shop where you can gain access to a range of tax, financial reporting, auditing and general business information by way of free articles and general updates (registration is free). It also contains lots of marketing tips for those of you who are running your own practice, or contemplating running a practice in the future. The website also has a dedicated forum where you can ask questions and get free advice on various matters from basic tax questions to more complex issues such as group accounts.

Association of Chartered Certified Accountants

The Association of Chartered Certified Accountants (ACCA) is one of the largest global professional bodies in the world. Its website, www.accaglobal.com, contains a wealth of information for students, professional accountants and auditors as well as information relating to the accountancy profession for the general public. For students (or potential students) of ACCA who are studying (or planning to study) for financial reporting papers, lots of articles are relevant to how you apply IFRS/IAS in studies as well as in real life.

Chartered Accountants Ireland

Chartered Accountants Ireland (CAI) (formerly known as the Institute of Chartered Accountants in Ireland, or ICAI) has a useful website that contains a range of information relating to IFRS as well as an e-library where you can source information relating to accountancy, taxation, business and management. It also has a shop online where you can purchase additional material to support your research or studies into IFRS and IAS. Visit www.chartered accountants.ie.

IAS Plus

Deloitte runs the IAS Plus website (www.iasplus.com). The website is a fantastic resource centre that contains all the latest IFRS and IAS in summary format. It also gives you details of the history of the standards including when they were first brought out, when they were amended and the dates they're effective from. This website is a brilliant resource if you're short of time and just need to clarify a technicality.

Institute of Chartered Accountants in England and Wales

The Institute of Chartered Accountants in England and Wales (ICAEW) has a great deal of input into the development of IFRS and IAS. Its website, www.icaew.com, has a wide range of technical material that provides additional information relating to accounting and auditing standards. The ICAEW also allows you to join various faculties (such as the financial reporting faculty or the audit faculty), and then you receive regular newsletters produced by the faculty staff that keep you abreast of developments in the world of financial reporting.

Institute of Chartered Accountants in Scotland

The Institute of Chartered Accountants in Scotland (ICAS) was the first institute to adopt the designation 'Chartered Accountant'. Its website, www.icas.org.uk, contains lots of relevant information relating to the development of international accounting standards and auditing standards. The ICAS also produces its own publications on various technical subjects, particularly financial reporting, which help subscribers keep up to date with what's going on in the profession.

International Accounting Standards Board

The International Accounting Standards Board (IASB) is the official standard-setter that creates and amends the standards. The website, www.ifrs.org, contains a mass of information that helps you if you need official guidance. On the website you can read the standards, find lots of detail about standards development and get clued up about future projects the IASB is embarking upon (I cover future developments in Chapter 19).

More Books on IFRS

Lots of books on IFRS and IAS are on the market. Some are written for those who don't have much experience in the subject, or are just starting out; others are for the more advanced who are perhaps technical partners in firms of accountants. Here's a selection of books I reckon you'll find interesting depending on your level and where you're going, or intend to go, in your career.

Interpretation and Application of International Financial Reporting Standards

Bruce Mackenzie and co's book, published by Wiley, is one of the best available on IFRS and IAS for those of you who want something a little more formal and high level to refer to for your IFRS research. This title is an excellent publication because (like the one in your hands and my ISA book) it provides practical illustrations as to how you apply the IFRS and IAS in real life. It also gives you lots of coverage of the IFRS and IAS that unfortunately is beyond the scope of this book. So if I've got you slightly hooked on IFRS and IAS (which does happen, by the way), then get yourself to www.wiley.com, put in the name of this publication, order it and see for yourself!

Interpretation and Application of International Standards on Auditing

Written by me and published by Wiley, this book is for the accountancy and auditing profession and contains a comprehensive interpretation of all the clarified International Standards on Auditing that are effective for audits of accounting periods starting on or after 15 December 2010. (Don't confuse an International Standard on Auditing, ISA, with an International Accounting Standard, IAS!) It also gives those of you who work in auditing lots of real-life, practical examples on how to apply ISAs. And the book provides a summary of the main technical content of the various IFRS and IAS, together with examples of how to apply them, audit tests and illustrative sets of financial statements. What more can you ask for? (Well, apart from the book you're reading right now!)

Wiley IFRS: Practical Implementation Guide and Workbook

Written by Abbas Ali Mirza and friends and published by Wiley, this book helps you develop and test your skills and knowledge of IFRS. You get thorough explanations of IFRS and other interpretations issued by the IASB, worked out illustrations and examples together with case studies, multiple-choice questions with answers (a great way to test your knowledge of IFRS, particularly for students) and extracts from published financial statements that show you how companies apply IFRS in practice.

Appendix B

IFRS for SMEs

. . . .

*T*his book focuses on the full International Financial Reporting Standards (IFRS). However, small and medium entities (SMEs) may use a condensed version of IFRS called IFRS for SMEs, which I outline in this appendix.

Understanding the Need for IFRS for SMEs

Organisations that use full IFRS as a basis for preparing their financial statements have to disclose a significant amount of information. Why? Well, the vast majority of organisations that prepare their financial statements to IFRS are *listed companies* (in other words, they trade their shares on a stock market). As a result, the chances are that they've a substantial number of shareholders.

Think about an organisation like Vodafone; it has hundreds of shareholders who are all keen on seeing results to know how much dividend (a form of return on investment) they're probably going to get based on the value of their shares. For this reason, Vodafone's financial statements run to hundreds of pages showing all different forms of disclosures needed in order to ensure that the user (the shareholder) has all the information he or she needs concerning Vodafone's profitability, financial position and cash flows.

Organisations that trade their shares on a stock market are publicly accountable. IFRS has no formal definition as to what *publicly accountable* is, but certainly companies that sell shares on a stock market to the general public are publicly accountable.

So you can see that full IFRS is really suited to those organisations that trade shares on stock market (usually referred to as *quoted* companies).

Smaller companies that don't necessarily trade their shares on a stock market and are smaller than the likes of Vodafone or Sony may find that applying full IFRS voluntarily would result in having to make far too many onerous disclosures in their financial statements. As a result, many organisations that were encouraged, but not mandated, to adopt full IFRS chose not do so simply because of the vast array of financial information they would need to disclose under full IFRS.

It became clear to the International Accounting Standards Board (IASB) that smaller companies just didn't need to make masses of disclosures in their financial statements; what they needed was something more user-friendly and less demanding. And so the IASB came up with IFRS for SMEs. This modified IFRS is quite user-friendly, running to about 250 pages long (some 85 per cent less than full IFRS, which is about 4,000 pages long!).

Seeing the Scope of IFRS for SMEs

The principal aim of IFRS for SMEs is to give those companies that are eligible to be classed as SMEs an international-based accounting framework on which to produce relevant, reliable and high-quality accounting information. 'Fantastic – problem solved!' I hear you say, but in the world of financial reporting, things are not exactly as straightforward as producing a framework for SMEs and then getting them on board!

Two main stumbling blocks exist:

- ✔ **Lack of a global definition of what constitutes an SME:** Because different countries have different rules, no exact definition can be a 'catch all'. Lots of countries (for example, the UK) determine whether a company is small, medium or large based on benchmarks such as levels of turnover, the value of gross assets (non-current plus current assets) and numbers of employees.

- ✔ **Lack of compliance with local legislation:** In some countries, IFRS for SMEs isn't compatible with domestic companies' legislation. So SMEs can't adopt the standards until amendments to the legislation or tweaks to IFRS for SMEs take place to make it compatible. Legislation always prevails over an accounting standard.

Because the IASB doesn't dictate which countries can and can't adopt IFRS for SMEs, this task is left to the national regulatory authorities and standard-setters who spell out exactly who can and can't use IFRS for SMEs in the country.

To find out whether your organisation/client is eligible to use IFRS for SMEs, you need to check out the legislation in your country as to what constitutes an SME. Your finance director or auditors can definitely tell you whether you're eligible to use IFRS for SMEs. Also, it's worth pointing out that if your company is an insurance company (or your client is) then you can't use IFRS for SMEs (boo!). This is because organisations that issue insurance contracts must use full IFRS instead.

Be warned – if your organisation is eligible to use IFRS for SMEs and chooses to go ahead and do so, it must adopt the standard in its entirety. You can't choose to account for some stuff under IFRS for SMEs and other bits using full IFRS – it doesn't work like that. IFRS for SMEs is all or nothing!

Knowing What IFRS for SMEs Doesn't Cover

In writing IFRS for SMEs, the IASB slashed the number of accounting practices and disclosures by some 85 per cent to make it more relevant to its target audience (SMEs). If a client, or your organisation, wants to adopt IFRS for SMEs and is eligible to do so, the good news is that you can absolutely forget about:

- ✔ IAS 33 *Earnings per Share*
- ✔ IAS 34 *Interim Financial Reporting*
- ✔ IFRS 8 *Operating Segments*
- ✔ IFRS 5 *Non-current Assets Held for Sale and Discontinued Operations*

Summarising the Main Differences between IFRS for SMEs and Full IFRS

Some notable differences exist between IFRS for SMEs and full IFRS, and here I take you through a couple of the more notable ones.

- ✔ **Amortising goodwill:** In Chapter 5, I tell you that under IFRS 3 *Business Combinations* you can't *amortise* goodwill – so write off the cost over its useful life; you've got to test it annually for impairment. But under IFRS for SMEs, you *can* amortise goodwill over its useful life. However, if management can't determine a reliable estimated useful life for the goodwill then you amortise goodwill over ten years.

- ✔ **Borrowing costs:** In IFRS, any interest you incur when you take out a loan to construct, say, your own building, you *capitalise* (you put the interest as part of the cost of the asset in the statement of financial position) – see Chapter 5 for details. Well, under IFRS for SMEs you can't do this. Instead, you write all such interest charges off to profit or loss in the period in which the interest charges are incurred.

✔ **Revaluing property, plant and equipment:** Under full IFRS (IAS 16 *Property, Plant and Equipment*), you've the option to carry your non-current assets in the statement of financial position at cost less depreciation charges (depreciated historic cost model) or carry some (or all) of them at market value (revaluation model). I discuss these various models in Chapter 4. Under IFRS for SMEs, you can't use the revaluation model at all.

✔ **Statement of compliance:** All organisations that adopt IFRS for SMEs must make a full and explicit statement of compliance with IFRS for SMEs in their financial statements. Organisations that adopt full IFRS must make a full and explicit statement of compliance with IFRS.

Remember, IFRS for SMEs is a one-stop shop – you don't mix and match IFRS for SMEs and full IFRS. Also, you don't go back to full IFRS if IFRS for SMEs doesn't cover a transaction or event; instead, management must develop an accounting policy in the same way I discuss in Chapter 2.

Of course, more differences exist between full IFRS and IFRS for SMEs, but they're a bit more complicated and detailed and therefore fall outside the scope of this book. Fear not: in Appendix A, I outline some resources where you can get lots more insight into the world of IFRS and how full IFRS differs from IFRS for SMEs. I also suggest that you visit the International Accounting Standards Board website at www.ifrs.org and download IFRS for SMEs so you can see for yourself what a set of IFRS for SME financial statements look like. It includes a useful set of illustrative financial statements and a disclosure checklist.

Appendix C

Glossary

· ·

accrual: An amount recognised in the financial statements in respect of goods or services received at (or before) the reporting date but for which a bill hasn't been received.

aggregate: The total (the sum of).

amortisation: The method of writing off the cost of an *intangible non-current asset* over its estimated useful life (the equivalent of *depreciation* for *tangible non-current assets*).

asset: Something that a business owns. An asset can be *non-current* or *current*.

average cost: The cost of a company's *inventory* based on the average cost of the goods available for sale during the accounting period.

carrying value: The amount at which an item is shown in the financial statements.

capital: Cash or goods used in a business to generate income.

capitalise: To include an item within *non-current assets* on the statement of financial position.

contingent consideration arrangements: An arrangement whereby the buyer pays a lump sum to the seller of a business at the time of the buyer's acquisition with a promise to pay more (contingent consideration) if the seller meets certain criteria within a specified time period.

current asset: An asset held in a company's statement of financial position that the company expects to turn into cash within 12 months.

depreciated historic cost model: Measures *non-current assets* in the statement of financial position at cost, which you then write off by way of *depreciation* over the asset's estimated useful life.

depreciation: The method of writing off the cost of a *tangible non-current asset* over its estimated useful life.

equity method: A method of accounting for an equity investment where the investor holds between 20 per cent and 50 per cent of the investee. You record the investment initially at cost and subsequently adjust it to reflect the investor's share of the investment's profit or loss.

fair value: An unbiased estimate of how much a good, service or other asset is worth.

first-in first-out: A method in which the *inventory* of a company that's produced or acquired first is sold, used or disposed of first.

gearing: The relationship between the amount of a company's borrowings and its equity. A company with high gearing is over-reliant on borrowings for a large proportion of its capital requirements.

going concern: The assumption that a company will continue to operate and not be forced into liquidation.

gross: Monetary amounts in the financial statements before any deductions.

gross profit: *Revenue* less cost of goods sold for the period.

held-for-sale: An asset (or disposal group) that you need to dispose of by way of sale.

impairment: A situation where the *carrying value* of an asset exceeds its recoverable amount (the amount that an unconnected third party would pay for the same asset).

inflows: Resources coming into the company, such as money or other assets.

intangible non-current asset: *Non-current assets* that are invisible, such as software and brands.

intrinsic value: The difference between the *fair value* of shares and the price that the counterparty pays for them.

inventory: Unsold goods owned by the company at the period end that the company expects to sell in the next accounting period.

last-in first-out: A method of *inventory* valuation where the most recently produced items are sold, used or disposed of first (opposite of *first-in first-out*).

net: Monetary amounts in the financial statements after deductions.

net assets: Sometimes called _net worth_; refers to shareholders' funds and is arrived at by deducting all liabilities (long- and short-term) from all long- and short-term assets.

net book value: The amount at which you state _non-current assets_ in the financial statements after charging _amortisation_ and _depreciation_.

net present value: Future monetary amounts stated at today's values.

net realisable value: The amount for which you can sell an asset, less the costs to sell it.

non-current asset: An asset used in the business that can't be easily turned into cash and isn't expected to be turned into cash within a year.

outflows: Resources going out of the company, such as cash or other forms of assets.

proportionate consolidation: A method to account for joint ventures by including items of income, expense, assets and liabilities of the venture in the investor's own financial statements according the investor's shareholding in the venture. In other words, if the investor owns 40 per cent of the venture, the investor includes 40 per cent of the investor's income, expense, assets and liabilities in with the investor's own income, expenses, assets and liabilities.

recoverable amount: The amount that's higher between an asset's _fair value_ less costs to sell and the asset's value in use. So if fair value less costs to sell is $100 and the assets' value in use is $200, the recoverable amount is $200.

residual value: The value of a _non-current asset_ after it's fully _depreciated_ or _amortised_.

retail method: A method to estimate the cost of a retailer's closing _inventory_ that involves using a cost-to-retail ratio in order to convert the closing inventory at retail back to its estimated cost.

retained earnings: Profits that are retained by the company and reinvested back into the business.

revaluation model: A method to adjust the _carrying value_ of _non-current assets_ and investment property to market value at each reporting date as opposed to charging _depreciation_.

revenue: Income generated by the company purely from its day-to-day business activities (sales).

standard cost: A pre-determined or estimated cost of producing goods that's allowed under IAS 2 *Inventories*, provided that the results approximate actual cost.

straight-line basis: Charging the income statement with equal amounts of income or expense over a specific period of time. It usually applies to *depreciation*, where you write off the cost of a *non-current asset* over a set number of years.

tangible non-current asset: A non-current asset used in the business that has a physical form such as a van or a computer.

tax base: The monetary amount of an asset or liability for the purposes of tax.

value in use: The *net present value* of a cash flow(s) or other forms of economic benefits that an asset generates for its owner.

vesting conditions: Conditions that an individual or a company must satisfy to receive an organisation's shares under a share-based payment arrangement.

weighted average exercise price: The average share price at which share options have been exercised during the year (in other words, the price at which the shares have been given). For example, if an option is granted for 1,000 shares at an exercise price of $2 and another option granted for 1,000 shares at an exercise price of $3, the weighted average exercise price granted during the period is (1,000 x $2) + (1,000 x $3) ÷ 2,000 = $2.50.

written-down value: The value of an asset after charging *depreciation* or *amortisation* (see also *net book value*).

Index

• *G* •

• H •

• I •

FOR DUMMIES®

Making Everything Easier! ™

UK editions

BUSINESS

Bookkeeping For Dummies
978-0-470-97626-5

Persuasion & Influence For Dummies
978-0-470-74737-7

Starting & Running a Business All-In-One For Dummies
978-1-119-97527-4

REFERENCE

British Politics For Dummies
978-0-470-68637-9

DIY For Dummies
978-0-470-97450-6

Dad's Guide to Pregnancy For Dummies
978-1-119-97660-8

HOBBIES

Growing Your Own Fruit & Veg For Dummies
978-0-470-69960-7

Keeping Chickens For Dummies
978-1-119-99417-6

Beekeeping For Dummies
978-1-119-97250-1

Asperger's Syndrome For Dummies
978-0-470-66087-4

Basic Maths For Dummies
978-1-119-97452-9

Body Language For Dummies, 2nd Edition
978-1-119-95351-7

Boosting Self-Esteem For Dummies
978-0-470-74193-1

British Sign Language For Dummies
978-0-470-69477-0

Cricket For Dummies
978-0-470-03454-5

Diabetes For Dummies, 3rd Edition
978-0-470-97711-8

Electronics For Dummies
978-0-470-68178-7

English Grammar For Dummies
978-0-470-05752-0

Flirting For Dummies
978-0-470-74259-4

IBS For Dummies
978-0-470-51737-6

Improving Your Relationship For Dummies
978-0-470-68472-6

ITIL For Dummies
978-1-119-95013-4

Management For Dummies, 2nd Edition
978-0-470-97769-9

Neuro-linguistic Programming For Dummies, 2nd Edition
978-0-470-66543-5

Nutrition For Dummies, 2nd Edition
978-0-470-97276-2

Organic Gardening For Dummies
978-1-119-97706-3

Available wherever books are sold. For more information or to order direct go to www.wiley.com or call +44 (0) 1243 843291

11-37870

FOR DUMMIES®

Making Everything Easier! ™

UK editions

SELF-HELP

Cognitive Behavioural Therapy For Dummies
978-0-470-66541-1

Creative Visualization For Dummies
978-1-119-99264-6

Mindfulness For Dummies
978-0-470-66086-7

Origami Kit For Dummies
978-0-470-75857-1

Overcoming Depression For Dummies
978-0-470-69430-5

Positive Psychology For Dummies
978-0-470-72136-0

PRINCE2 For Dummies, 2009 Edition
978-0-470-71025-8

STUDENTS

Philosophy For Dummies
978-0-470-68820-5

Student Cookbook For Dummies
978-0-470-974711-7

Sociology For Dummies
978-1-119-99134-2

Project Management For Dummies
978-0-470-71119-4

Psychometric Tests For Dummies
978-0-470-75366-8

Renting Out Your Property For Dummies, 3rd Edition
978-1-119-97640-0

Ruby Union For Dummies, 3rd Edition
978-1-119-99092-5

Sage One For Dummies
978-1-119-95236-7

Self-Hypnosis For Dummies
978-0-470-66073-7

Storing and Preserving Garden Produce For Dummies
978-1-119-95156-8

HISTORY

The Tudors For Dummies
978-0-470-68792-5

Medieval History For Dummies
978-0-470-74783-4

British History For Dummies
978-0-470-97819-1

Study Skills For Dummies
978-0-470-74047-7

Teaching English as a Foreign Language For Dummies
978-0-470-74576-2

Time Management For Dummies
978-0-470-77765-7

Training Your Brain For Dummies
978-0-470-97449-0

Work-Life Balance For Dummies
978-0-470-71380-8

Available wherever books are sold. For more information or to order direct go to www.wiley.com or call +44 (0) 1243 843291

11–37870